CHRISTOPHER SEBELA

HAYDEN SHERMAN

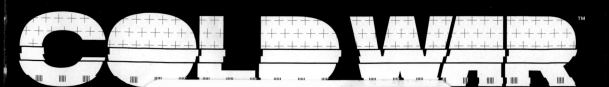
COLD WAR™

DISCARD

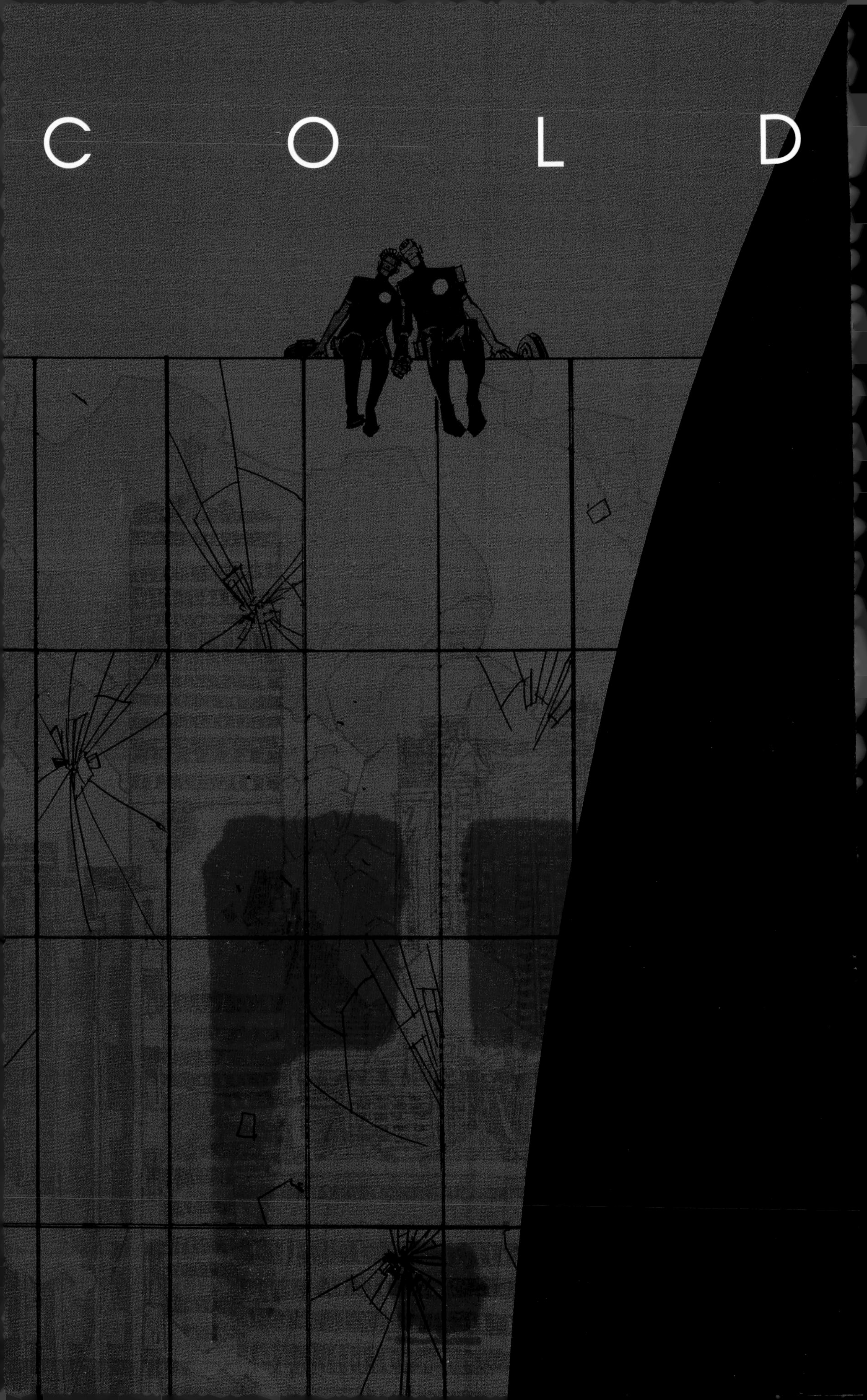
C O L D

WAR

VOLUME 1

DEAD FUTURE

CHRISTOPHER SEBELA co-creator & writer

HAYDEN SHERMAN co-creator & artist

HAYDEN SHERMAN letterer

HAYDEN SHERMAN original covers

JUAN DOE, HAYDEN SHERMAN variant covers

DYLAN TODD logo designer

COREY BREEN book designer

MIKE MARTS editor

AFTERSHOCK™

MIKE MARTS - Editor-in-Chief • **JOE PRUETT** - Publisher/ Chief Creative Officer • **LEE KRAMER** - President
JON KRAMER - Chief Executive Officer • **STEVE ROTTERDAM** - SVP, Sales & Marketing • **LISA Y. WU** - Retailer/Fan Relations Manager
CHRISTINA HARRINGTON - Managing Editor • **JAY BEHLING** - Chief Financial Officer • **JAWAD QURESHI** - SVP, Investor Relations
AARON MARION - Publicist • **CHRIS LA TORRE** - Sales Associate • **KIM PAGNOTTA** - Sales Associate • **LISA MOODY** - Finance
CHARLES PRITCHETT - Comics Production • **COREY BREEN** - Collections Production • **TEDDY LEO** - Editorial Assistant

AfterShock Trade Dress by **JOHN J. HILL** • AfterShock Logo Design by **COMICRAFT**
Publicity: contact **AARON MARION** (aaron@publichausagency.com) & **RYAN CROY** (ryan@publichausagency.com) at **PUBLICHAUS**
Special thanks to: **IRA KURGAN, STEPHAN NILSON, JULIE PIFHER** and **SARAH PRUETT**

AFTERSHOCKCOMICS.COM Follow us on social media 🐦 📷 f

COLD WAR was always a fun nightmare. From the moment it was born to the long process to make it a real story, it fought me every step of the way. The only real solution in the end was to get another pair of hands to wrangle it, and I was lucky when those came in the form of Hayden Sherman. For all the characters I birthed and the strange weapons I puzzled out, nothing about COLD WAR truly existed until Hayden sent those first designs over. I had no idea what this book would look like with the two of us running it, but I had to see. I leaned into the mystery and came out with what you hold in your hands.

Writing is mostly a quiet, insular thing. You nurture your strange monsters until they grow up and wander out into the world. Maybe they're strong enough to face what's out there. Maybe they'll crawl back into their memories and lay down to die. But COLD WAR was an explosive series of trust falls, each issue hoping the next would hold up, too—each page a marvel to behold as it came in, a tightrope walk all the way to the last page. I wouldn't change a thing if I could.

CHRISTOPHER SEBELA
June 2018

I N T R O D U C T I O N S

When I started working on COLD WAR, I had no idea what it was going to look like. Not a clue. But the pitch had me hooked. Chris had created something that was weird, out there, fun and perfect for comics. So I at least knew that however I was going to interpret that story to the page, it had to carry that energy with it. The book couldn't look flat or dead. It had to be pulsing and weird and dark and chaotic. There had to be a level of "what?" to the whole thing. And thankfully, this is something that Chris and I seemed to sync up on from the beginning. We knew how "out there" the premise was and decided to play it as oddly and sincerely as it felt.

The result is a book that I am immensely proud to have been a part of. It's a playground of ink and color where every page I challenged myself to push beyond what I'd usually do. But it wouldn't have been even half of what it became without the constant encouragement of Chris, editor Mike Marts and certainly my partner, Hanna Cha. No Cryonaut would make it alone, and I surely wouldn't have made it to this point without their wholehearted support.

HAYDEN SHERMAN
June 2018

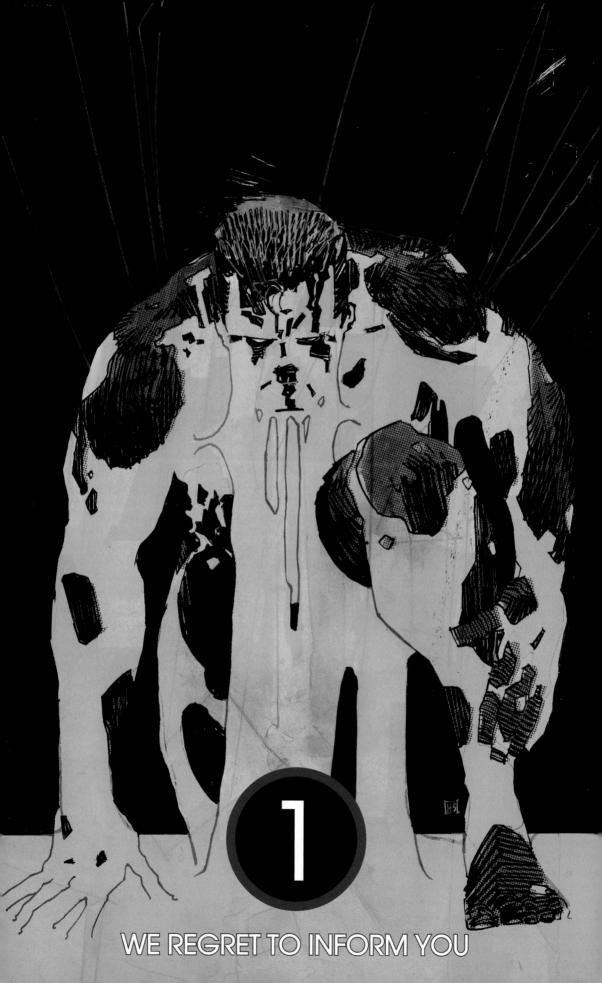

1

WE REGRET TO INFORM YOU

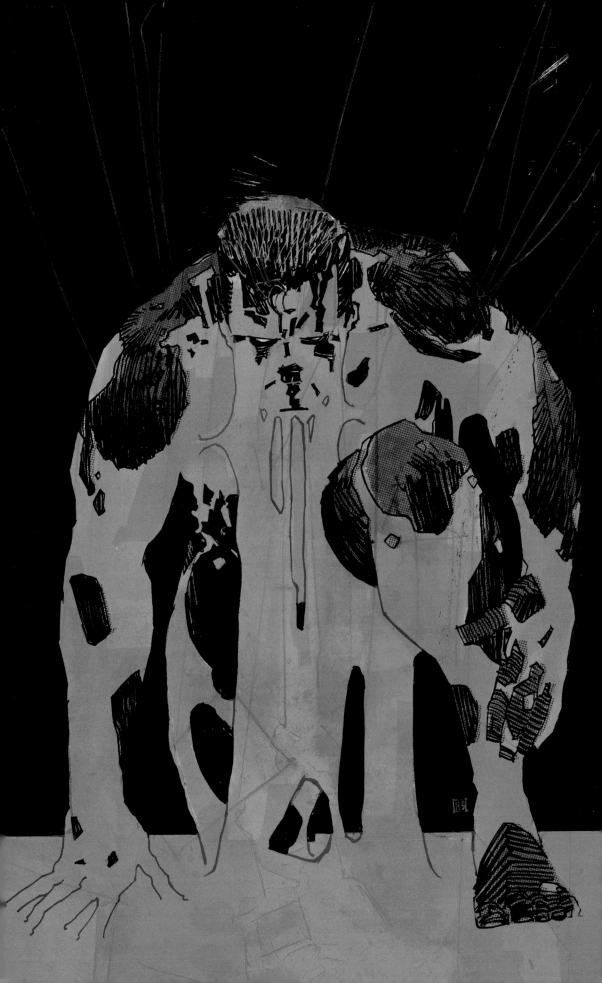

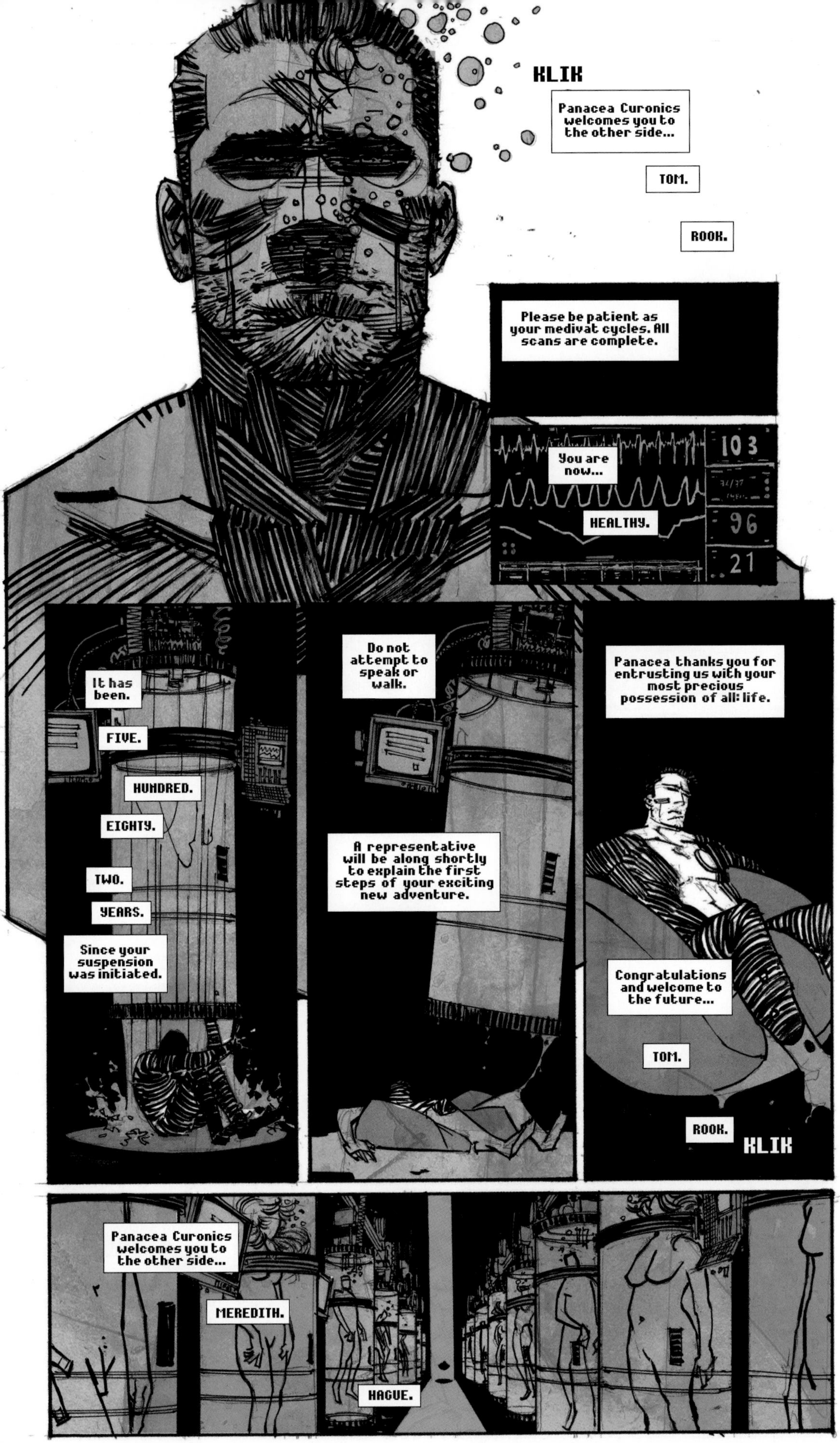
KLIK
Panacea Curonics welcomes you to the other side...
TOM.
ROOK.
Please be patient as your medivat cycles. All scans are complete.
You are now...
HEALTHY.
103
96
21
It has been.
FIVE.
HUNDRED.
EIGHTY.
TWO.
YEARS.
Since your suspension was initiated.
Do not attempt to speak or walk.
A representative will be along shortly to explain the first steps of your exciting new adventure.
Panacea thanks you for entrusting us with your most precious possession of all: life.
Congratulations and welcome to the future...
TOM.
ROOK.
KLIK
Panacea Curonics welcomes you to the other side...
MEREDITH.
HAGUE.

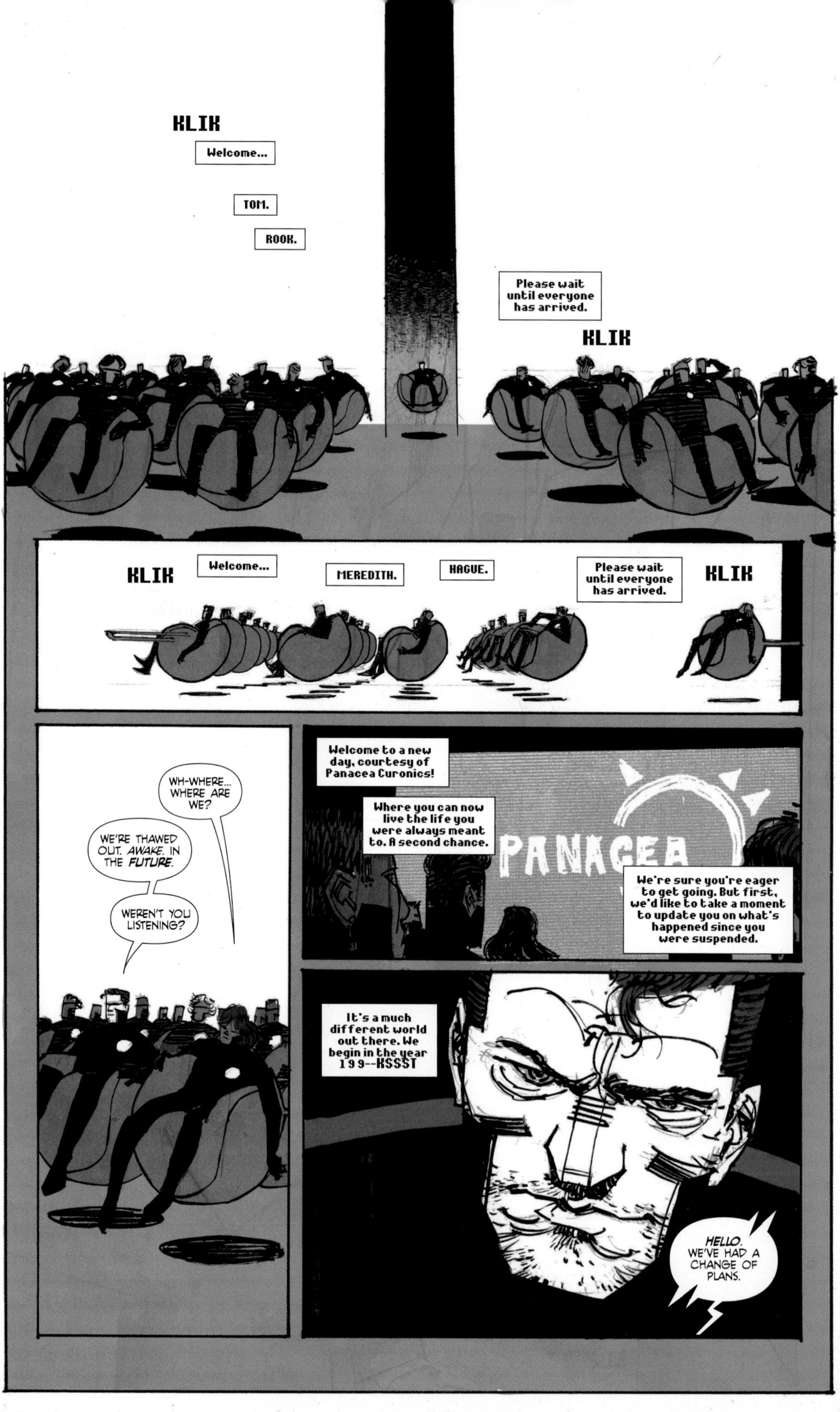
KLIK
Welcome...
TOM.
ROOK.
Please wait until everyone has arrived.
KLIK
KLIK
Welcome...
MEREDITH.
HAGUE.
Please wait until everyone has arrived.
KLIK
WH-WHERE... WHERE ARE WE?
WE'RE THAWED OUT. *AWAKE*. IN THE *FUTURE*.
WEREN'T YOU LISTENING?
Welcome to a new day, courtesy of Panacea Curonics!
Where you can now live the life you were always meant to. A second chance.
PANACEA
We're sure you're eager to get going. But first, we'd like to take a moment to update you on what's happened since you were suspended.
It's a much different world out there. We begin in the year 199--KSSST
HELLO. WE'VE HAD A CHANGE OF PLANS.

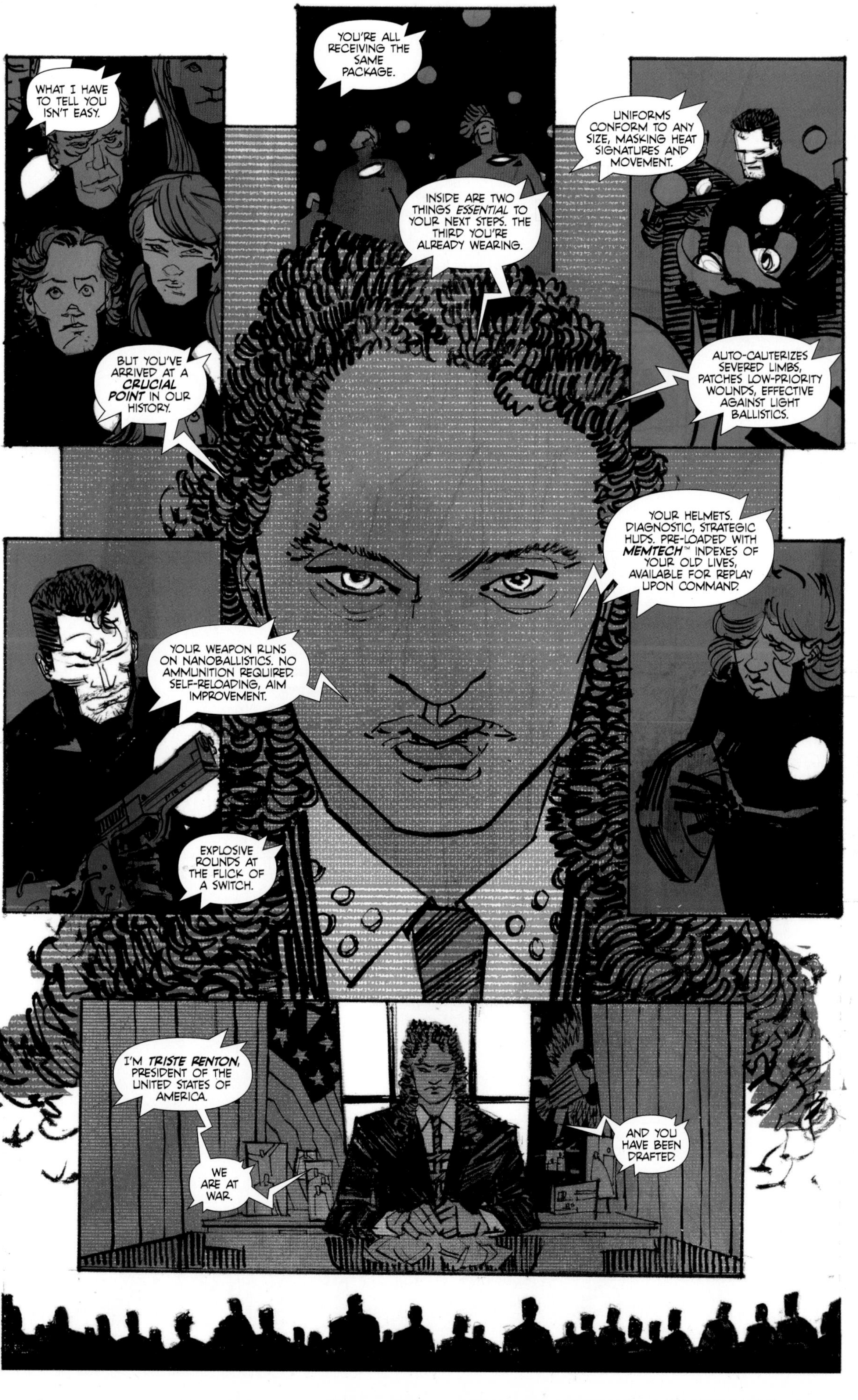
WHAT I HAVE TO TELL YOU ISN'T EASY.
BUT YOU'VE ARRIVED AT A CRUCIAL POINT IN OUR HISTORY.
YOU'RE ALL RECEIVING THE SAME PACKAGE.
INSIDE ARE TWO THINGS ESSENTIAL TO YOUR NEXT STEPS. THE THIRD YOU'RE ALREADY WEARING.
UNIFORMS CONFORM TO ANY SIZE, MASKING HEAT SIGNATURES AND MOVEMENT.
AUTO-CAUTERIZES SEVERED LIMBS, PATCHES LOW-PRIORITY WOUNDS, EFFECTIVE AGAINST LIGHT BALLISTICS.
YOUR WEAPON RUNS ON NANOBALLISTICS. NO AMMUNITION REQUIRED. SELF-RELOADING, AIM IMPROVEMENT.
EXPLOSIVE ROUNDS AT THE FLICK OF A SWITCH.
YOUR HELMETS. DIAGNOSTIC, STRATEGIC HUDS. PRE-LOADED WITH MEMTECH™ INDEXES OF YOUR OLD LIVES, AVAILABLE FOR REPLAY UPON COMMAND.
I'M TRISTE RENTON, PRESIDENT OF THE UNITED STATES OF AMERICA.
WE ARE AT WAR.
AND YOU HAVE BEEN DRAFTED.

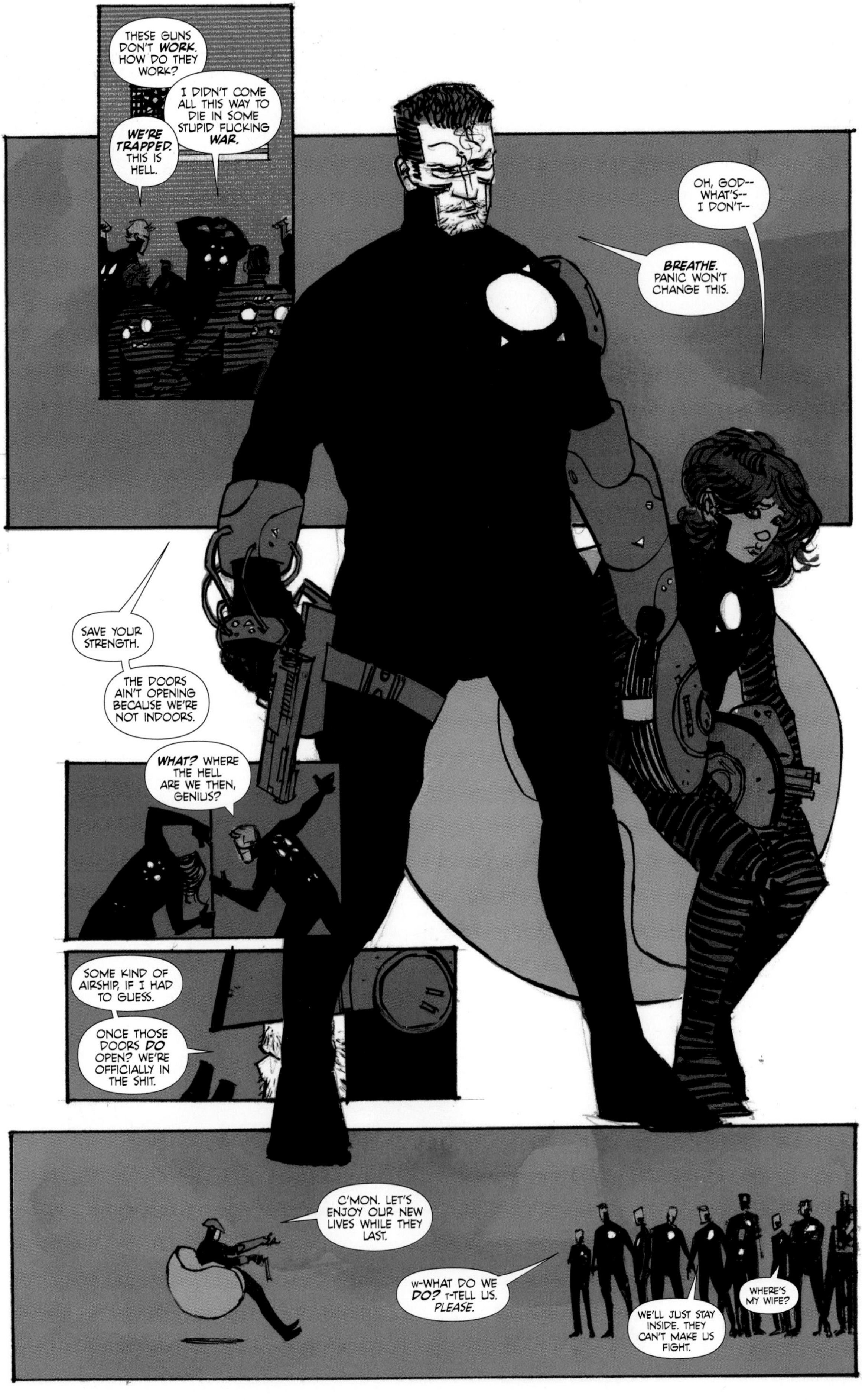
THESE GUNS DON'T **WORK**. HOW DO THEY WORK?
I DIDN'T COME ALL THIS WAY TO DIE IN SOME STUPID FUCKING **WAR**.
WE'RE TRAPPED. THIS IS HELL.
OH, GOD-- WHAT'S-- I DON'T--
BREATHE. PANIC WON'T CHANGE THIS.
SAVE YOUR STRENGTH.
THE DOORS AIN'T OPENING BECAUSE WE'RE NOT INDOORS.
WHAT? WHERE THE HELL ARE WE THEN, GENIUS?
SOME KIND OF AIRSHIP, IF I HAD TO GUESS.
ONCE THOSE DOORS **DO** OPEN? WE'RE OFFICIALLY IN THE SHIT.
C'MON. LET'S ENJOY OUR NEW LIVES WHILE THEY LAST.
W-WHAT DO WE **DO?** T-TELL US. *PLEASE*.
WE'LL JUST STAY INSIDE. THEY CAN'T MAKE US FIGHT.
WHERE'S MY WIFE?

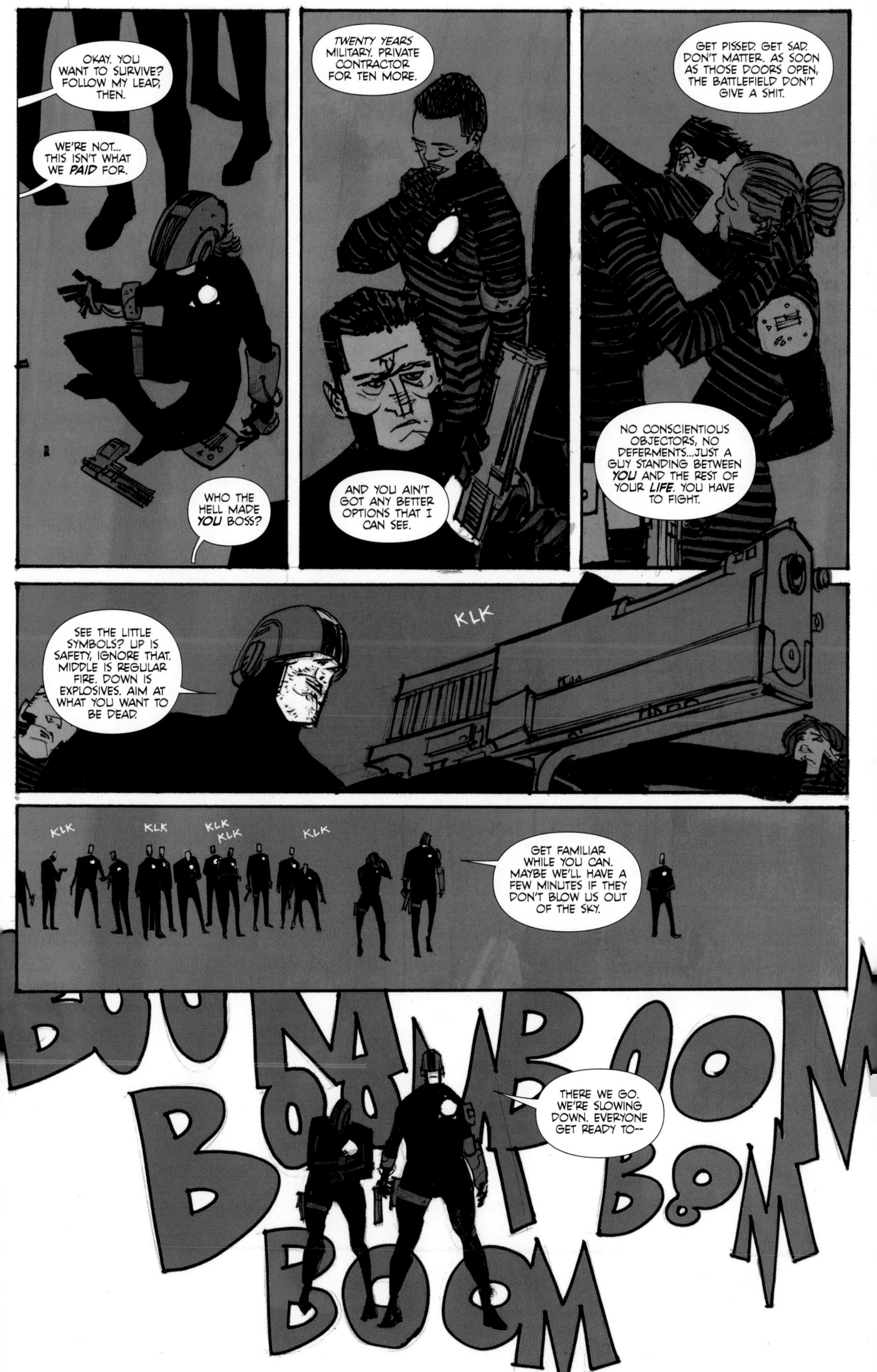
OKAY. YOU WANT TO SURVIVE? FOLLOW MY LEAD, THEN.
WE'RE NOT... THIS ISN'T WHAT WE *PAID* FOR.
WHO THE HELL MADE *YOU* BOSS?
TWENTY YEARS MILITARY. PRIVATE CONTRACTOR FOR TEN MORE.
AND YOU AIN'T GOT ANY BETTER OPTIONS THAT I CAN SEE.
GET PISSED. GET SAD. DON'T MATTER. AS SOON AS THOSE DOORS OPEN, THE BATTLEFIELD DON'T GIVE A SHIT.
NO CONSCIENTIOUS OBJECTORS, NO DEFERMENTS...JUST A GUY STANDING BETWEEN *YOU* AND THE REST OF YOUR *LIFE*. YOU HAVE TO FIGHT.
SEE THE LITTLE SYMBOLS? UP IS SAFETY, IGNORE THAT. MIDDLE IS REGULAR FIRE. DOWN IS EXPLOSIVES. AIM AT WHAT YOU WANT TO BE DEAD.
KLK
KLK
KLK
KLK
KLK
KLK
GET FAMILIAR WHILE YOU CAN. MAYBE WE'LL HAVE A FEW MINUTES IF THEY DON'T BLOW US OUT OF THE SKY.
BOOM BOOM BOOM BOOM BOOM BOOM BOOM
THERE WE GO. WE'RE SLOWING DOWN. EVERYONE GET READY TO--

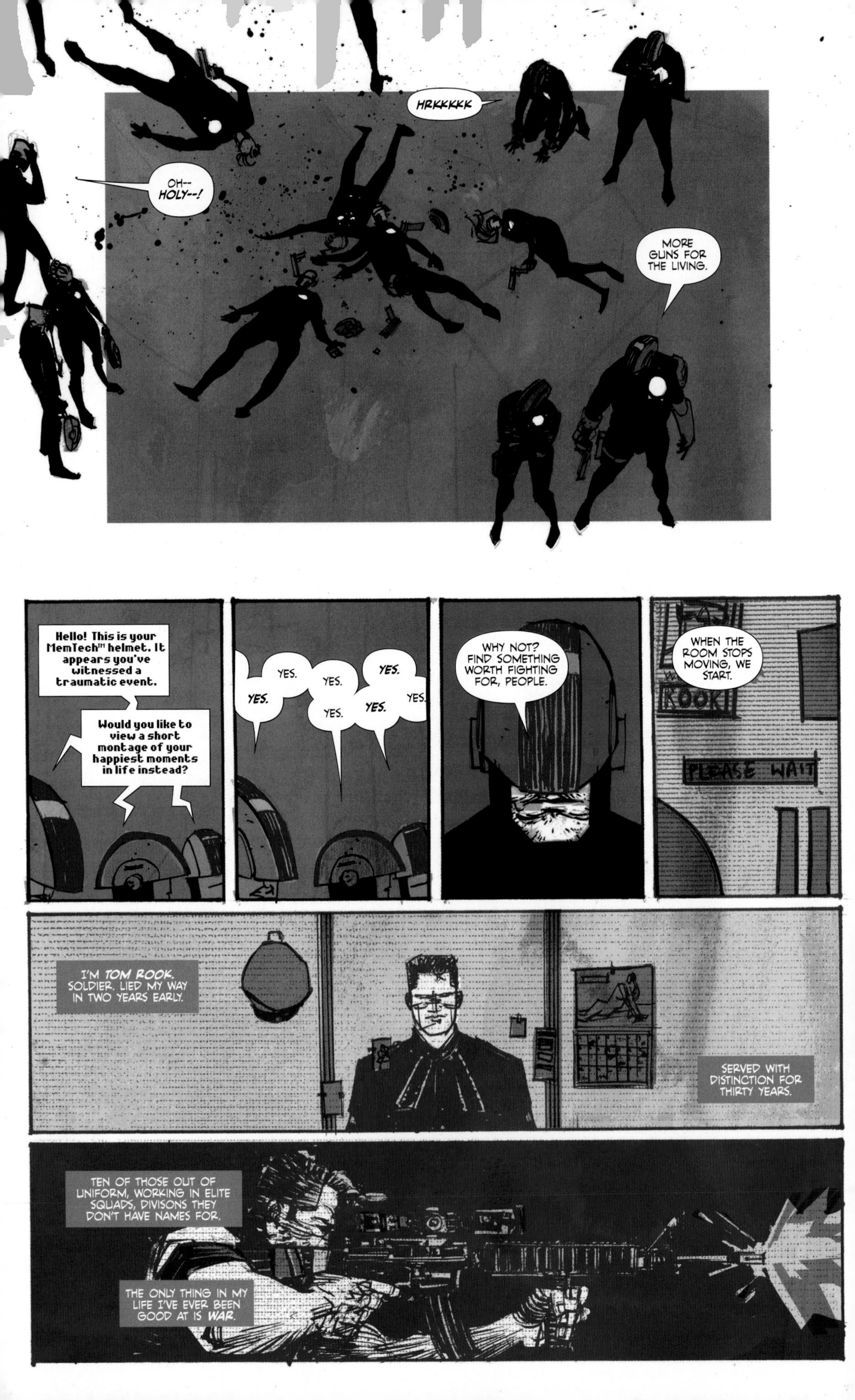

OH-- HOLY--!
HRKKKKK
MORE GUNS FOR THE LIVING.
Hello! This is your MemTech™ helmet. It appears you've witnessed a traumatic event.
Would you like to view a short montage of your happiest moments in life instead?
YES.
YES.
YES.
YES.
YES.
YES.
YES.
WHY NOT? FIND SOMETHING WORTH FIGHTING FOR, PEOPLE.
ROOK
WHEN THE ROOM STOPS MOVING, WE START.
PLEASE WAIT
I'M TOM ROOK. SOLDIER. LIED MY WAY IN TWO YEARS EARLY.
SERVED WITH DISTINCTION FOR THIRTY YEARS.
TEN OF THOSE OUT OF UNIFORM, WORKING IN ELITE SQUADS, DIVISONS THEY DON'T HAVE NAMES FOR.
THE ONLY THING IN MY LIFE I'VE EVER BEEN GOOD AT IS WAR.

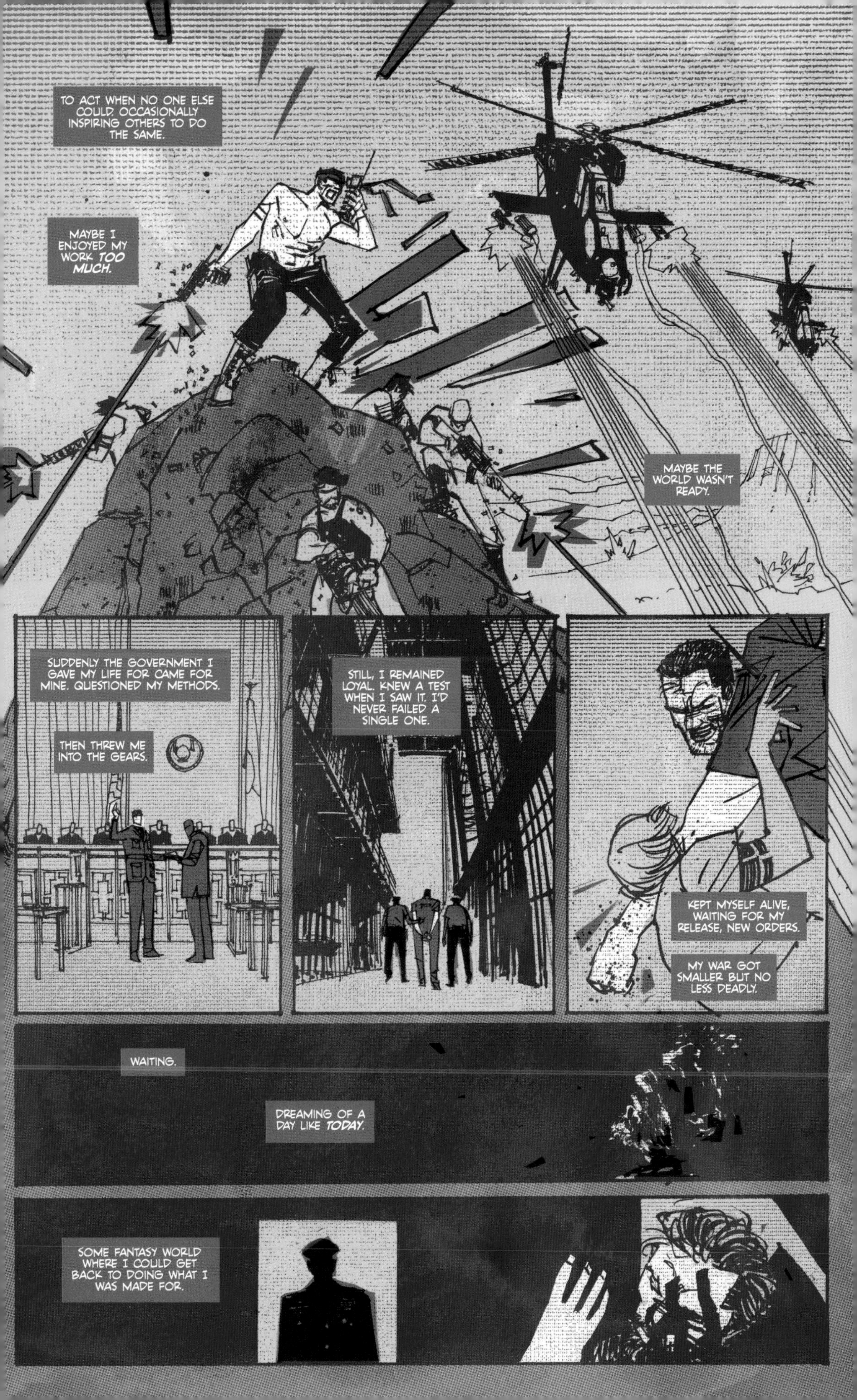
TO ACT WHEN NO ONE ELSE COULD. OCCASIONALLY INSPIRING OTHERS TO DO THE SAME.
MAYBE I ENJOYED MY WORK *TOO MUCH.*
MAYBE THE WORLD WASN'T READY.
SUDDENLY THE GOVERNMENT I GAVE MY LIFE FOR CAME FOR MINE. QUESTIONED MY METHODS.
THEN THREW ME INTO THE GEARS.
STILL, I REMAINED LOYAL. KNEW A TEST WHEN I SAW IT. I'D NEVER FAILED A SINGLE ONE.
KEPT MYSELF ALIVE, WAITING FOR MY RELEASE, NEW ORDERS.
MY WAR GOT SMALLER BUT NO LESS DEADLY.
WAITING.
DREAMING OF A DAY LIKE *TODAY.*
SOME FANTASY WORLD WHERE I COULD GET BACK TO DOING WHAT I WAS MADE FOR.

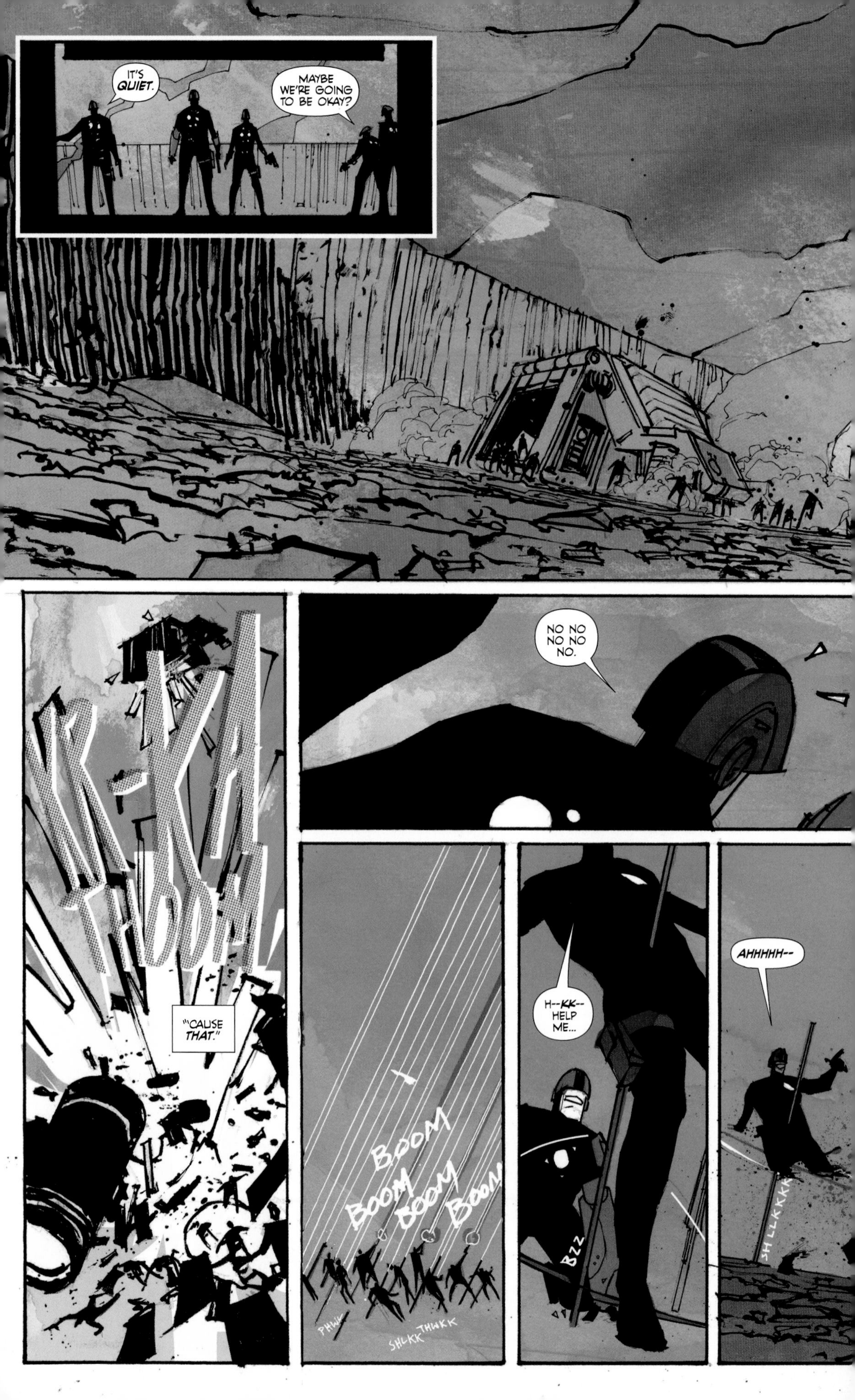
IT'S QUIET.
MAYBE WE'RE GOING TO BE OKAY?
'CAUSE THAT.
NO NO NO NO NO.
BOOM BOOM BOOM BOOM
PHWK
SHLKK
THWKK
H--KK-- HELP ME...
BZZ
AHHHHH--
SHLLKKKK

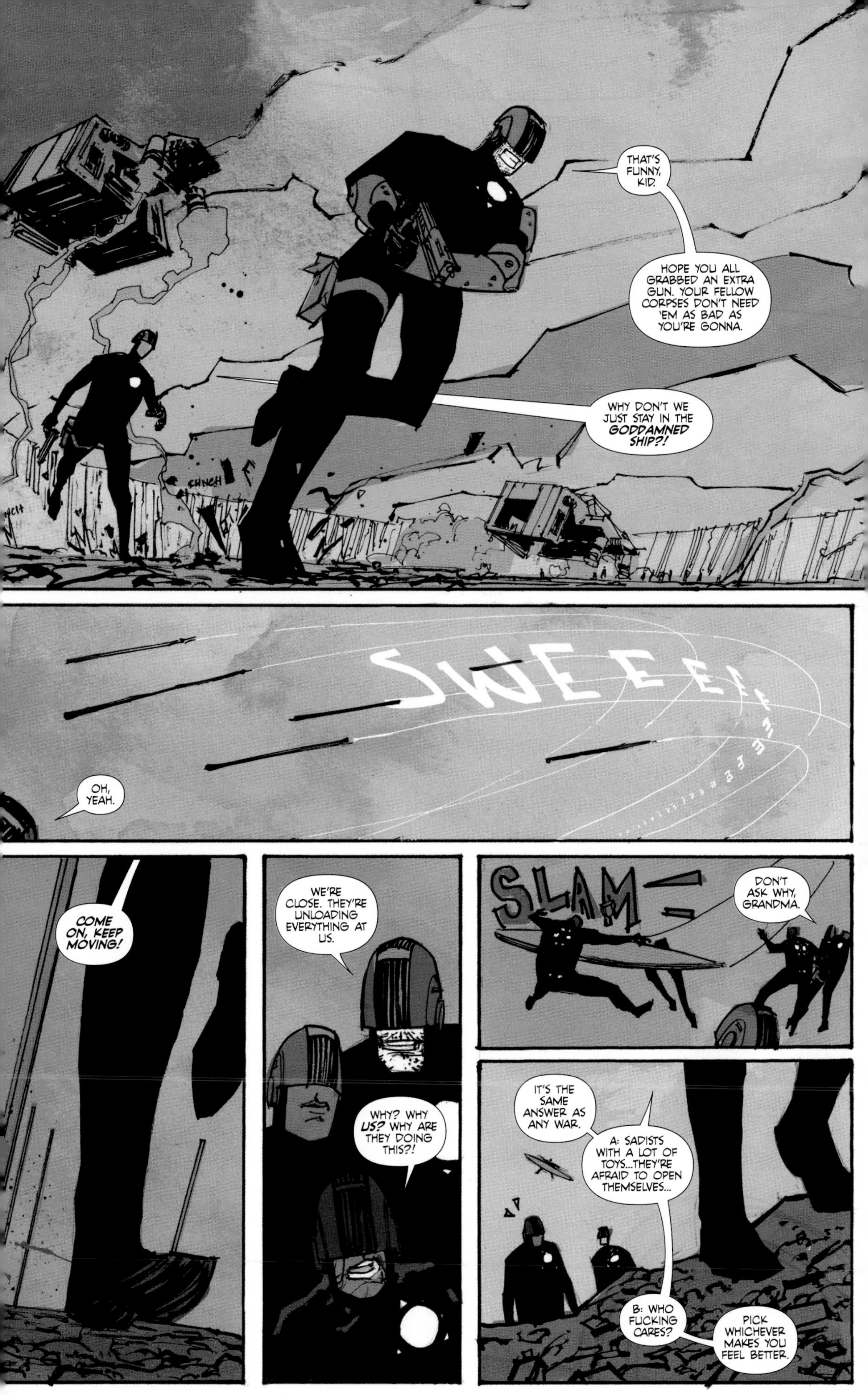
THAT'S FUNNY, KID.
HOPE YOU ALL GRABBED AN EXTRA GUN. YOUR FELLOW CORPSES DON'T NEED 'EM AS BAD AS YOU'RE GONNA.
WHY DON'T WE JUST STAY IN THE *GODDAMNED SHIP?!*
SWEEE
OH, YEAH.
COME ON, KEEP MOVING!
WE'RE CLOSE. THEY'RE UNLOADING EVERYTHING AT US.
WHY? WHY *US?* WHY ARE THEY DOING THIS?!
SLAM
DON'T ASK WHY, GRANDMA.
IT'S THE SAME ANSWER AS ANY WAR.
A: SADISTS WITH A LOT OF TOYS...THEY'RE AFRAID TO OPEN THEMSELVES...
B: WHO FUCKING CARES?
PICK WHICHEVER MAKES YOU FEEL BETTER.

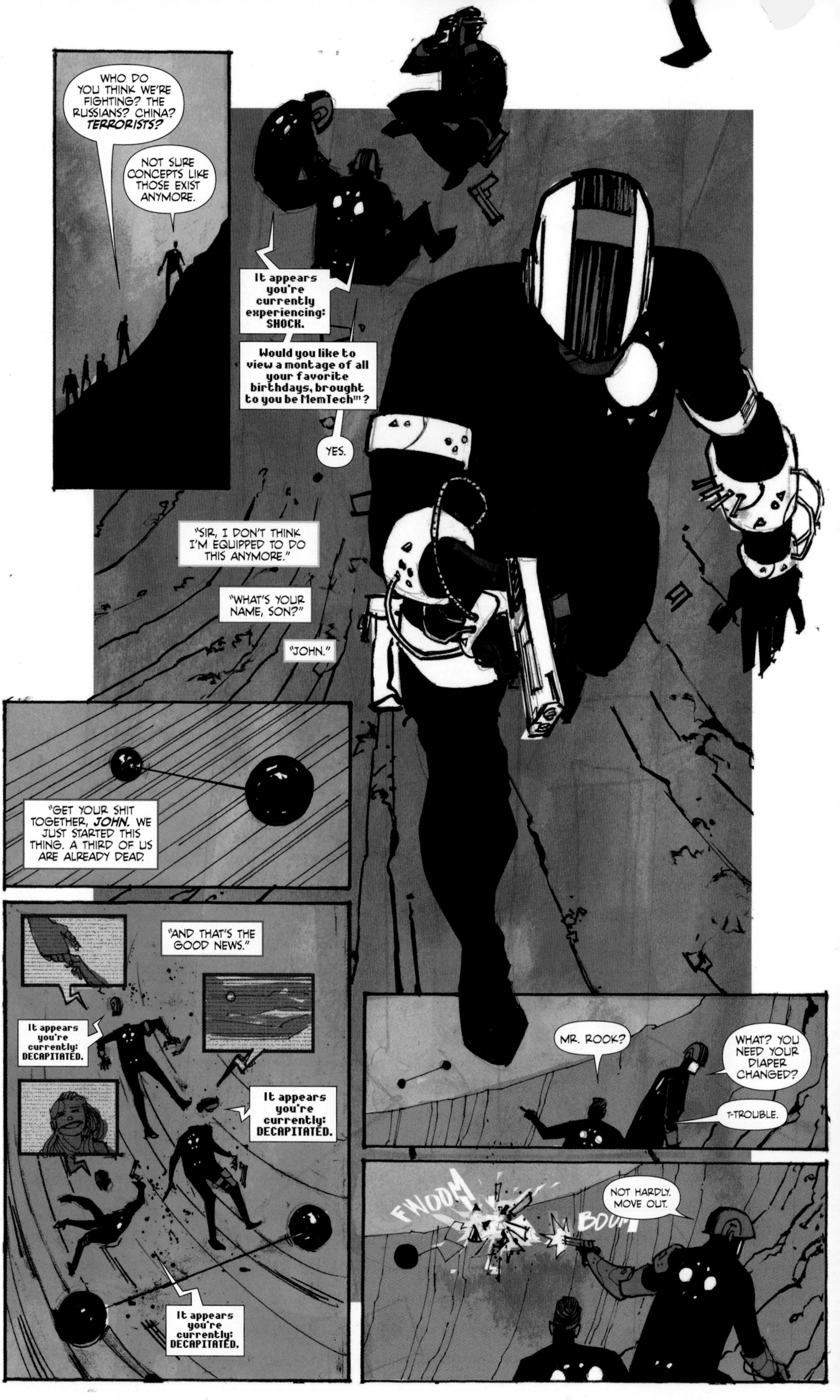

WHO DO YOU THINK WE'RE FIGHTING? THE RUSSIANS? CHINA? *TERRORISTS?*
NOT SURE CONCEPTS LIKE THOSE EXIST ANYMORE.
It appears you're currently experiencing: SHOCK.
Would you like to view a montage of all your favorite birthdays, brought to you be MemTech™?
YES.
"SIR, I DON'T THINK I'M EQUIPPED TO DO THIS ANYMORE."
"WHAT'S YOUR NAME, SON?"
"JOHN."
"GET YOUR SHIT TOGETHER, *JOHN.* WE JUST STARTED THIS THING. A THIRD OF US ARE ALREADY DEAD.
"AND THAT'S THE GOOD NEWS."
It appears you're currently: DECAPITATED.
It appears you're currently: DECAPITATED.
It appears you're currently: DECAPITATED.
MR. ROOK?
WHAT? YOU NEED YOUR DIAPER CHANGED?
T-TROUBLE.
FWOOM
BOOM
NOT HARDLY. MOVE OUT.

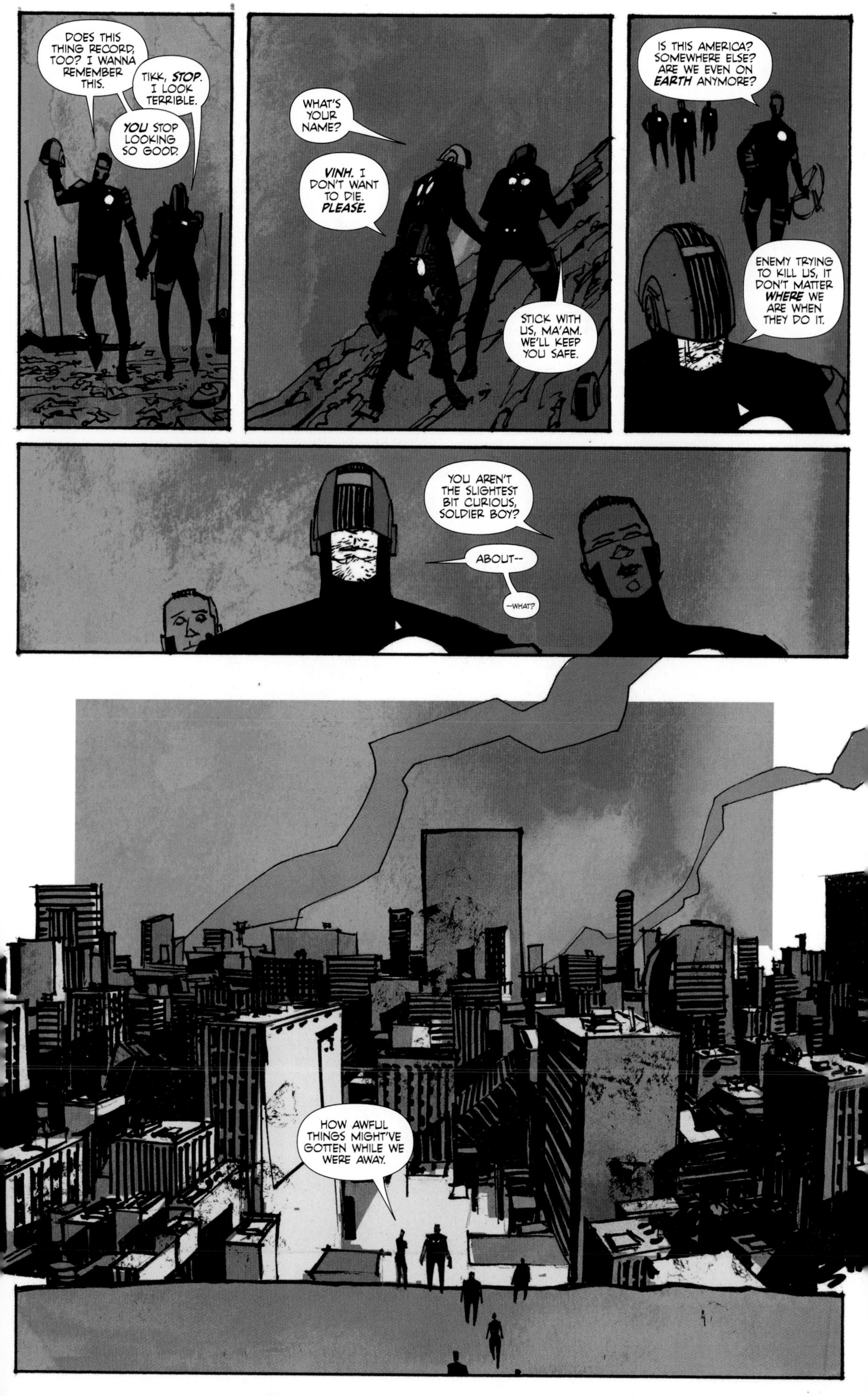
DOES THIS THING RECORD, TOO? I WANNA REMEMBER THIS.
TIKK, STOP. I LOOK TERRIBLE.
YOU STOP LOOKING SO GOOD.
WHAT'S YOUR NAME?
VINH. I DON'T WANT TO DIE. PLEASE.
STICK WITH US, MA'AM. WE'LL KEEP YOU SAFE.
IS THIS AMERICA? SOMEWHERE ELSE? ARE WE EVEN ON EARTH ANYMORE?
ENEMY TRYING TO KILL US, IT DON'T MATTER WHERE WE ARE WHEN THEY DO IT.
YOU AREN'T THE SLIGHTEST BIT CURIOUS, SOLDIER BOY?
ABOUT--
--WHAT?
HOW AWFUL THINGS MIGHT'VE GOTTEN WHILE WE WERE AWAY.

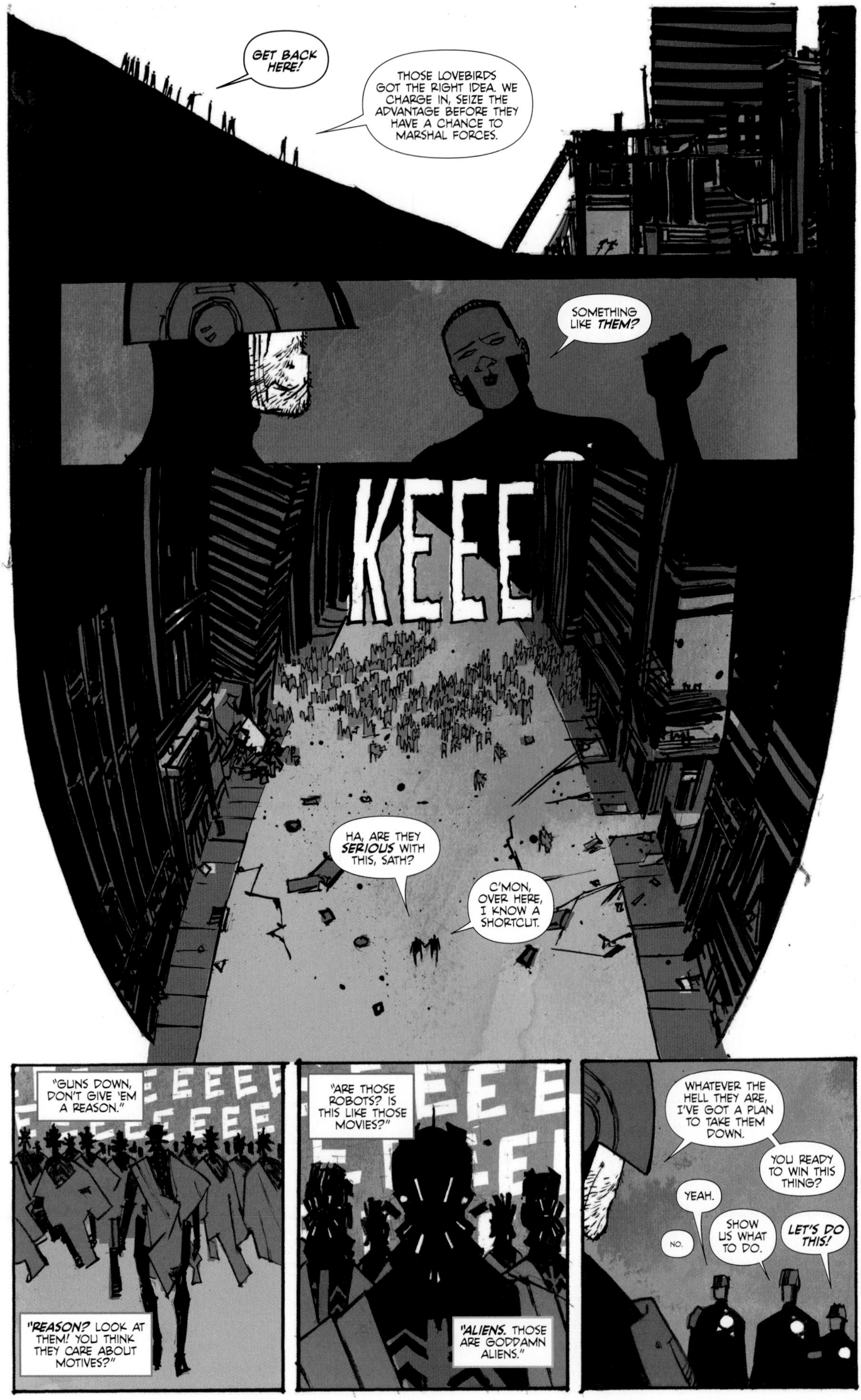
GET BACK HERE!
THOSE LOVEBIRDS GOT THE RIGHT IDEA. WE CHARGE IN, SEIZE THE ADVANTAGE BEFORE THEY HAVE A CHANCE TO MARSHAL FORCES.
SOMETHING LIKE *THEM?*
KEEE
HA, ARE THEY *SERIOUS* WITH THIS, SATH?
C'MON, OVER HERE, I KNOW A SHORTCUT.
"GUNS DOWN, DON'T GIVE 'EM A REASON."
"*REASON?* LOOK AT THEM! YOU THINK THEY CARE ABOUT MOTIVES?"
"ARE THOSE ROBOTS? IS THIS LIKE THOSE MOVIES?"
"*ALIENS.* THOSE ARE GODDAMN ALIENS."
WHATEVER THE HELL THEY ARE, I'VE GOT A PLAN TO TAKE THEM DOWN.
YOU READY TO WIN THIS THING?
YEAH.
NO.
SHOW US WHAT TO DO.
LET'S DO THIS!

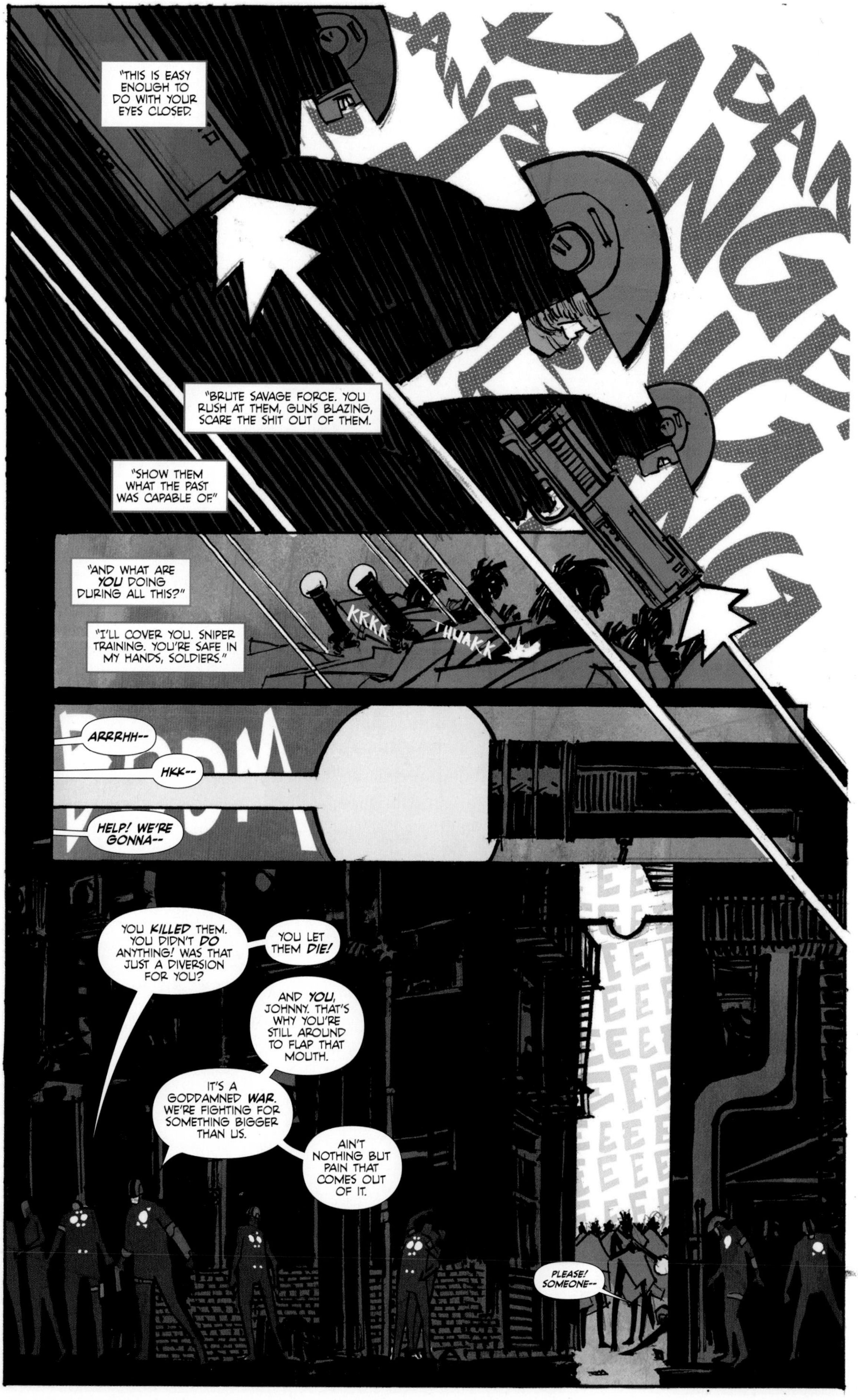

"THIS IS EASY ENOUGH TO DO WITH YOUR EYES CLOSED.
"BRUTE SAVAGE FORCE. YOU RUSH AT THEM, GUNS BLAZING, SCARE THE SHIT OUT OF THEM.
"SHOW THEM WHAT THE PAST WAS CAPABLE OF."
"AND WHAT ARE YOU DOING DURING ALL THIS?"
"I'LL COVER YOU. SNIPER TRAINING. YOU'RE SAFE IN MY HANDS, SOLDIERS."
KRKK
THUAKK
ARRRHH--
HKK--
HELP! WE'RE GONNA--
YOU KILLED THEM. YOU DIDN'T DO ANYTHING! WAS THAT JUST A DIVERSION FOR YOU?
YOU LET THEM DIE!
AND YOU, JOHNNY. THAT'S WHY YOU'RE STILL AROUND TO FLAP THAT MOUTH.
IT'S A GODDAMNED WAR. WE'RE FIGHTING FOR SOMETHING BIGGER THAN US.
AIN'T NOTHING BUT PAIN THAT COMES OUT OF IT.
PLEASE! SOMEONE--

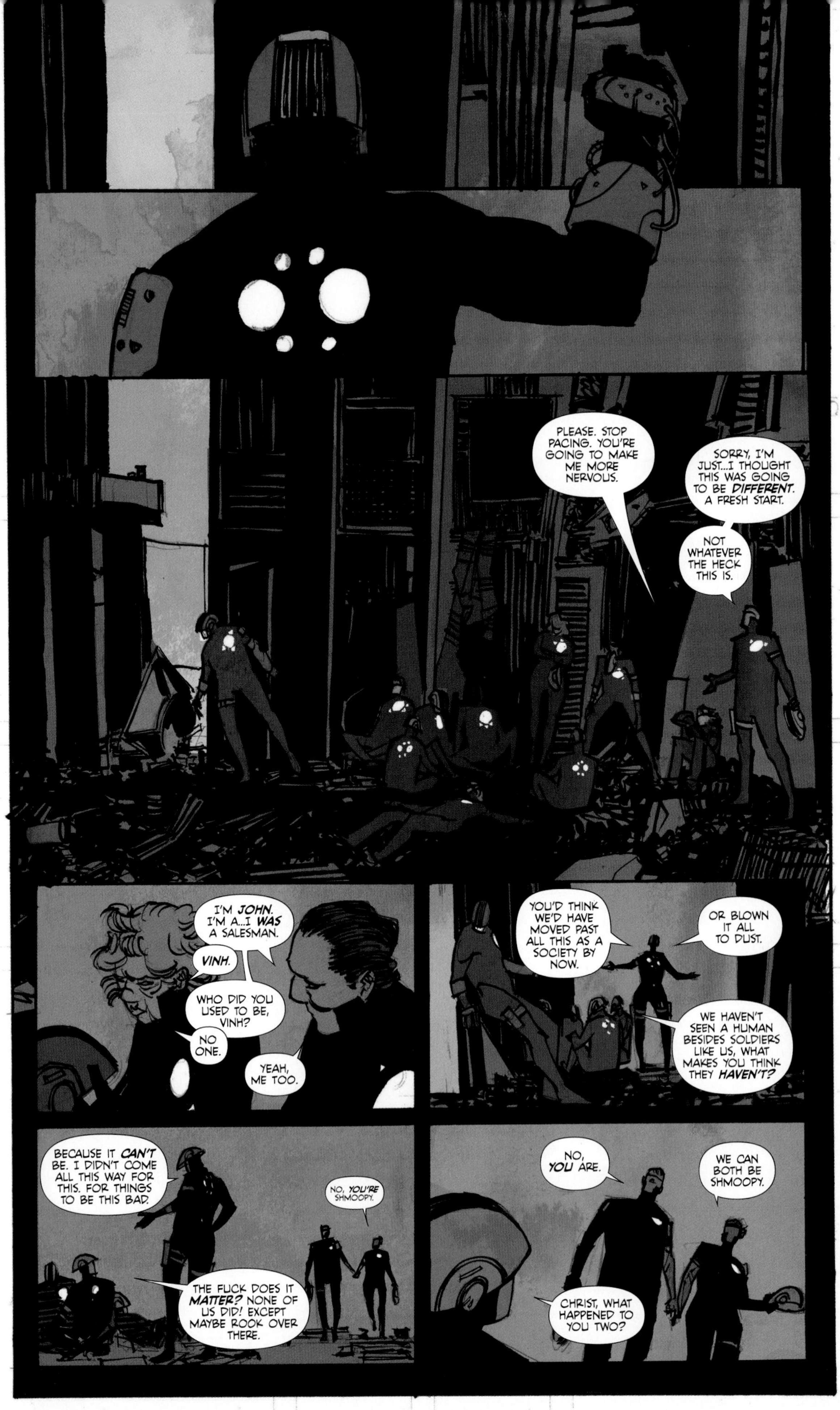
PLEASE. STOP PACING. YOU'RE GOING TO MAKE ME MORE NERVOUS.
SORRY, I'M JUST...I THOUGHT THIS WAS GOING TO BE DIFFERENT. A FRESH START.
NOT WHATEVER THE HECK THIS IS.
I'M JOHN. I'M A...I WAS A SALESMAN.
VINH.
WHO DID YOU USED TO BE, VINH?
NO ONE.
YEAH, ME TOO.
YOU'D THINK WE'D HAVE MOVED PAST ALL THIS AS A SOCIETY BY NOW.
OR BLOWN IT ALL TO DUST.
WE HAVEN'T SEEN A HUMAN BESIDES SOLDIERS LIKE US, WHAT MAKES YOU THINK THEY HAVEN'T?
BECAUSE IT CAN'T BE. I DIDN'T COME ALL THIS WAY FOR THIS. FOR THINGS TO BE THIS BAD.
NO, YOU'RE SHMOOPY.
THE FUCK DOES IT MATTER? NONE OF US DID! EXCEPT MAYBE ROOK OVER THERE.
NO, YOU ARE.
WE CAN BOTH BE SHMOOPY.
CHRIST, WHAT HAPPENED TO YOU TWO?

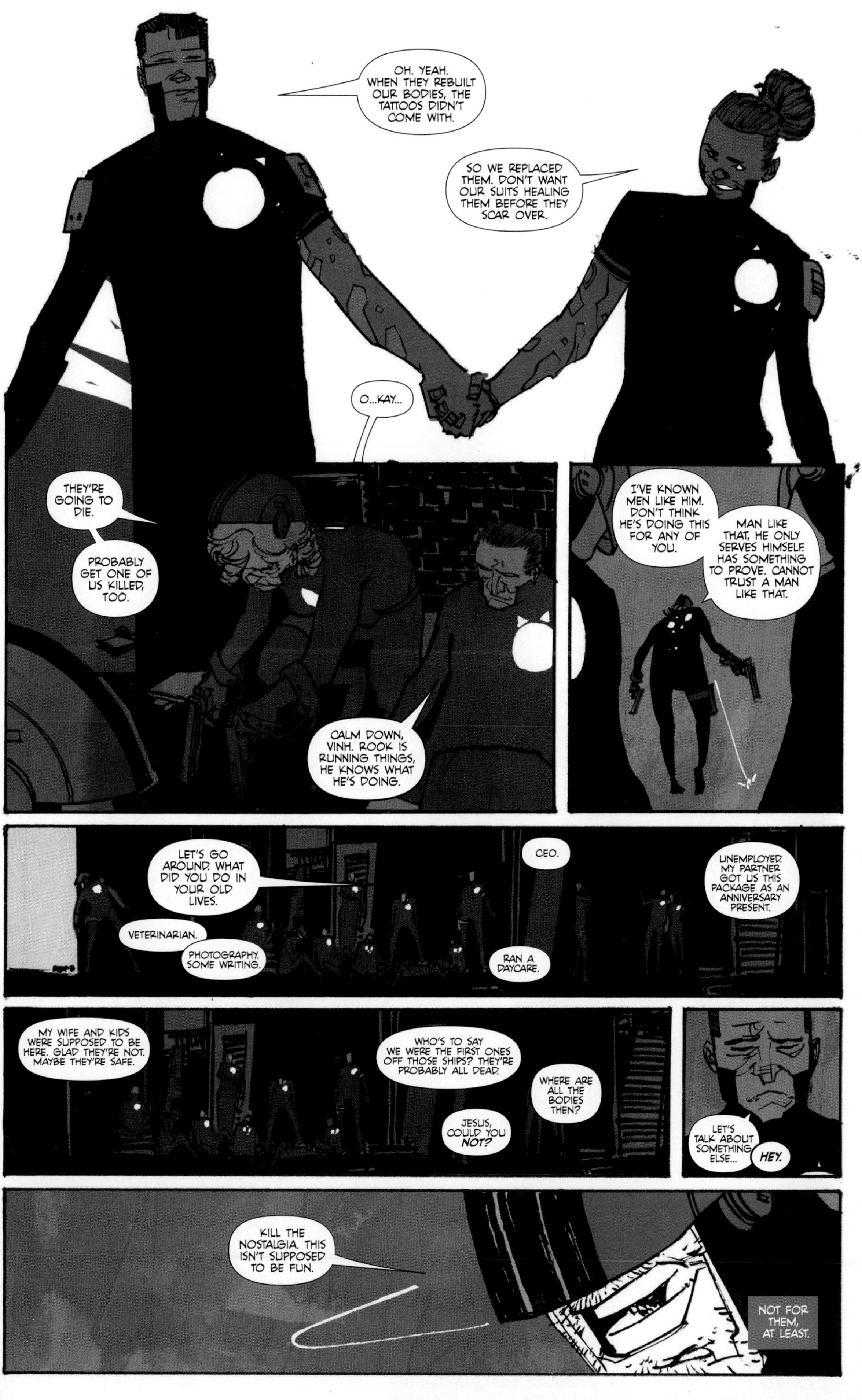
OH. YEAH. WHEN THEY REBUILT OUR BODIES, THE TATTOOS DIDN'T COME WITH.
SO WE REPLACED THEM. DON'T WANT OUR SUITS HEALING THEM BEFORE THEY SCAR OVER.
O...KAY...
THEY'RE GOING TO DIE.
PROBABLY GET ONE OF US KILLED, TOO.
CALM DOWN, VINH. ROOK IS RUNNING THINGS, HE KNOWS WHAT HE'S DOING.
I'VE KNOWN MEN LIKE HIM. DON'T THINK HE'S DOING THIS FOR ANY OF YOU.
MAN LIKE THAT, HE ONLY SERVES HIMSELF. HAS SOMETHING TO PROVE. CANNOT TRUST A MAN LIKE THAT.
LET'S GO AROUND. WHAT DID YOU DO IN YOUR OLD LIVES.
VETERINARIAN.
PHOTOGRAPHY. SOME WRITING.
CEO.
RAN A DAYCARE.
UNEMPLOYED. MY PARTNER GOT US THIS PACKAGE AS AN ANNIVERSARY PRESENT.
MY WIFE AND KIDS WERE SUPPOSED TO BE HERE. GLAD THEY'RE NOT. MAYBE THEY'RE SAFE.
WHO'S TO SAY WE WERE THE FIRST ONES OFF THOSE SHIPS? THEY'RE PROBABLY ALL DEAD.
JESUS, COULD YOU *NOT?*
WHERE ARE ALL THE BODIES THEN?
LET'S TALK ABOUT SOMETHING ELSE...
HEY.
KILL THE NOSTALGIA. THIS ISN'T SUPPOSED TO BE FUN.
NOT FOR THEM, AT LEAST.

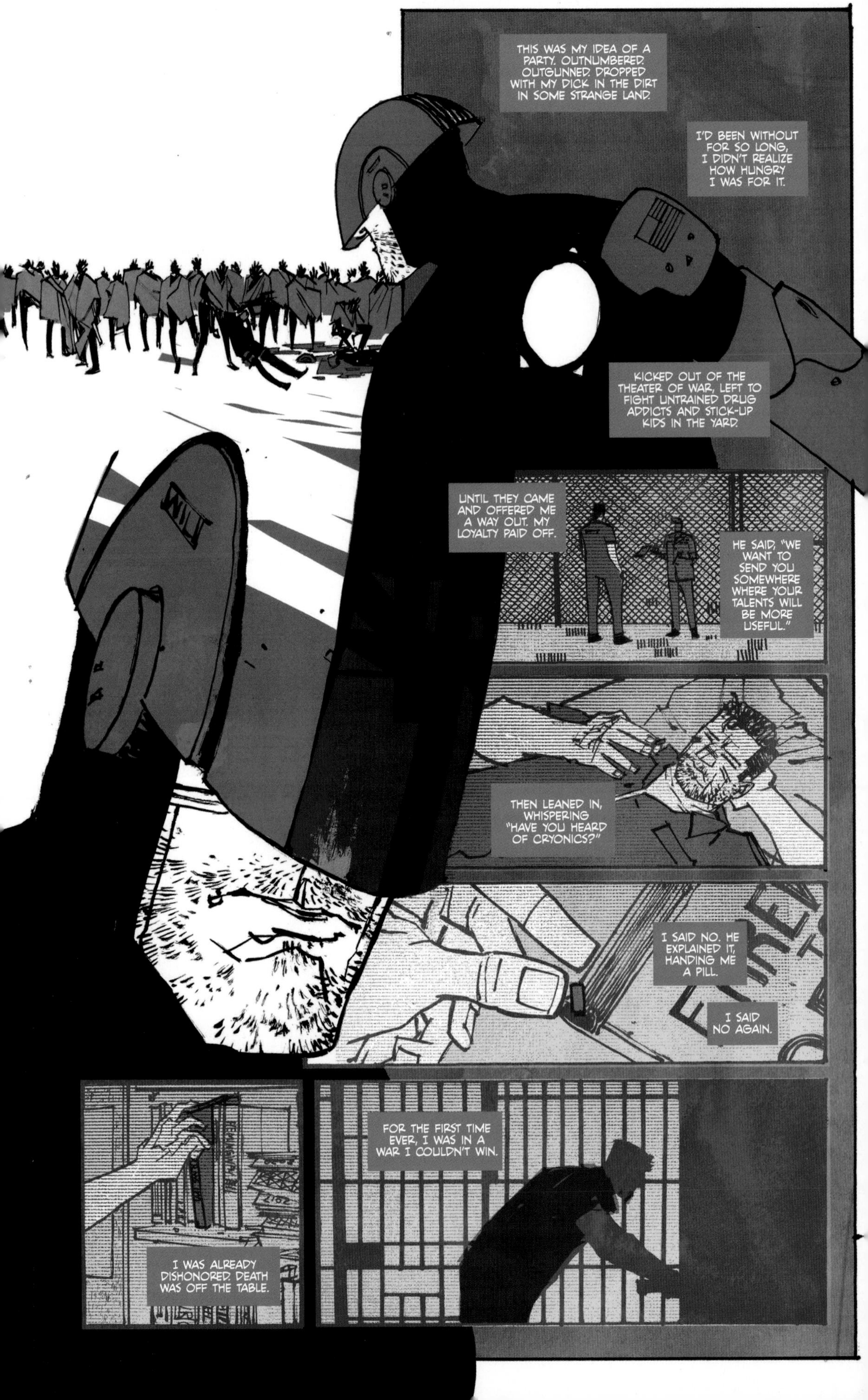
THIS WAS MY IDEA OF A PARTY. OUTNUMBERED. OUTGUNNED. DROPPED WITH MY DICK IN THE DIRT IN SOME STRANGE LAND.
I'D BEEN WITHOUT FOR SO LONG, I DIDN'T REALIZE HOW HUNGRY I WAS FOR IT.
KICKED OUT OF THE THEATER OF WAR, LEFT TO FIGHT UNTRAINED DRUG ADDICTS AND STICK-UP KIDS IN THE YARD.
UNTIL THEY CAME AND OFFERED ME A WAY OUT. MY LOYALTY PAID OFF.
HE SAID, "WE WANT TO SEND YOU SOMEWHERE WHERE YOUR TALENTS WILL BE MORE USEFUL."
THEN LEANED IN, WHISPERING "HAVE YOU HEARD OF CRYONICS?"
I SAID NO. HE EXPLAINED IT, HANDING ME A PILL.
I SAID NO AGAIN.
I WAS ALREADY DISHONORED. DEATH WAS OFF THE TABLE.
FOR THE FIRST TIME EVER, I WAS IN A WAR I COULDN'T WIN.

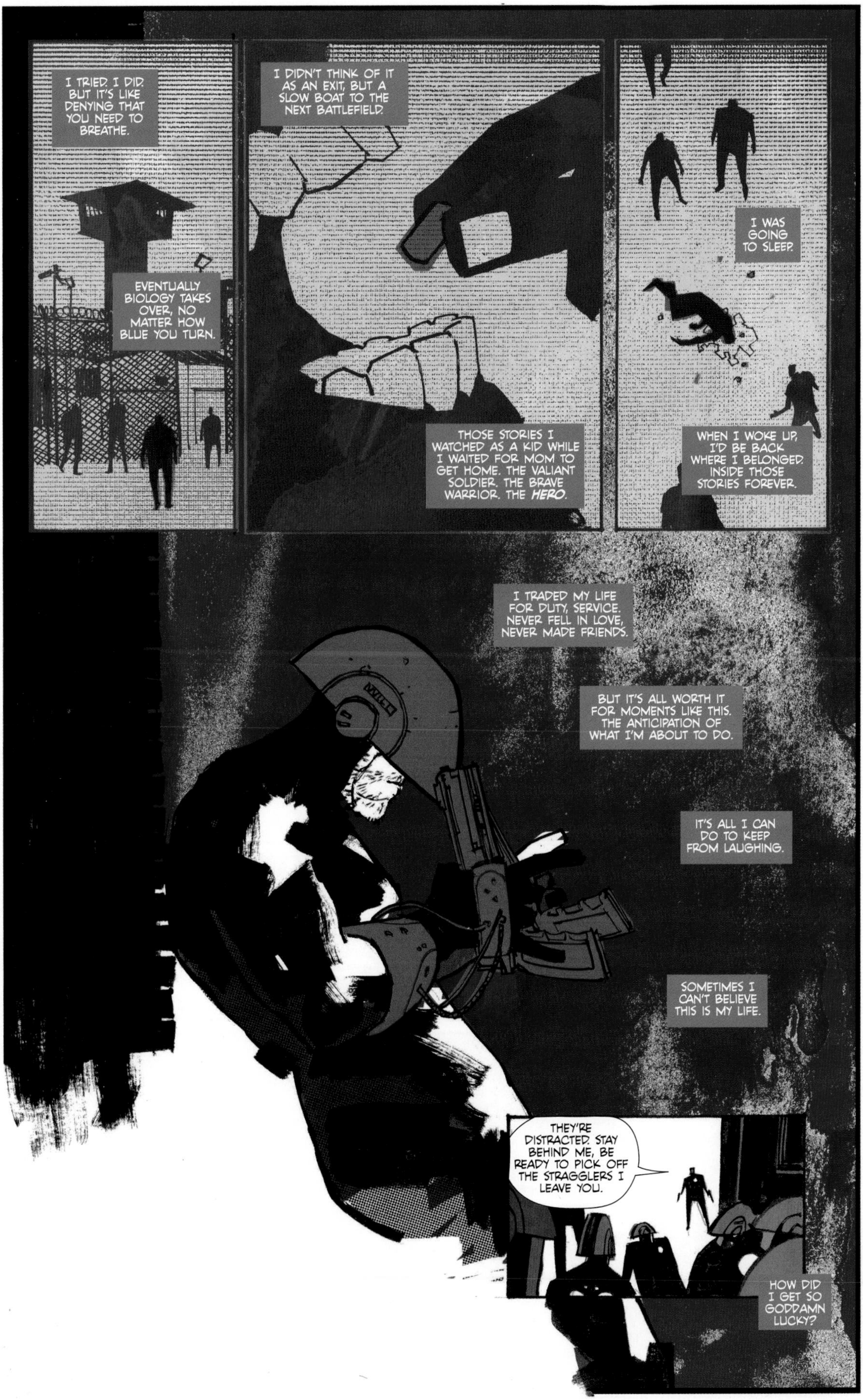
I TRIED. I DID. BUT IT'S LIKE DENYING THAT YOU NEED TO BREATHE.
EVENTUALLY BIOLOGY TAKES OVER, NO MATTER HOW BLUE YOU TURN.
I DIDN'T THINK OF IT AS AN EXIT, BUT A SLOW BOAT TO THE NEXT BATTLEFIELD.
THOSE STORIES I WATCHED AS A KID WHILE I WAITED FOR MOM TO GET HOME. THE VALIANT SOLDIER. THE BRAVE WARRIOR. THE *HERO*.
I WAS GOING TO SLEEP.
WHEN I WOKE UP, I'D BE BACK WHERE I BELONGED. INSIDE THOSE STORIES FOREVER.
I TRADED MY LIFE FOR DUTY, SERVICE. NEVER FELL IN LOVE, NEVER MADE FRIENDS.
BUT IT'S ALL WORTH IT FOR MOMENTS LIKE THIS. THE ANTICIPATION OF WHAT I'M ABOUT TO DO.
IT'S ALL I CAN DO TO KEEP FROM LAUGHING.
SOMETIMES I CAN'T BELIEVE THIS IS MY LIFE.
THEY'RE DISTRACTED. STAY BEHIND ME, BE READY TO PICK OFF THE STRAGGLERS I LEAVE YOU.
HOW DID I GET SO GODDAMN LUCKY?

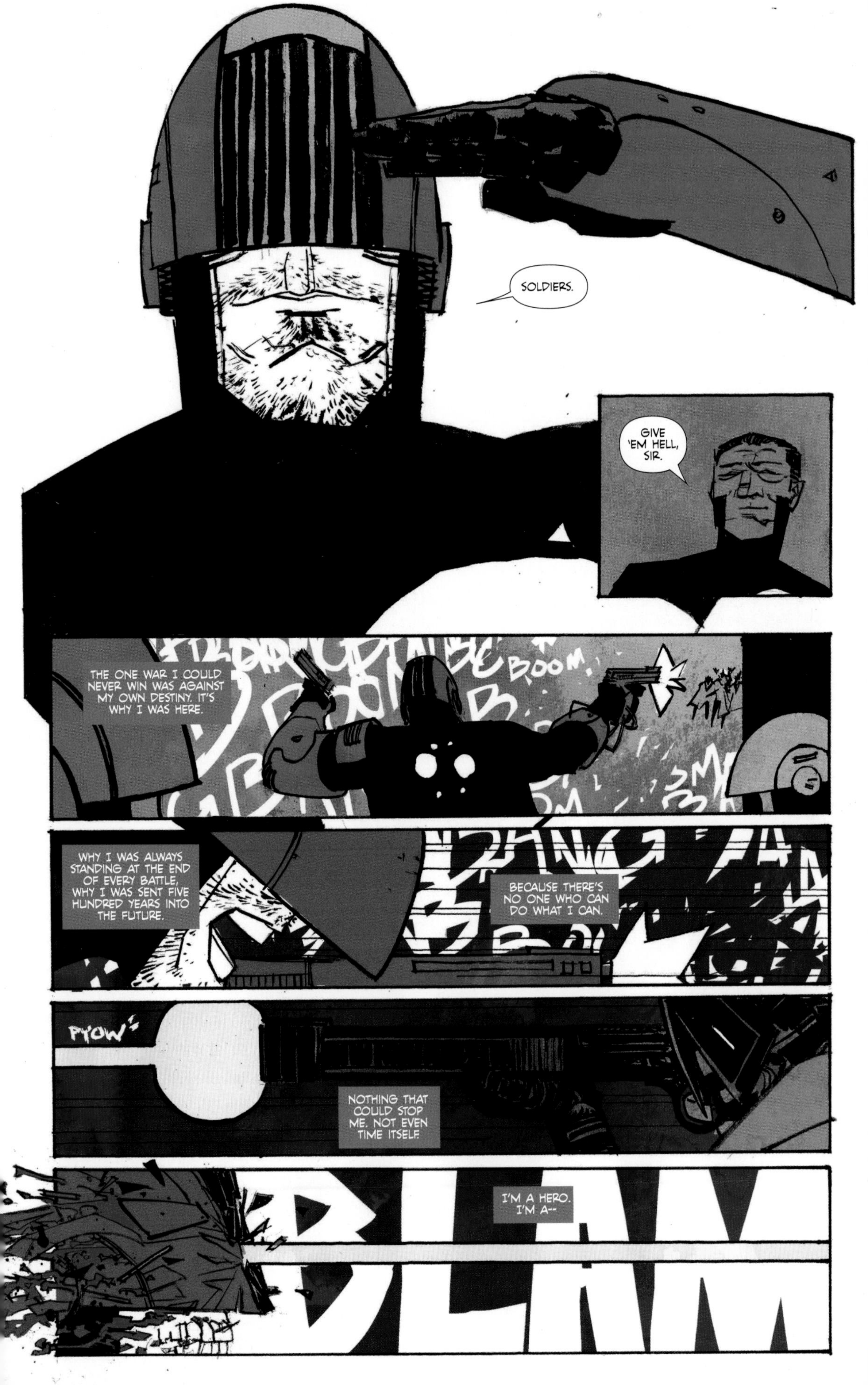
SOLDIERS.
GIVE 'EM HELL, SIR.
THE ONE WAR I COULD NEVER WIN WAS AGAINST MY OWN DESTINY. IT'S WHY I WAS HERE.
BOOM
WHY I WAS ALWAYS STANDING AT THE END OF EVERY BATTLE, WHY I WAS SENT FIVE HUNDRED YEARS INTO THE FUTURE.
BECAUSE THERE'S NO ONE WHO CAN DO WHAT I CAN.
PYOW
NOTHING THAT COULD STOP ME. NOT EVEN TIME ITSELF.
I'M A HERO. I'M A--
BLAM
BLAM

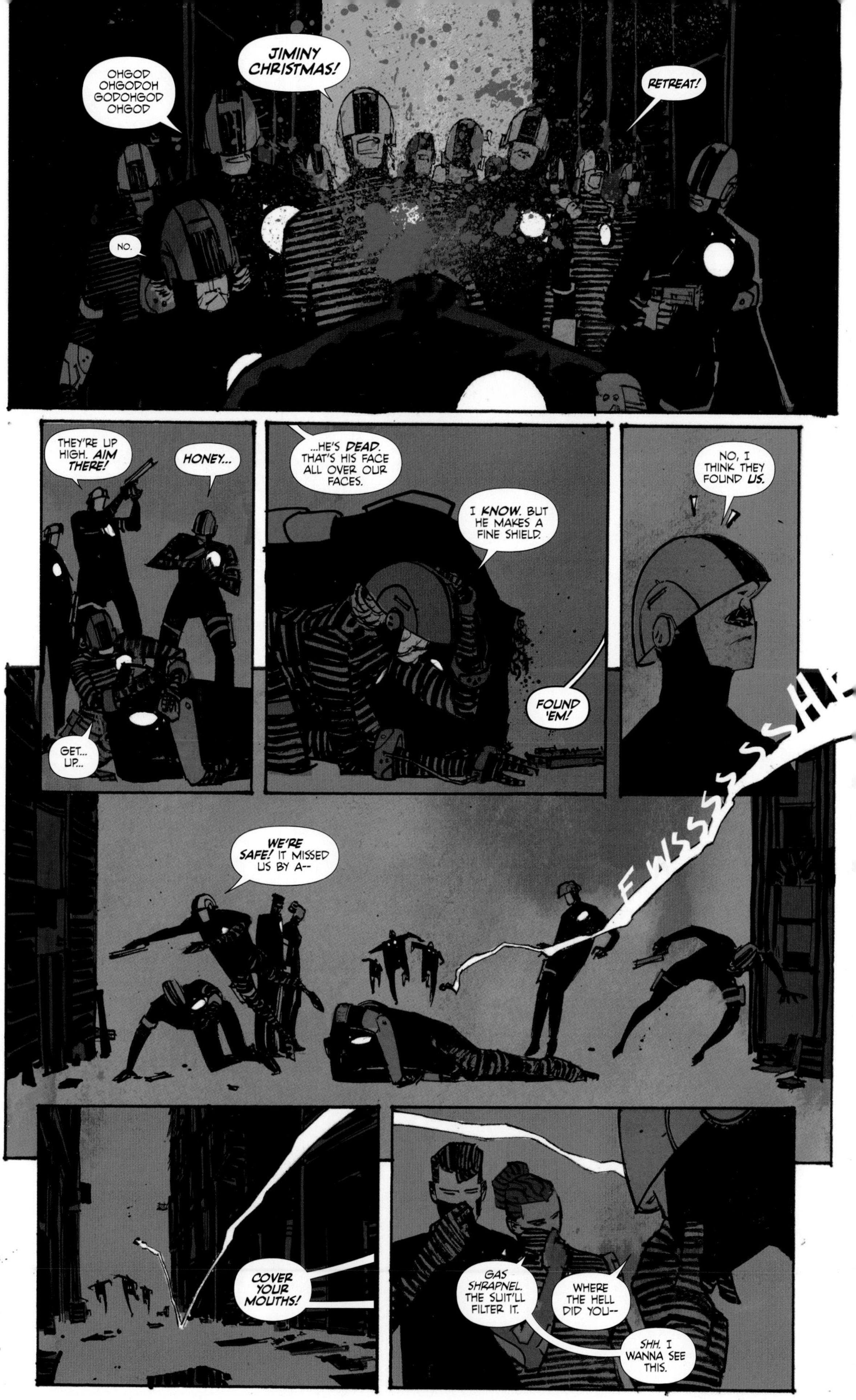
OHGOD OHGODOH GODOHGOD OHGOD
JIMINY CHRISTMAS!
RETREAT!
NO.
THEY'RE UP HIGH. AIM THERE!
HONEY...
GET... UP...
...HE'S DEAD. THAT'S HIS FACE ALL OVER OUR FACES.
I KNOW. BUT HE MAKES A FINE SHIELD.
FOUND 'EM!
NO, I THINK THEY FOUND US.
EWSSSSSSH
WE'RE SAFE! IT MISSED US BY A--
COVER YOUR MOUTHS!
GAS SHRAPNEL. THE SUIT'LL FILTER IT.
WHERE THE HELL DID YOU--
SHH. I WANNA SEE THIS.

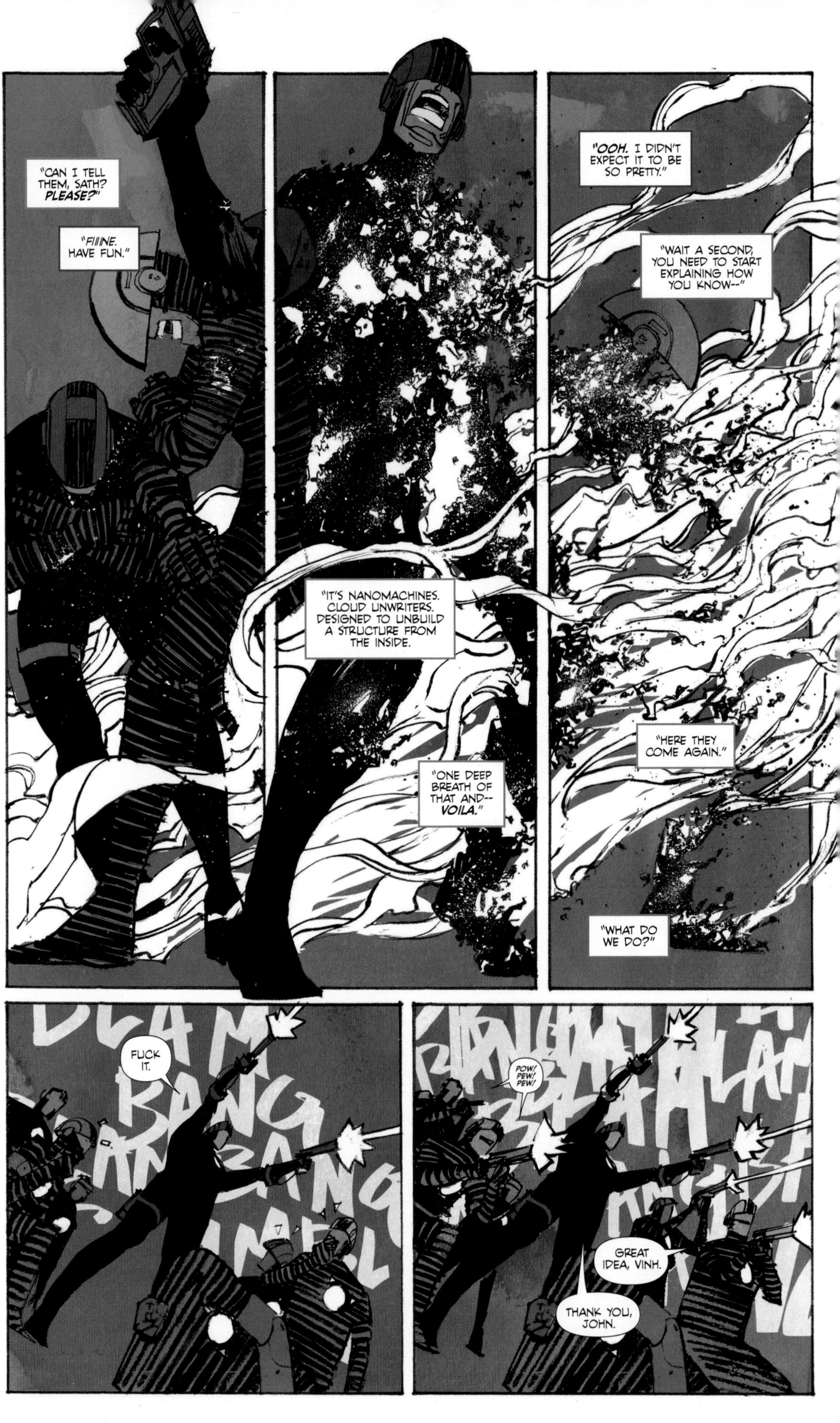
"CAN I TELL THEM, SATH? PLEASE?"
"FIIIINE. HAVE FUN."
"IT'S NANOMACHINES. CLOUD UNWRITERS. DESIGNED TO UNBUILD A STRUCTURE FROM THE INSIDE.
"ONE DEEP BREATH OF THAT AND-- VOILA."
"OOH. I DIDN'T EXPECT IT TO BE SO PRETTY."
"WAIT A SECOND, YOU NEED TO START EXPLAINING HOW YOU KNOW--"
"HERE THEY COME AGAIN."
"WHAT DO WE DO?"
FUCK IT.
BANG
POW! PEW! PEW!
GREAT IDEA, VINH.
THANK YOU, JOHN.

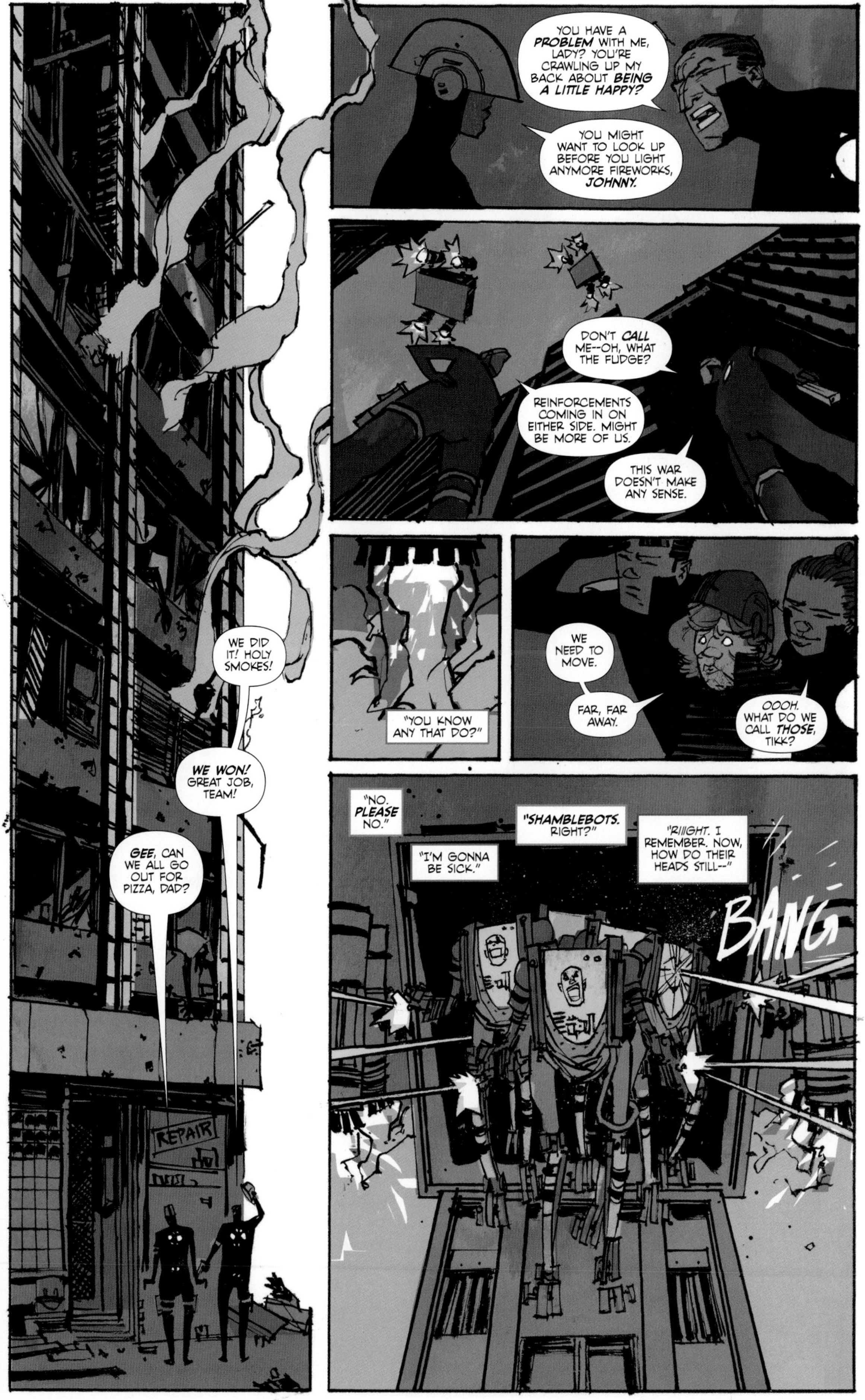
WE DID IT! HOLY SMOKES!
WE WON! GREAT JOB, TEAM!
GEE, CAN WE ALL GO OUT FOR PIZZA, DAD?
REPAIR
YOU HAVE A PROBLEM WITH ME, LADY? YOU'RE CRAWLING UP MY BACK ABOUT BEING A LITTLE HAPPY?
YOU MIGHT WANT TO LOOK UP BEFORE YOU LIGHT ANYMORE FIREWORKS, JOHNNY.
DON'T CALL ME--OH, WHAT THE FUDGE?
REINFORCEMENTS COMING IN ON EITHER SIDE. MIGHT BE MORE OF US.
THIS WAR DOESN'T MAKE ANY SENSE.
"YOU KNOW ANY THAT DO?"
WE NEED TO MOVE.
FAR, FAR AWAY.
OOOH. WHAT DO WE CALL THOSE, TIKK?
"NO. PLEASE NO."
"I'M GONNA BE SICK."
"SHAMBLEBOTS. RIGHT?"
"RIIIGHT. I REMEMBER. NOW, HOW DO THEIR HEADS STILL--"
BANG

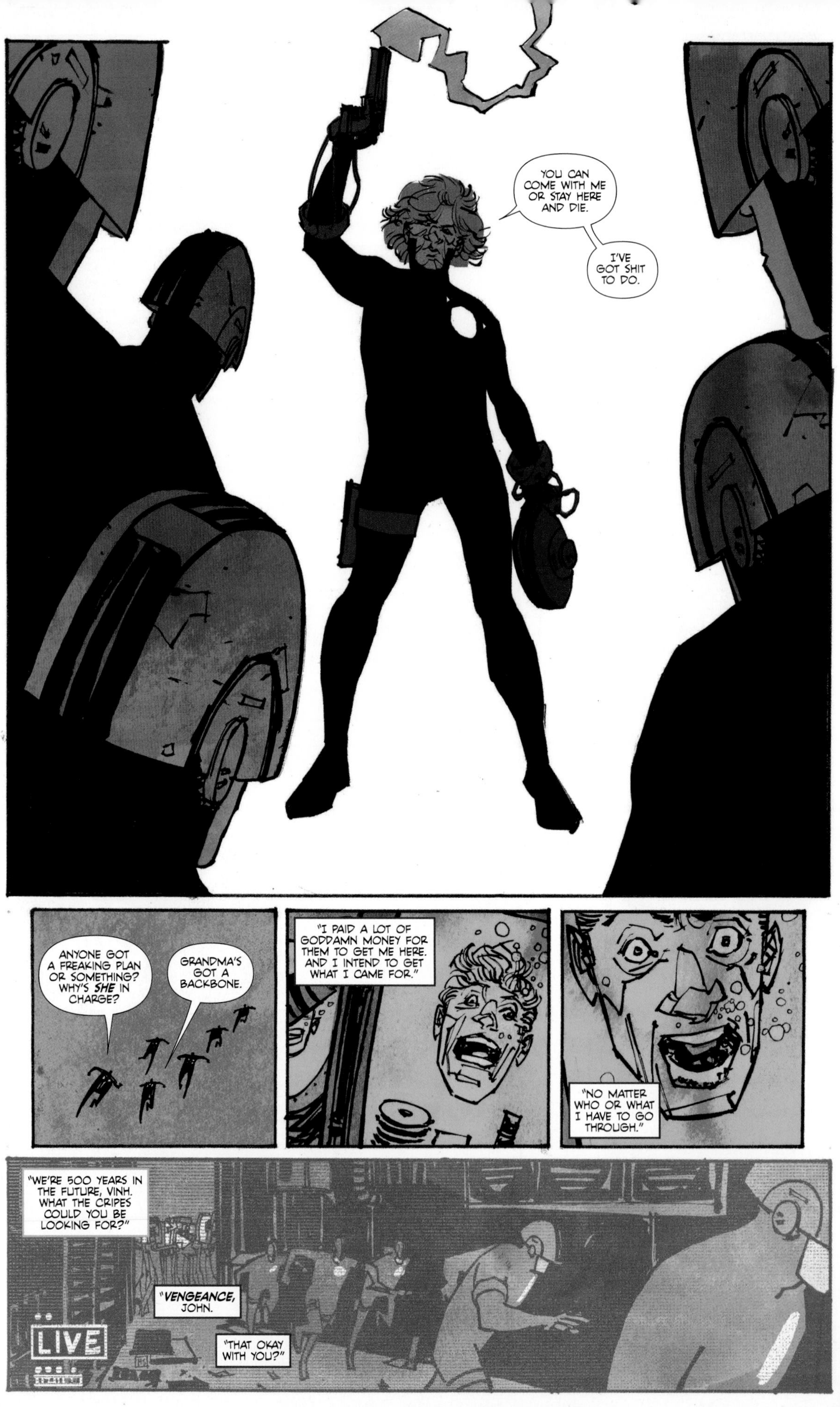
YOU CAN COME WITH ME OR STAY HERE AND DIE.
I'VE GOT SHIT TO DO.
ANYONE GOT A FREAKING PLAN OR SOMETHING? WHY'S *SHE* IN CHARGE?
GRANDMA'S GOT A BACKBONE.
"I PAID A LOT OF GODDAMN MONEY FOR THEM TO GET ME HERE. AND I INTEND TO GET WHAT I CAME FOR."
"NO MATTER WHO OR WHAT I HAVE TO GO THROUGH."
"WE'RE 500 YEARS IN THE FUTURE, VINH. WHAT THE CRIPES COULD YOU BE LOOKING FOR?"
"*VENGEANCE*, JOHN.
"THAT OKAY WITH YOU?"
LIVE

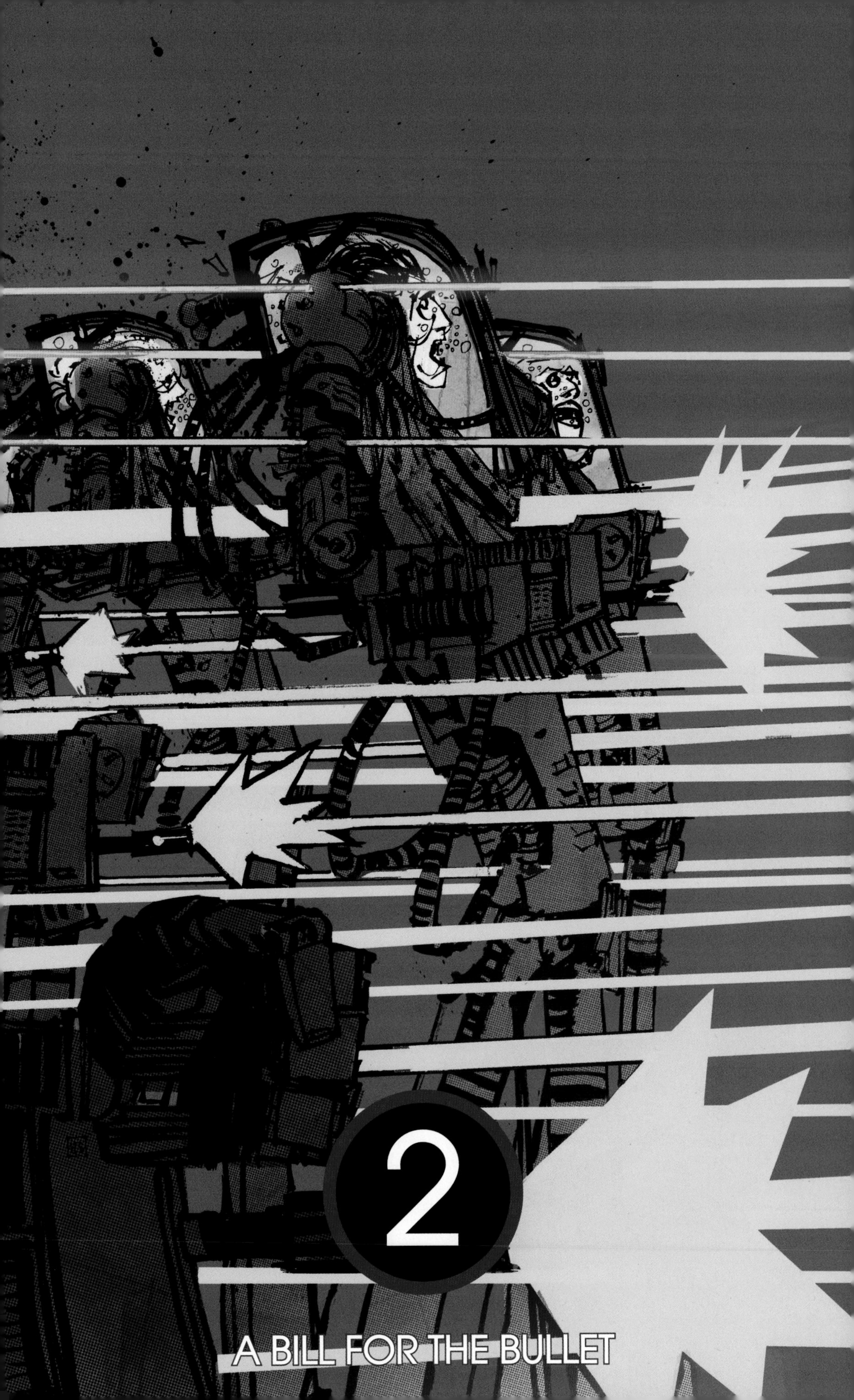

2

A BILL FOR THE BULLET

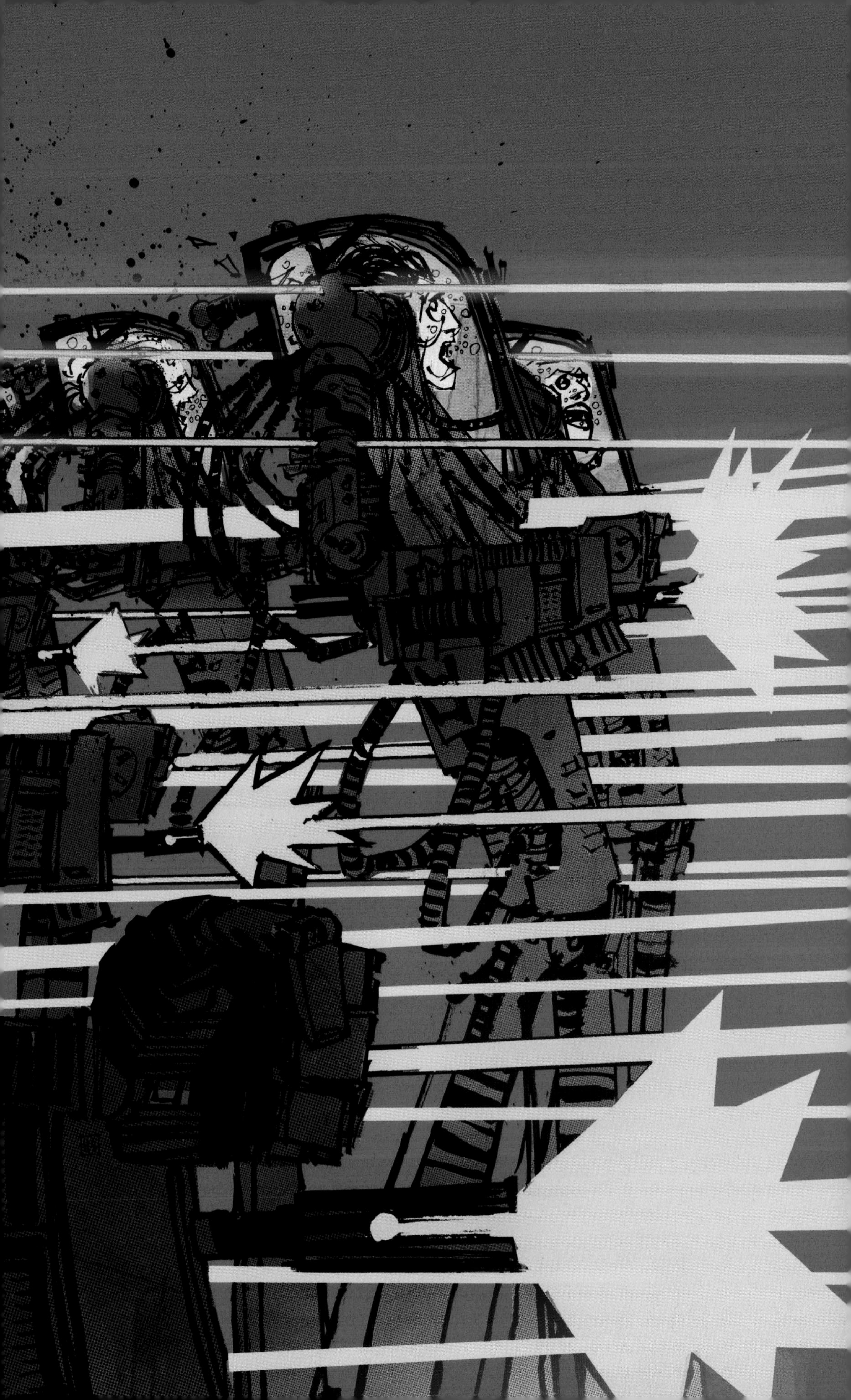

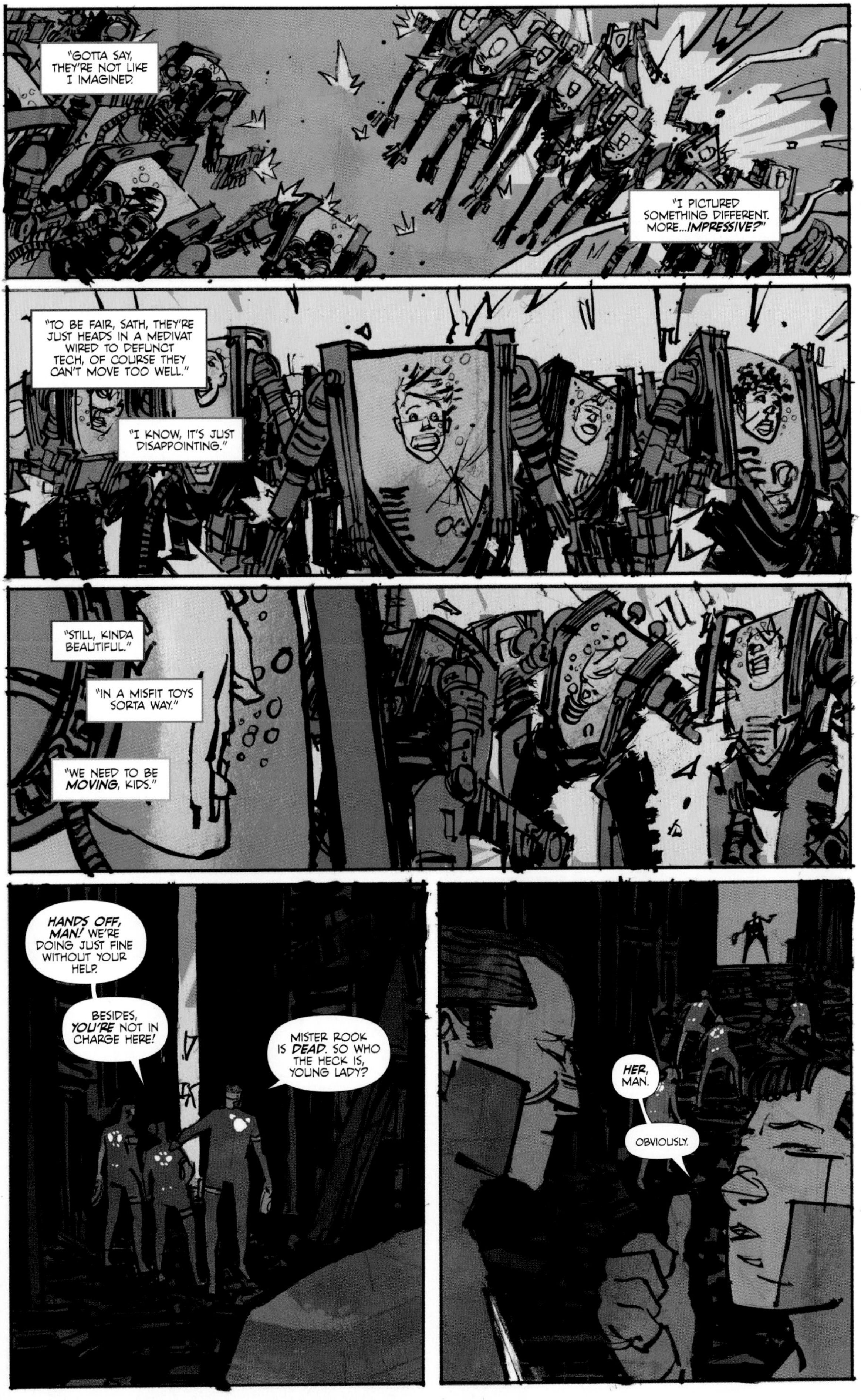
"GOTTA SAY, THEY'RE NOT LIKE I IMAGINED.
"I PICTURED SOMETHING DIFFERENT. MORE...IMPRESSIVE?"
"TO BE FAIR, SATH, THEY'RE JUST HEADS IN A MEDIVAT WIRED TO DEFUNCT TECH, OF COURSE THEY CAN'T MOVE TOO WELL."
"I KNOW, IT'S JUST DISAPPOINTING."
"STILL, KINDA BEAUTIFUL."
"IN A MISFIT TOYS SORTA WAY."
"WE NEED TO BE MOVING, KIDS."
HANDS OFF, MAN! WE'RE DOING JUST FINE WITHOUT YOUR HELP.
BESIDES, YOU'RE NOT IN CHARGE HERE!
MISTER ROOK IS DEAD. SO WHO THE HECK IS, YOUNG LADY?
HER, MAN.
OBVIOUSLY.

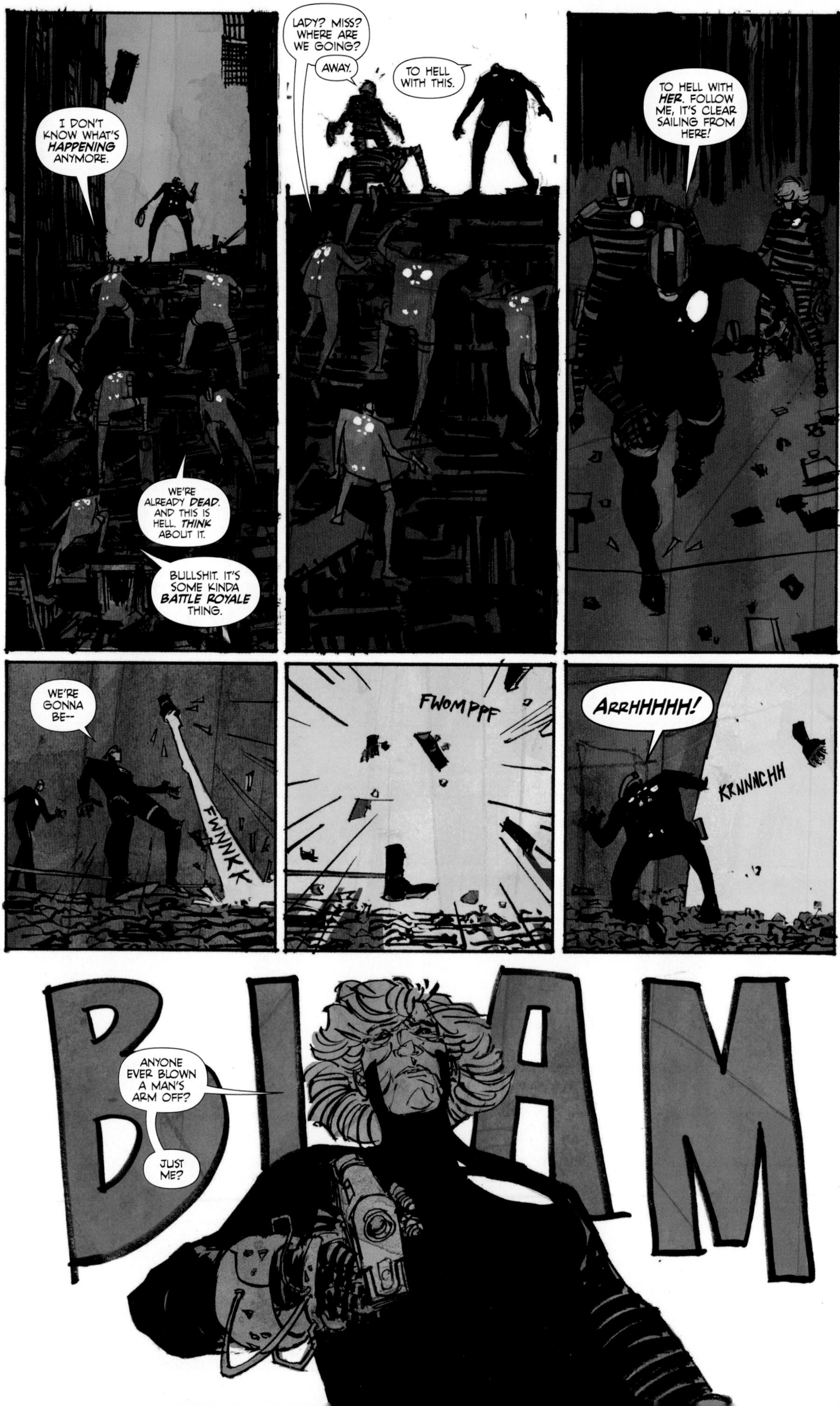
I DON'T KNOW WHAT'S HAPPENING ANYMORE.
WE'RE ALREADY DEAD. AND THIS IS HELL. THINK ABOUT IT.
BULLSHIT. IT'S SOME KINDA BATTLE ROYALE THING.
LADY? MISS? WHERE ARE WE GOING?
AWAY.
TO HELL WITH THIS.
TO HELL WITH HER. FOLLOW ME, IT'S CLEAR SAILING FROM HERE!
WE'RE GONNA BE--
FWNNKK
FWOMPPF
ARRHHHHH!
KRNNNCHH
BLAM
ANYONE EVER BLOWN A MAN'S ARM OFF?
JUST ME?

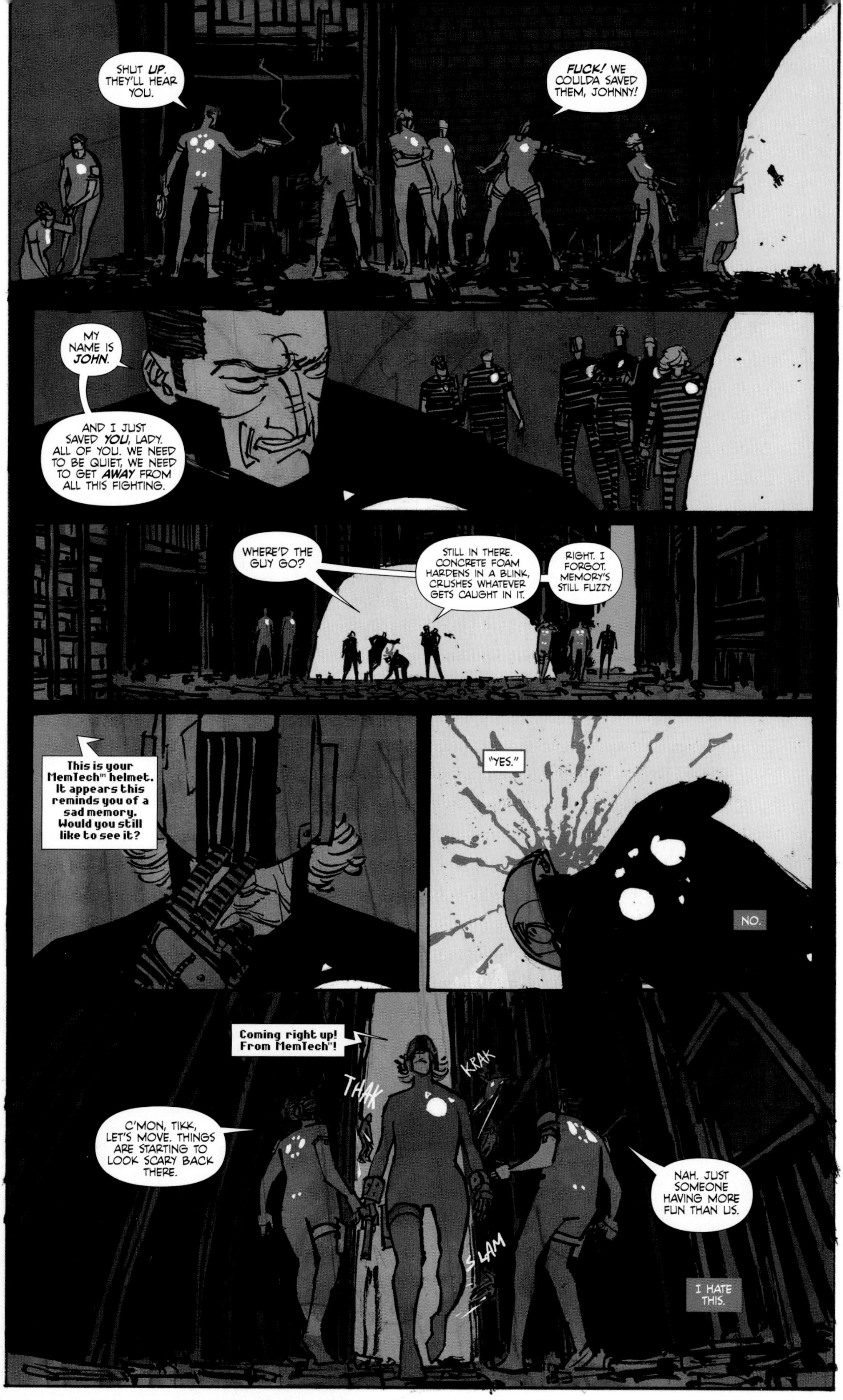
SHUT UP. THEY'LL HEAR YOU.
FUCK! WE COULDA SAVED THEM, JOHNNY!
MY NAME IS JOHN.
AND I JUST SAVED YOU, LADY. ALL OF YOU. WE NEED TO BE QUIET, WE NEED TO GET AWAY FROM ALL THIS FIGHTING.
WHERE'D THE GUY GO?
STILL IN THERE. CONCRETE FOAM HARDENS IN A BLINK, CRUSHES WHATEVER GETS CAUGHT IN IT.
RIGHT. I FORGOT. MEMORY'S STILL FUZZY.
This is your MemTech™ helmet. It appears this reminds you of a sad memory. Would you still like to see it?
"YES."
NO.
Coming right up! From MemTech™!
THAK
KRAK
C'MON, TIKK, LET'S MOVE. THINGS ARE STARTING TO LOOK SCARY BACK THERE.
NAH. JUST SOMEONE HAVING MORE FUN THAN US.
SLAM
I HATE THIS.

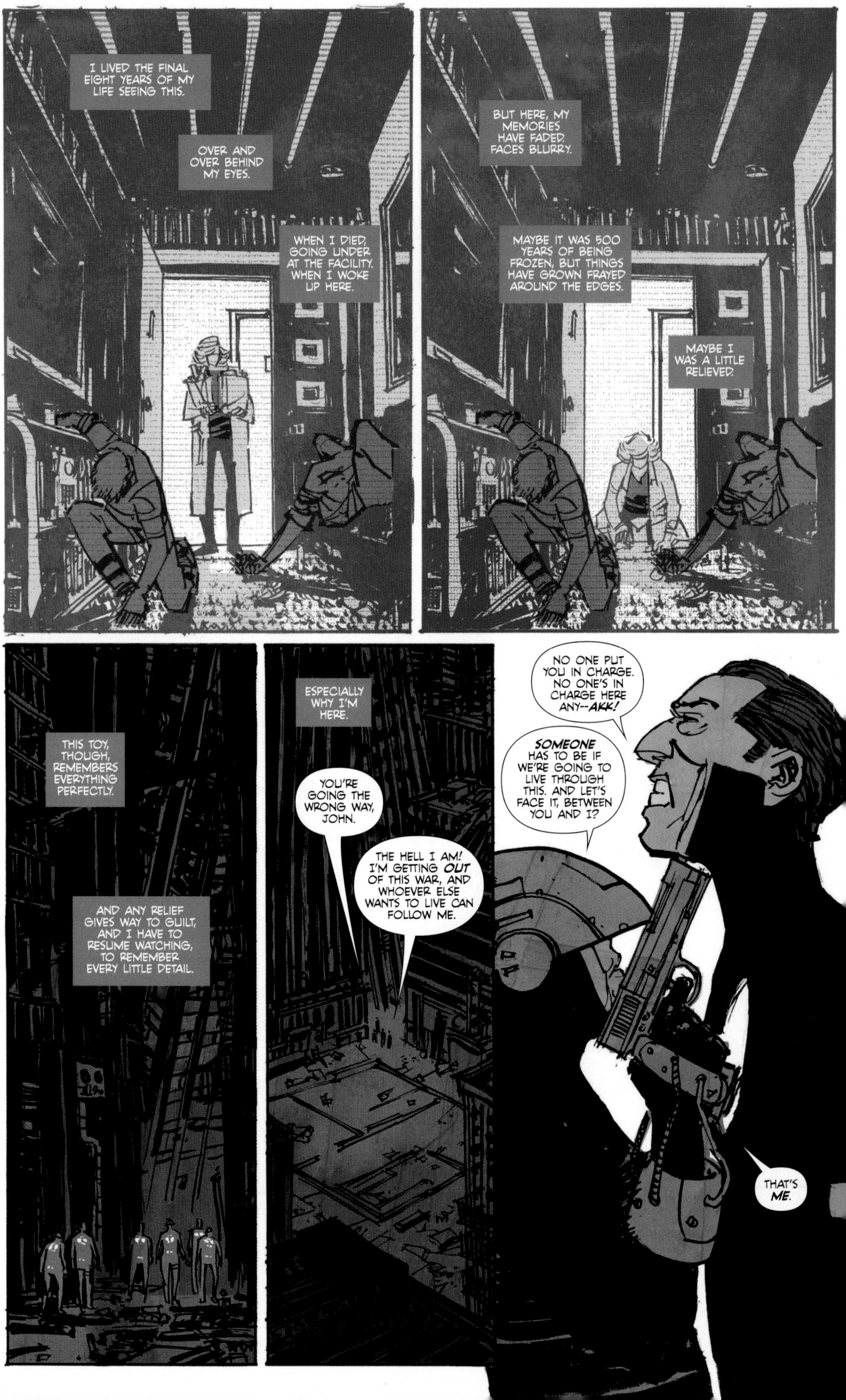
I LIVED THE FINAL EIGHT YEARS OF MY LIFE SEEING THIS.
OVER AND OVER BEHIND MY EYES.
WHEN I DIED, GOING UNDER AT THE FACILITY. WHEN I WOKE UP HERE.
BUT HERE, MY MEMORIES HAVE FADED. FACES BLURRY.
MAYBE IT WAS 500 YEARS OF BEING FROZEN, BUT THINGS HAVE GROWN FRAYED AROUND THE EDGES.
MAYBE I WAS A LITTLE RELIEVED.
THIS TOY, THOUGH, REMEMBERS EVERYTHING PERFECTLY.
AND ANY RELIEF GIVES WAY TO GUILT, AND I HAVE TO RESUME WATCHING, TO REMEMBER EVERY LITTLE DETAIL.
ESPECIALLY WHY I'M HERE.
YOU'RE GOING THE WRONG WAY, JOHN.
THE HELL I AM! I'M GETTING *OUT* OF THIS WAR, AND WHOEVER ELSE WANTS TO LIVE CAN FOLLOW ME.
NO ONE PUT YOU IN CHARGE. NO ONE'S IN CHARGE HERE ANY--*AKK!*
SOMEONE HAS TO BE IF WE'RE GOING TO LIVE THROUGH THIS. AND LET'S FACE IT, BETWEEN YOU AND I?
THAT'S *ME*.

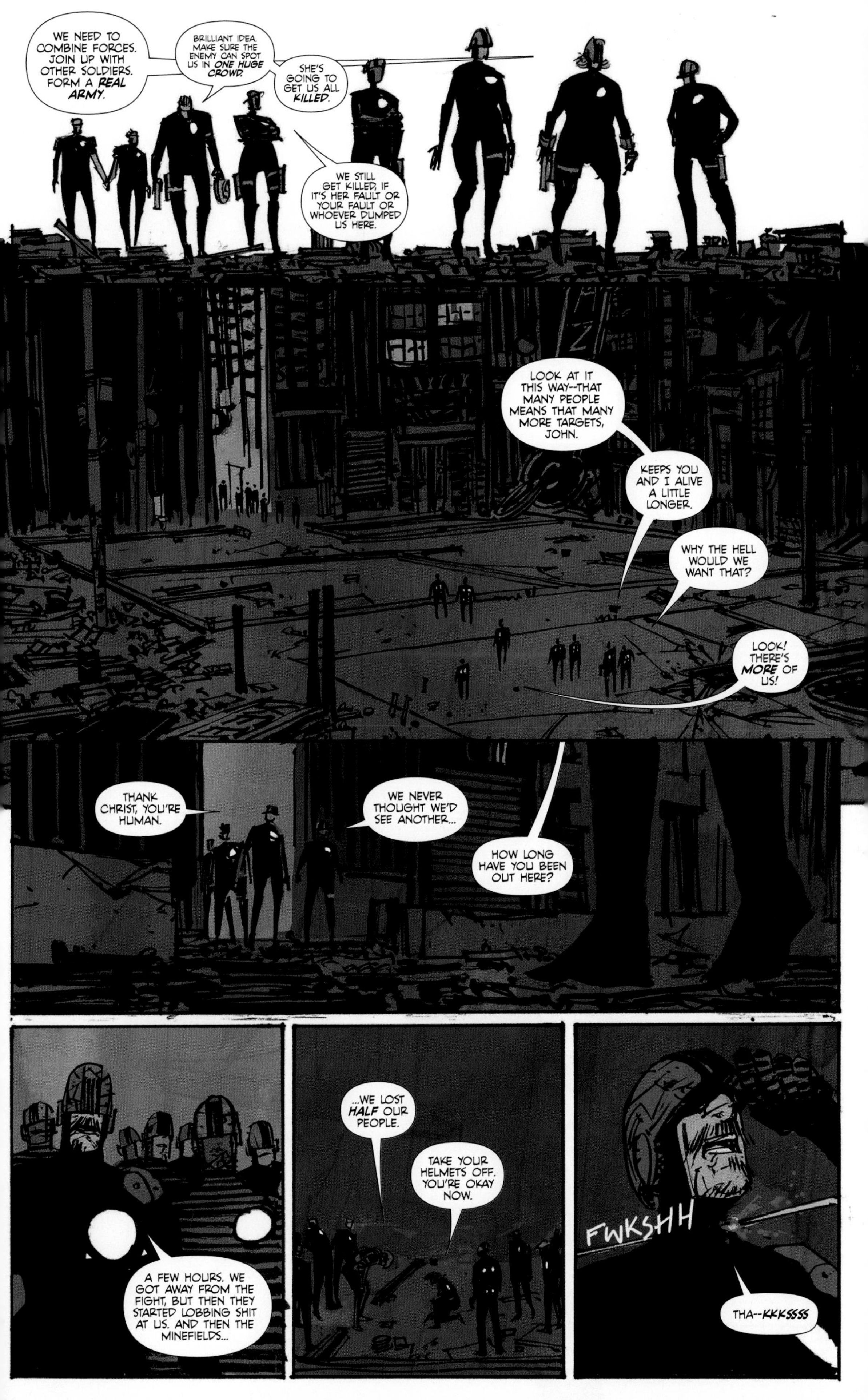
WE NEED TO COMBINE FORCES. JOIN UP WITH OTHER SOLDIERS. FORM A **REAL ARMY**.
BRILLIANT IDEA. MAKE SURE THE ENEMY CAN SPOT US IN **ONE HUGE CROWD**.
SHE'S GOING TO GET US ALL **KILLED**.
WE STILL GET KILLED, IF IT'S HER FAULT OR YOUR FAULT OR WHOEVER DUMPED US HERE.
LOOK AT IT THIS WAY--THAT MANY PEOPLE MEANS THAT MANY MORE TARGETS, JOHN.
KEEPS YOU AND I ALIVE A LITTLE LONGER.
WHY THE HELL WOULD WE WANT THAT?
LOOK! THERE'S **MORE** OF US!
THANK CHRIST, YOU'RE HUMAN.
WE NEVER THOUGHT WE'D SEE ANOTHER...
HOW LONG HAVE YOU BEEN OUT HERE?
A FEW HOURS. WE GOT AWAY FROM THE FIGHT, BUT THEN THEY STARTED LOBBING SHIT AT US. AND THEN THE MINEFIELDS...
...WE LOST **HALF** OUR PEOPLE.
TAKE YOUR HELMETS OFF. YOU'RE OKAY NOW.
FWKSHH
THA--**KKKSSSS**

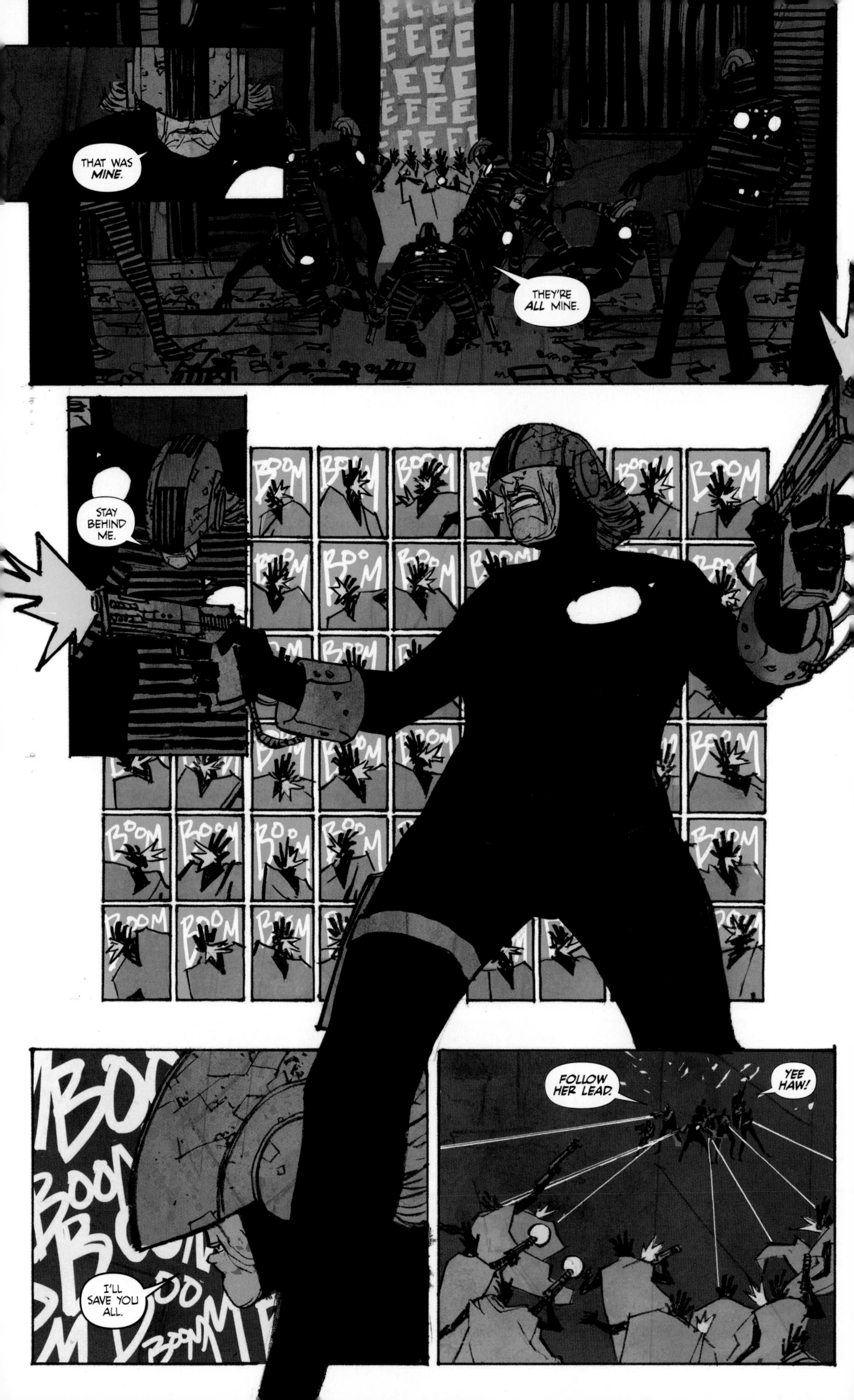
EEEEE
THAT WAS MINE.
THEY'RE ALL MINE.
STAY BEHIND ME.
BOOM
I'LL SAVE YOU ALL.
FOLLOW HER LEAD.
YEE HAW!

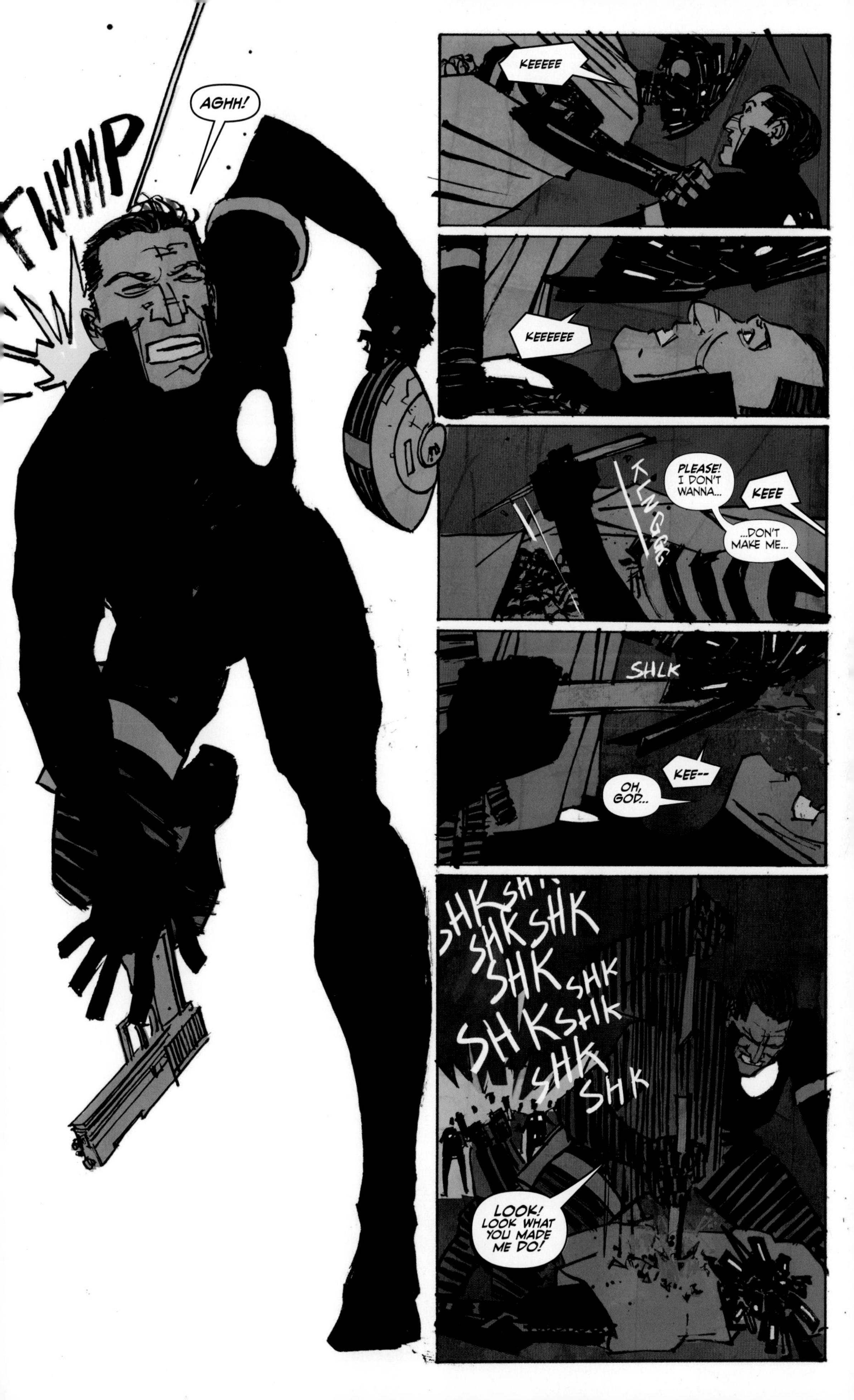
FWMMP
AGHH!
KEEEEE
KEEEEEE
KLNGGG
PLEASE! I DON'T WANNA...
KEEE
...DON'T MAKE ME...
SHLK
KEE--
OH, GOD...
SHK SHK SHK SHK SHK SHK SHK SHK SHK SHK SHK
LOOK! LOOK WHAT YOU MADE ME DO!

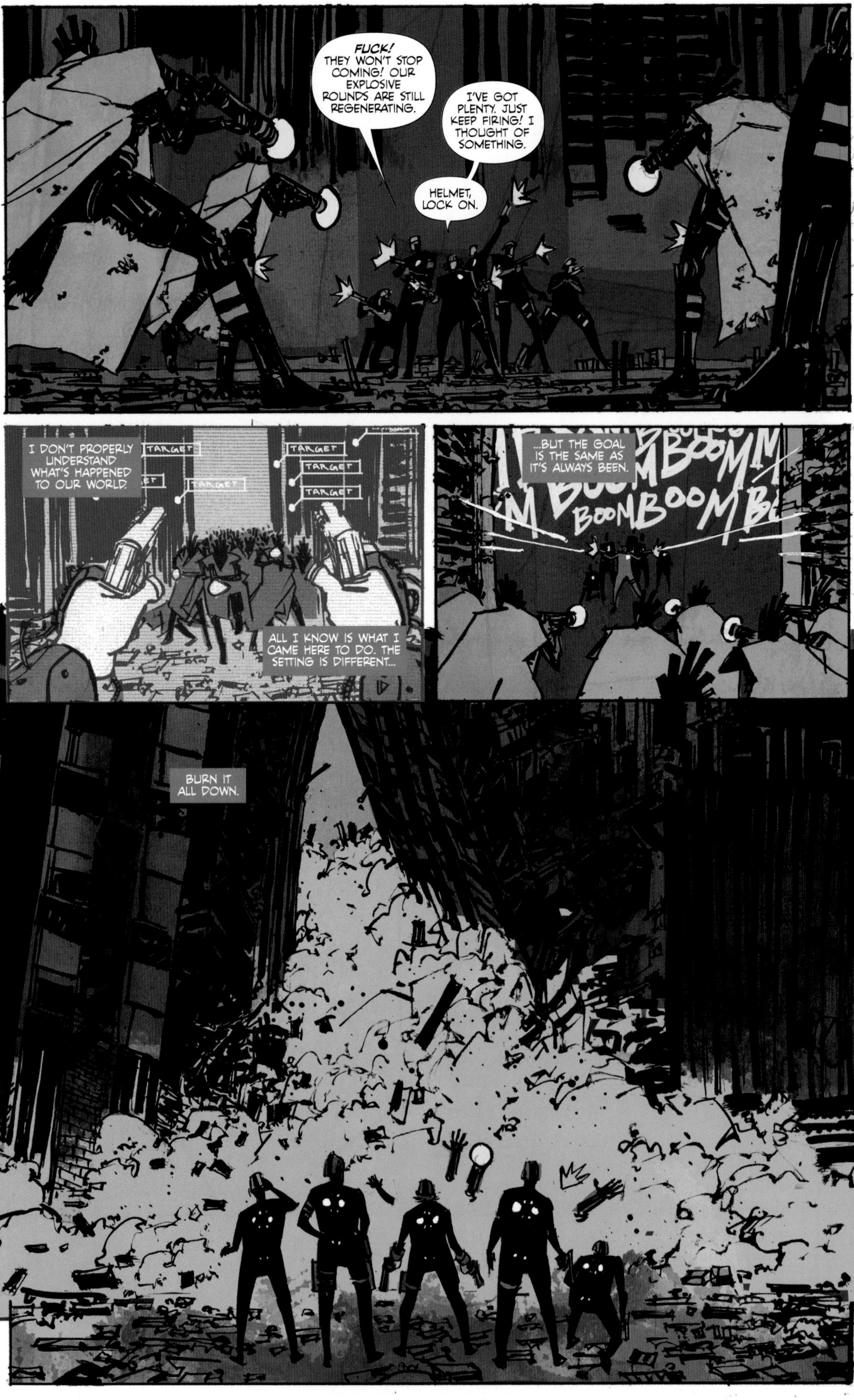

FUCK! THEY WON'T STOP COMING! OUR EXPLOSIVE ROUNDS ARE STILL REGENERATING.
I'VE GOT PLENTY. JUST KEEP FIRING! I THOUGHT OF SOMETHING.
HELMET, LOCK ON.
I DON'T PROPERLY UNDERSTAND WHAT'S HAPPENED TO OUR WORLD.
TARGET
TARGET
TARGET
TARGET
TARGET
ALL I KNOW IS WHAT I CAME HERE TO DO. THE SETTING IS DIFFERENT...
...BUT THE GOAL IS THE SAME AS IT'S ALWAYS BEEN.
BOOMBOOM
BOOMBOOM
BURN IT ALL DOWN.

I HAVE TO SAY, VINH, YOU'RE AN ABSOLUTE TERROR.

AND I *LOVE* IT.

WHAT DID YOU DO IN YOUR OLD LIFE ANYWAY?

I KEPT A HOME. I RAISED TWO BEAUTIFUL CHILDREN.

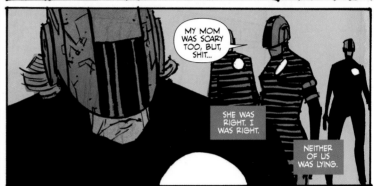

MY MOM WAS SCARY TOO, BUT, SHIT...

SHE WAS RIGHT. I WAS RIGHT.

NEITHER OF US WAS LYING.

I WAS AN ABSOLUTE TERROR.

THE POWER BEHIND THE THRONE.

MY HUSBAND'S THRONE.

HE OPENED HIS MOUTH, TOLD MEN WHERE TO GO, WHAT TO STEAL, WHO TO KILL.

BUT IT WAS I WHO PUT THE THOUGHT IN HIS HEAD, POINTED HIM TO THE NEXT PLATEAU.

TO THE WORLD, BY DESIGN, I WAS ONLY A MOTHER, A WIFE. A DISGUISE I GREW TO ACCEPT.

BUT ONE I NEVER STOPPED RESENTING.

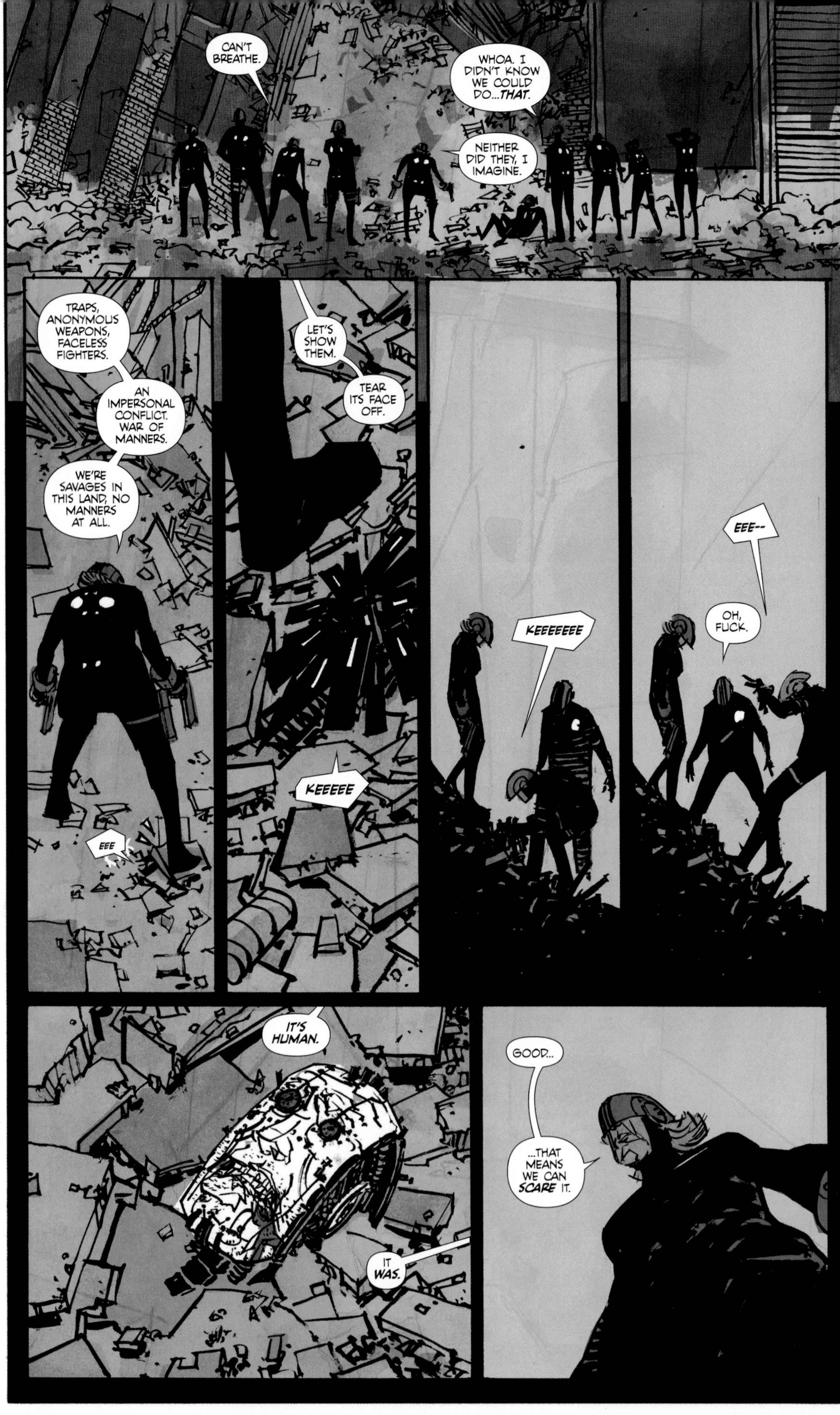
CAN'T BREATHE.
WHOA. I DIDN'T KNOW WE COULD DO...THAT.
NEITHER DID THEY, I IMAGINE.
TRAPS, ANONYMOUS WEAPONS, FACELESS FIGHTERS.
AN IMPERSONAL CONFLICT. WAR OF MANNERS.
WE'RE SAVAGES IN THIS LAND, NO MANNERS AT ALL.
EEE
LET'S SHOW THEM.
TEAR ITS FACE OFF.
KEEEEE
KEEEEEEE
EEE--
OH, FUCK.
IT'S HUMAN.
IT WAS.
GOOD...
...THAT MEANS WE CAN SCARE IT.

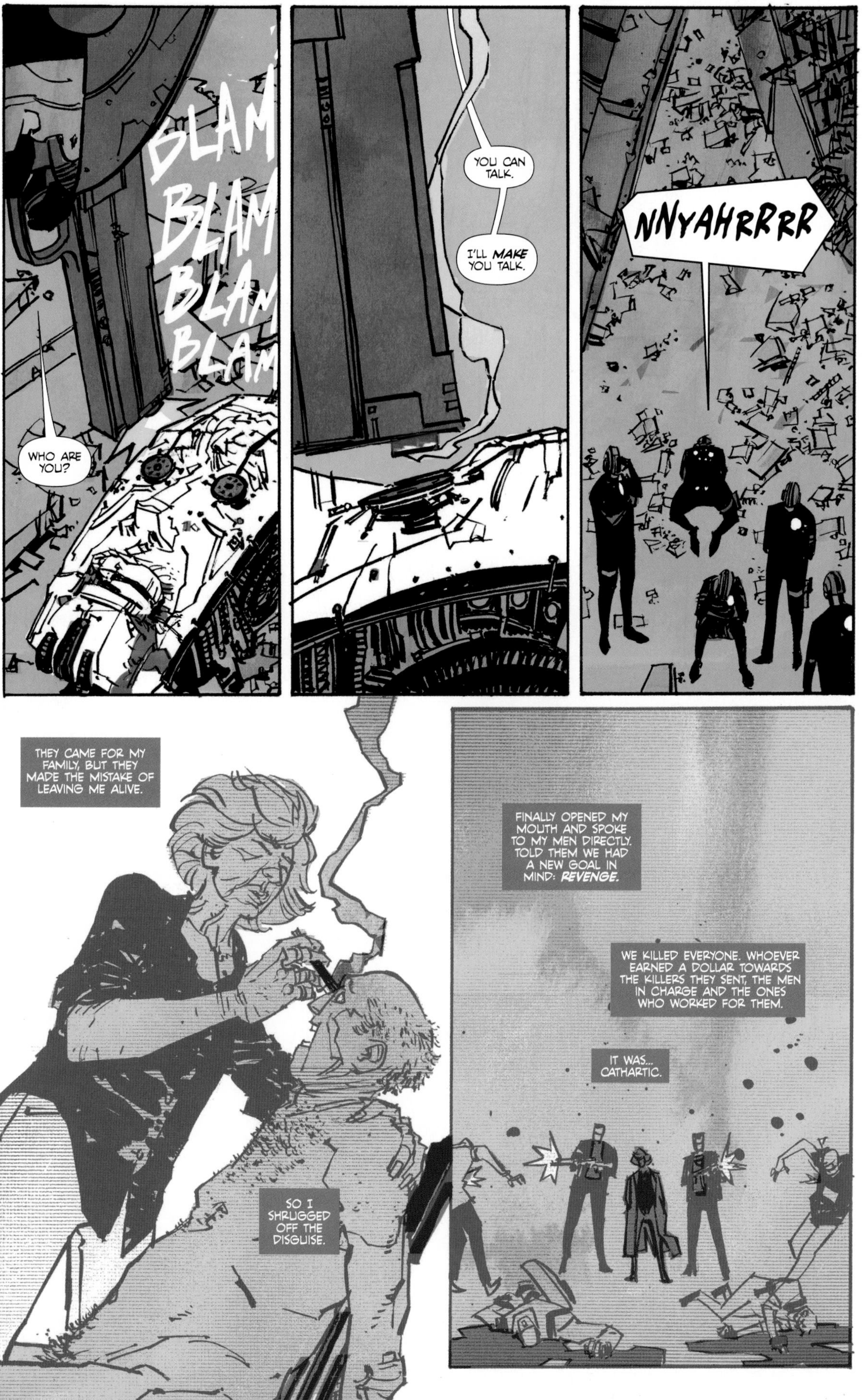
BLAM BLAM BLAM BLAM
WHO ARE YOU?
YOU CAN TALK.
I'LL *MAKE* YOU TALK.
NNYAHRRRR
THEY CAME FOR MY FAMILY, BUT THEY MADE THE MISTAKE OF LEAVING ME ALIVE.
SO I SHRUGGED OFF THE DISGUISE.
FINALLY OPENED MY MOUTH AND SPOKE TO MY MEN DIRECTLY. TOLD THEM WE HAD A NEW GOAL IN MIND: *REVENGE.*
WE KILLED EVERYONE. WHOEVER EARNED A DOLLAR TOWARDS THE KILLERS THEY SENT, THE MEN IN CHARGE AND THE ONES WHO WORKED FOR THEM.
IT WAS... CATHARTIC.

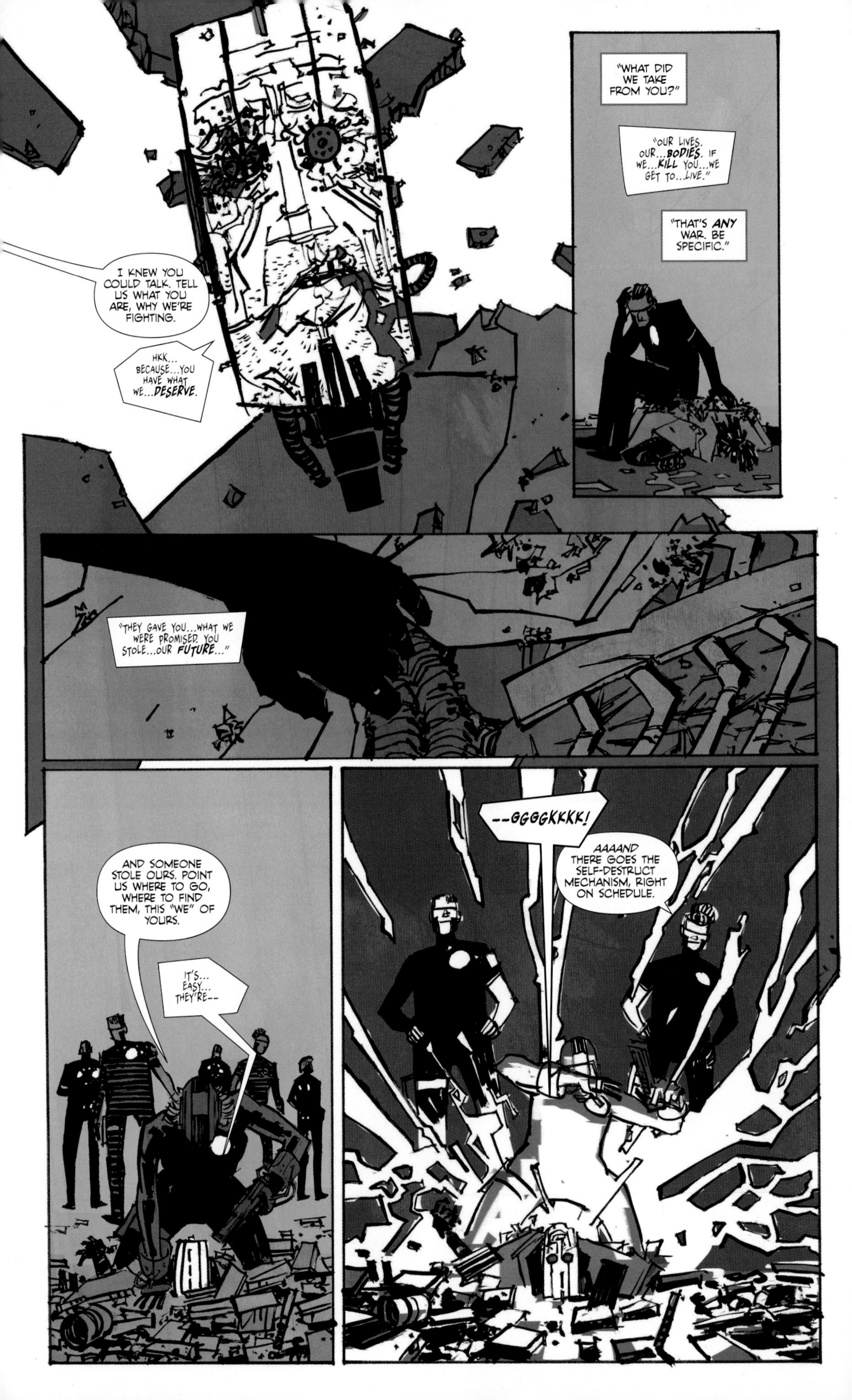
I KNEW YOU COULD TALK. TELL US WHAT YOU ARE, WHY WE'RE FIGHTING.
HKK... BECAUSE...YOU HAVE WHAT WE...DESERVE.
"WHAT DID WE TAKE FROM YOU?"
"OUR LIVES. OUR...BODIES. IF WE...KILL YOU...WE GET TO...LIVE."
"THAT'S ANY WAR. BE SPECIFIC."
"THEY GAVE YOU...WHAT WE WERE PROMISED. YOU STOLE...OUR FUTURE..."
AND SOMEONE STOLE OURS. POINT US WHERE TO GO, WHERE TO FIND THEM, THIS "WE" OF YOURS.
IT'S... EASY... THEY'RE--
--GGGGKKKK!
AAAAND THERE GOES THE SELF-DESTRUCT MECHANISM, RIGHT ON SCHEDULE.

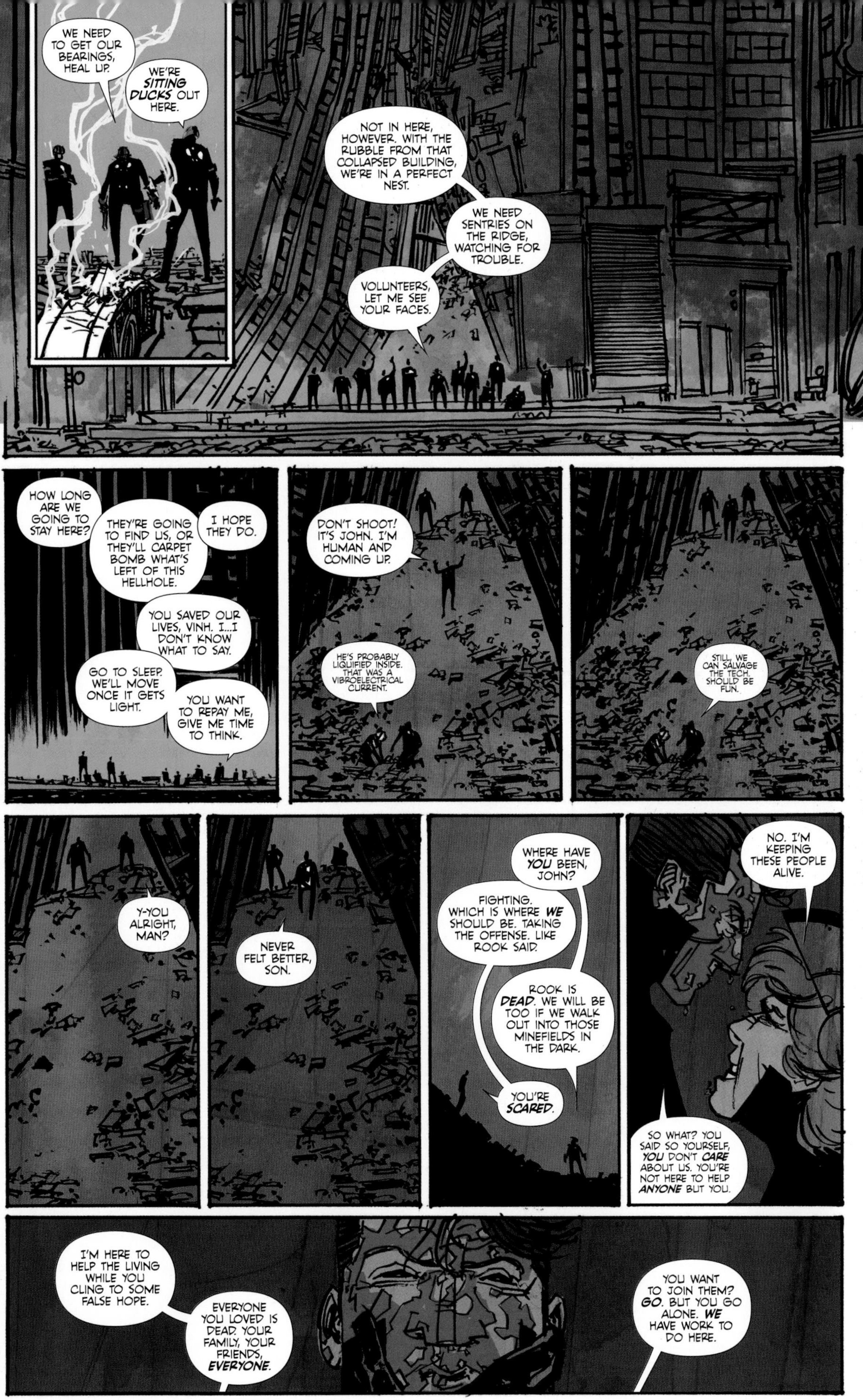

WE NEED TO GET OUR BEARINGS, HEAL UP.
WE'RE *SITTING DUCKS* OUT HERE.
NOT IN HERE, HOWEVER. WITH THE RUBBLE FROM THAT COLLAPSED BUILDING, WE'RE IN A PERFECT NEST.
WE NEED SENTRIES ON THE RIDGE, WATCHING FOR TROUBLE.
VOLUNTEERS, LET ME SEE YOUR FACES.
HOW LONG ARE WE GOING TO STAY HERE?
THEY'RE GOING TO FIND US, OR THEY'LL CARPET BOMB WHAT'S LEFT OF THIS HELLHOLE.
I HOPE THEY DO.
YOU SAVED OUR LIVES, VINH. I...I DON'T KNOW WHAT TO SAY.
GO TO SLEEP. WE'LL MOVE ONCE IT GETS LIGHT.
YOU WANT TO REPAY ME, GIVE ME TIME TO THINK.
DON'T SHOOT! IT'S JOHN. I'M HUMAN AND COMING UP.
HE'S PROBABLY LIQUIFIED INSIDE. THAT WAS A VIBROELECTRICAL CURRENT.
STILL, WE CAN SALVAGE THE TECH. SHOULD BE FUN.
Y-YOU ALRIGHT, MAN?
NEVER FELT BETTER, SON.
WHERE HAVE *YOU* BEEN, JOHN?
FIGHTING. WHICH IS WHERE *WE* SHOULD BE. TAKING THE OFFENSE. LIKE ROOK SAID.
ROOK IS *DEAD*. WE WILL BE TOO IF WE WALK OUT INTO THOSE MINEFIELDS IN THE DARK.
YOU'RE *SCARED*.
NO. I'M KEEPING THESE PEOPLE ALIVE.
SO WHAT? YOU SAID SO YOURSELF, *YOU* DON'T *CARE* ABOUT US. YOU'RE NOT HERE TO HELP *ANYONE* BUT YOU.
I'M HERE TO HELP THE LIVING WHILE YOU CLING TO SOME FALSE HOPE.
EVERYONE YOU LOVED IS DEAD. YOUR FAMILY, YOUR FRIENDS, *EVERYONE*.
YOU WANT TO JOIN THEM? *GO*. BUT YOU GO ALONE. *WE* HAVE WORK TO DO HERE.

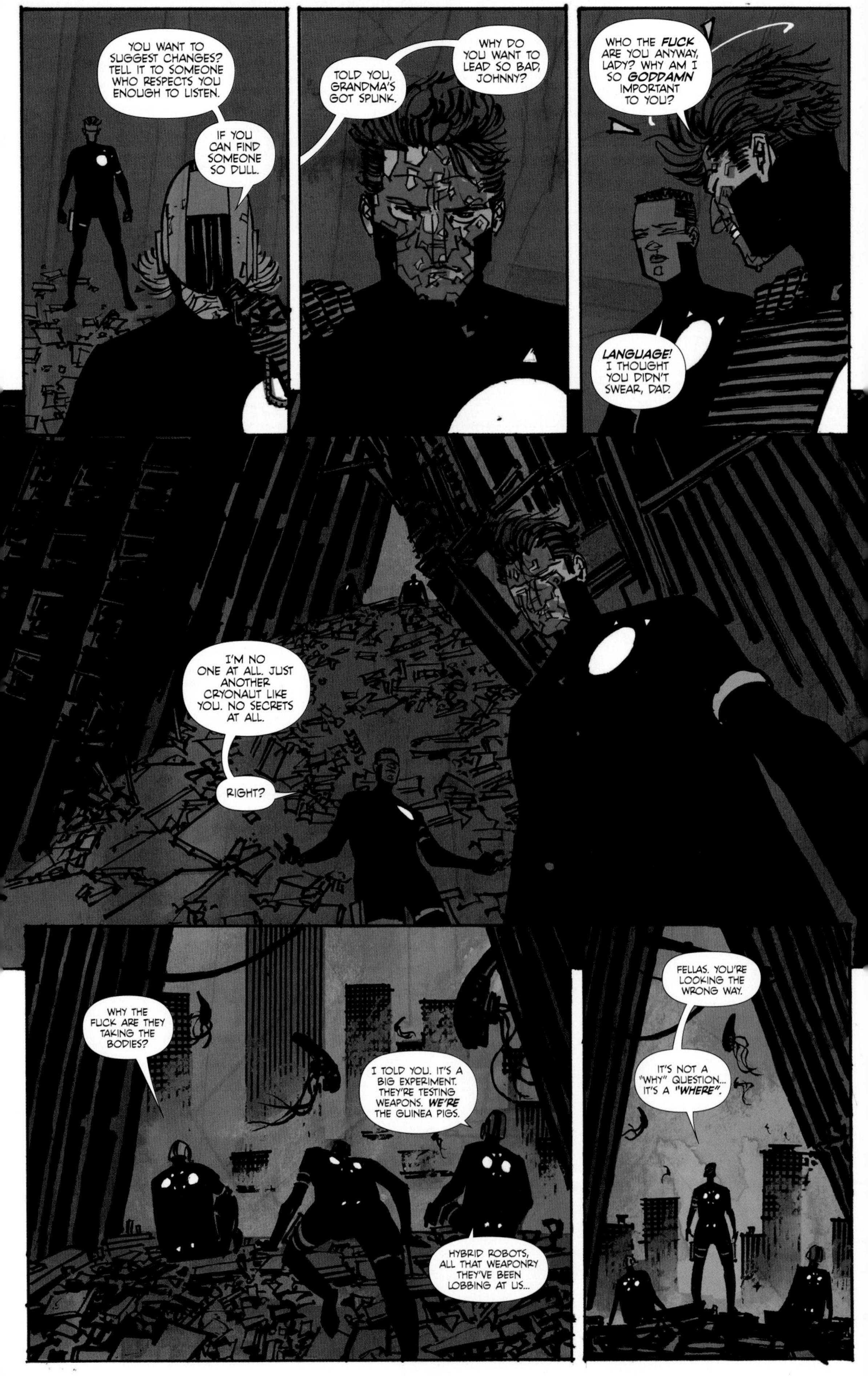

YOU WANT TO SUGGEST CHANGES? TELL IT TO SOMEONE WHO RESPECTS YOU ENOUGH TO LISTEN.
IF YOU CAN FIND SOMEONE SO DULL.
TOLD YOU, GRANDMA'S GOT SPUNK.
WHY DO YOU WANT TO LEAD SO BAD, JOHNNY?
WHO THE **FUCK** ARE YOU ANYWAY, LADY? WHY AM I SO **GODDAMN** IMPORTANT TO YOU?
LANGUAGE! I THOUGHT YOU DIDN'T SWEAR, DAD.
I'M NO ONE AT ALL. JUST ANOTHER CRYONAUT LIKE YOU. NO SECRETS AT ALL.
RIGHT?
WHY THE FUCK ARE THEY TAKING THE BODIES?
I TOLD YOU. IT'S A BIG EXPERIMENT. THEY'RE TESTING WEAPONS. ***WE'RE*** THE GUINEA PIGS.
HYBRID ROBOTS, ALL THAT WEAPONRY THEY'VE BEEN LOBBING AT US...
FELLAS. YOU'RE LOOKING THE WRONG WAY.
IT'S NOT A "WHY" QUESTION... IT'S A ***"WHERE"***.

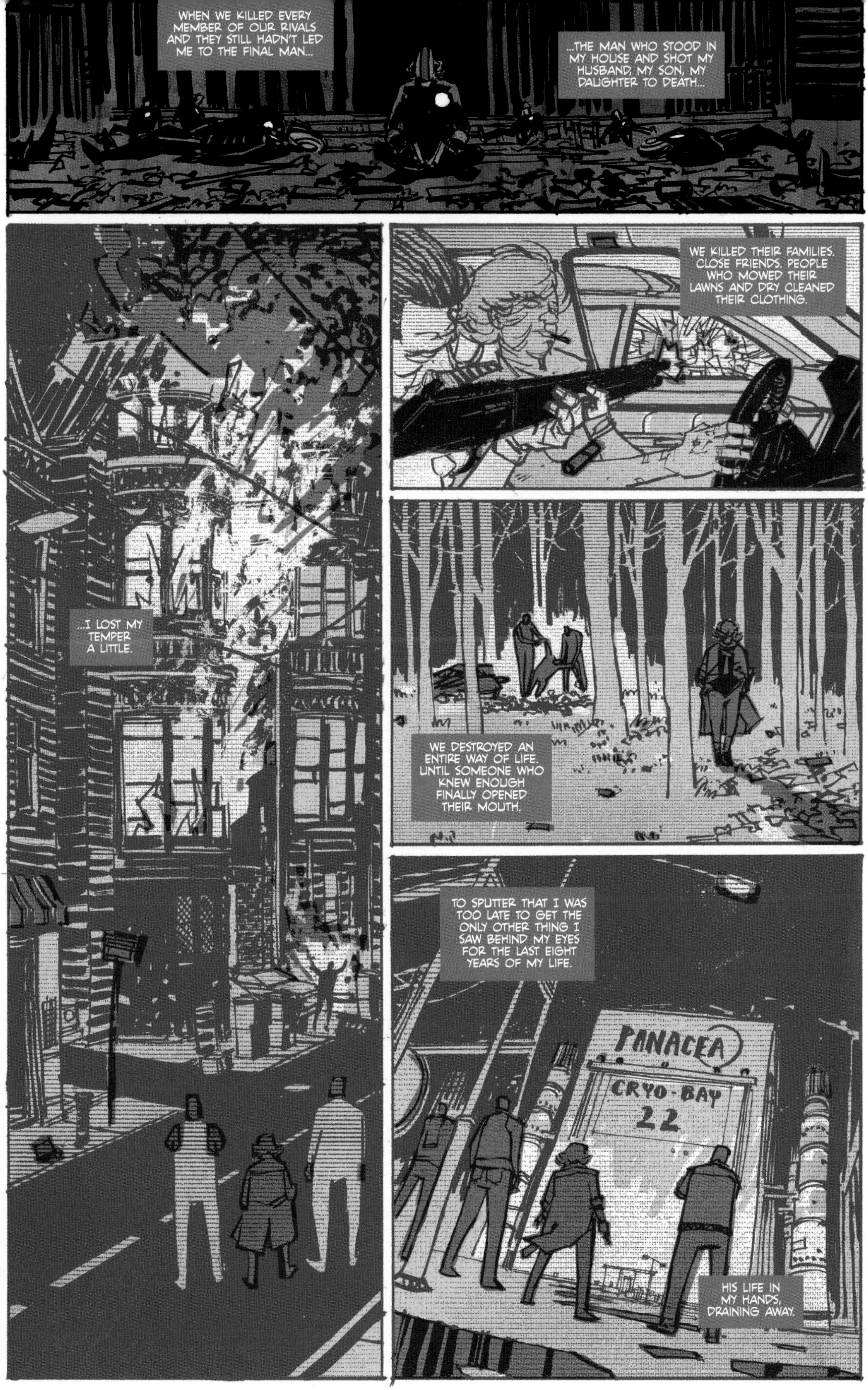
WHEN WE KILLED EVERY MEMBER OF OUR RIVALS AND THEY STILL HADN'T LED ME TO THE FINAL MAN...
...THE MAN WHO STOOD IN MY HOUSE AND SHOT MY HUSBAND, MY SON, MY DAUGHTER TO DEATH...
...I LOST MY TEMPER A LITTLE.
WE KILLED THEIR FAMILIES. CLOSE FRIENDS. PEOPLE WHO MOWED THEIR LAWNS AND DRY CLEANED THEIR CLOTHING.
WE DESTROYED AN ENTIRE WAY OF LIFE. UNTIL SOMEONE WHO KNEW ENOUGH FINALLY OPENED THEIR MOUTH.
TO SPUTTER THAT I WAS TOO LATE TO GET THE ONLY OTHER THING I SAW BEHIND MY EYES FOR THE LAST EIGHT YEARS OF MY LIFE.
PANACEA
CRYO-BAY
22
HIS LIFE IN MY HANDS, DRAINING AWAY.

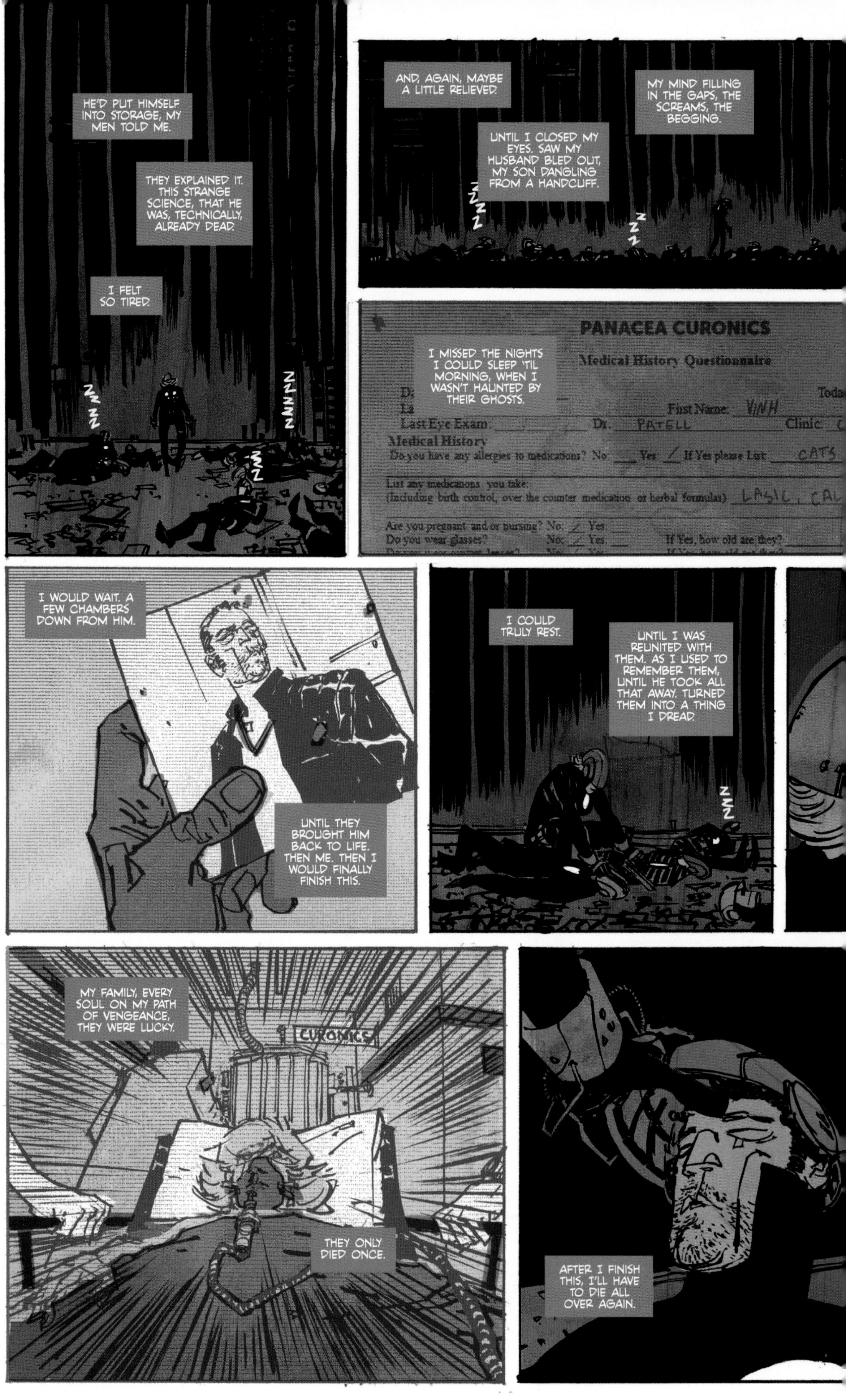
HE'D PUT HIMSELF INTO STORAGE, MY MEN TOLD ME.
THEY EXPLAINED IT. THIS STRANGE SCIENCE, THAT HE WAS, TECHNICALLY, ALREADY DEAD.
I FELT SO TIRED.
AND, AGAIN, MAYBE A LITTLE RELIEVED.
UNTIL I CLOSED MY EYES. SAW MY HUSBAND BLED OUT, MY SON DANGLING FROM A HANDCUFF.
MY MIND FILLING IN THE GAPS, THE SCREAMS, THE BEGGING.
PANACEA CURONICS
I MISSED THE NIGHTS I COULD SLEEP 'TIL MORNING, WHEN I WASN'T HAUNTED BY THEIR GHOSTS.
Medical History Questionnaire
First Name: VINH
Last Eye Exam: Dr. PATELL Clinic:
Medical History
Do you have any allergies to medications? No: Yes: If Yes please List: CATS
List any medications you take:
(Including birth control, over the counter medication or herbal formulas)
Are you pregnant and/or nursing? No: Yes:
Do you wear glasses? No: Yes: If Yes, how old are they?
I WOULD WAIT. A FEW CHAMBERS DOWN FROM HIM.
UNTIL THEY BROUGHT HIM BACK TO LIFE. THEN ME. THEN I WOULD FINALLY FINISH THIS.
I COULD TRULY REST.
UNTIL I WAS REUNITED WITH THEM. AS I USED TO REMEMBER THEM, UNTIL HE TOOK ALL THAT AWAY. TURNED THEM INTO A THING I DREAD.
MY FAMILY, EVERY SOUL ON MY PATH OF VENGEANCE, THEY WERE LUCKY.
CURONICS
THEY ONLY DIED ONCE.
AFTER I FINISH THIS, I'LL HAVE TO DIE ALL OVER AGAIN.

I *WANTED* TO FORGET. I *WANTED* TO PRETEND.

I WANTED TO FADE OUT OF THE WORLD AND ALL MY RESPONSIBILITIES.

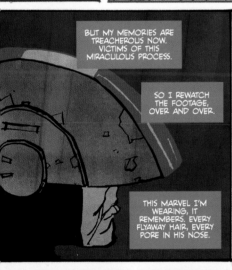

BUT MY MEMORIES ARE TREACHEROUS NOW. VICTIMS OF THIS MIRACULOUS PROCESS.

SO I REWATCH THE FOOTAGE, OVER AND OVER.

THIS MARVEL I'M WEARING, IT REMEMBERS. EVERY FLYAWAY HAIR, EVERY PORE IN HIS NOSE.

I CAN FEEL HIM OUT HERE, ALIVE. RIGHT UNDER MY NOSE.

IT'S WHY I PROTECTED THESE STRANGERS, WHY I BROUGHT THEM HERE.

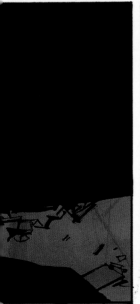

KRAK

AND HOPE MY SOUL STILL KNOWS THE WAY HOME.

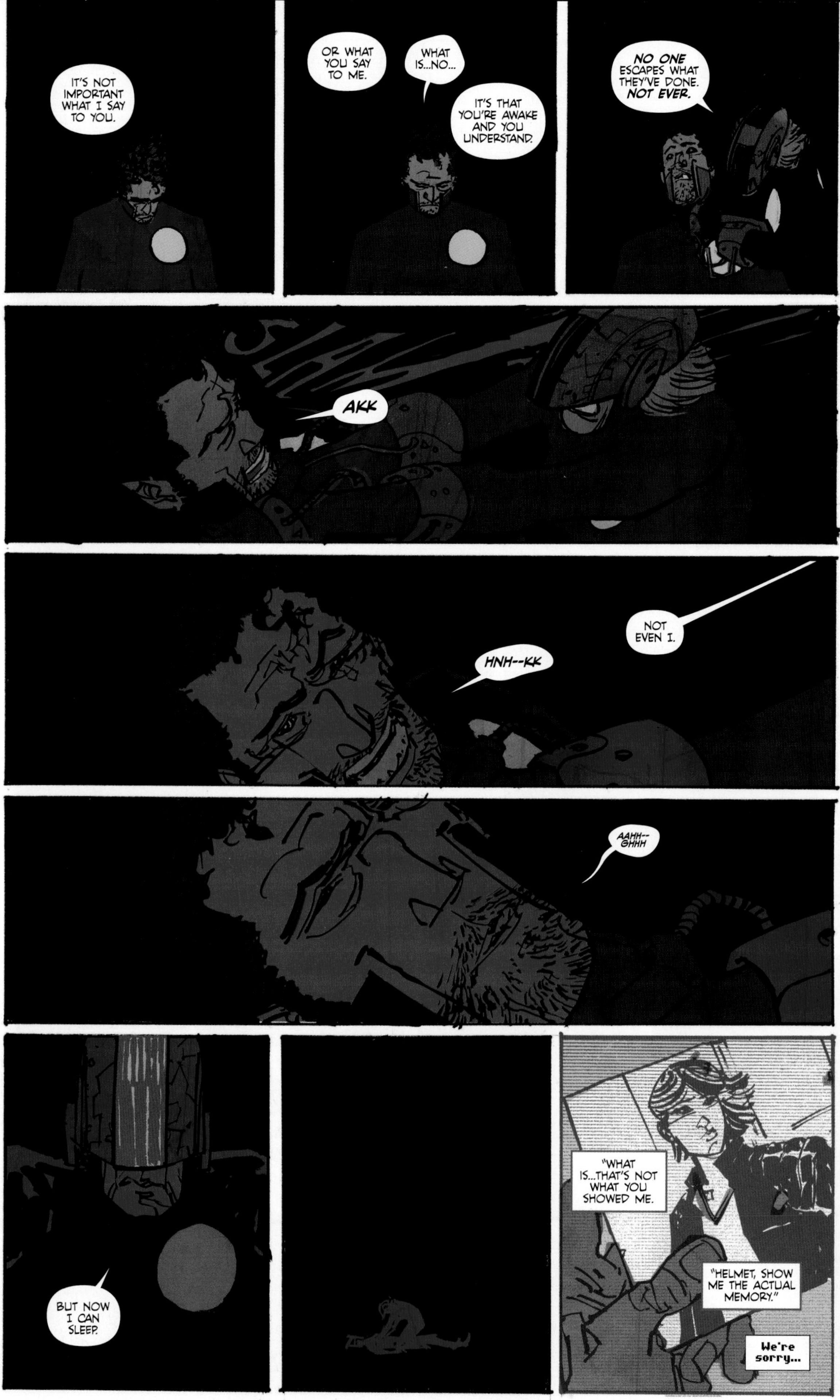
IT'S NOT IMPORTANT WHAT I SAY TO YOU.
OR WHAT YOU SAY TO ME.
WHAT IS...NO...
IT'S THAT YOU'RE AWAKE AND YOU UNDERSTAND.
NO ONE ESCAPES WHAT THEY'VE DONE. NOT EVER.
AKK
HNH--KK
NOT EVEN I.
AAHH--GHHH
BUT NOW I CAN SLEEP.
"WHAT IS...THAT'S NOT WHAT YOU SHOWED ME.
"HELMET, SHOW ME THE ACTUAL MEMORY."
We're sorry...

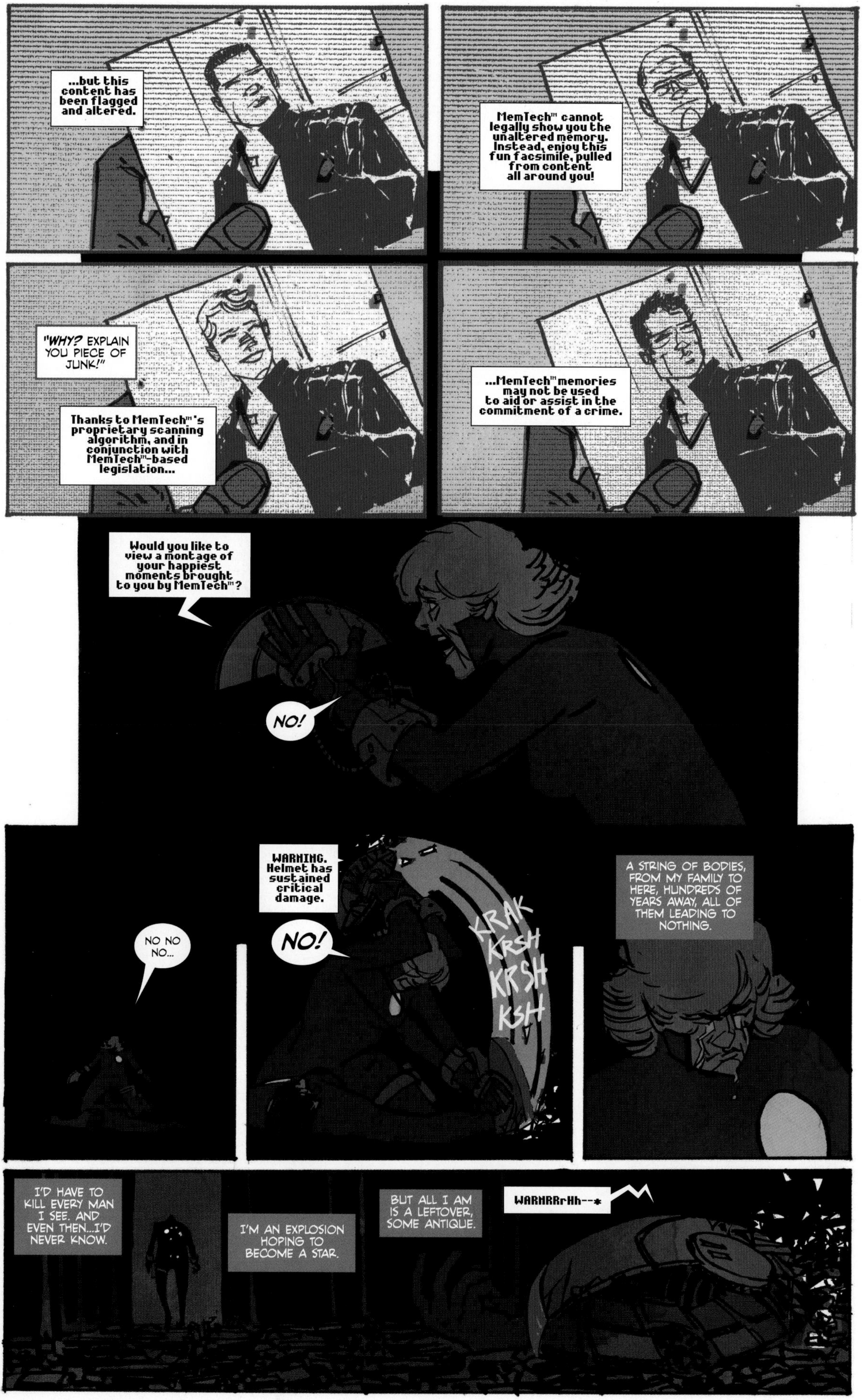
...but this content has been flagged and altered.
MemTech™ cannot legally show you the unaltered memory. Instead, enjoy this fun facsimile, pulled from content all around you!
"WHY? EXPLAIN YOU PIECE OF JUNK!"
Thanks to MemTech™'s proprietary scanning algorithm, and in conjunction with MemTech™-based legislation...
...MemTech™ memories may not be used to aid or assist in the commitment of a crime.
Would you like to view a montage of your happiest moments brought to you by MemTech™?
NO!
NO NO NO...
WARNING. Helmet has sustained critical damage.
NO!
KRAK
KRSH
KRSH
KSH
A STRING OF BODIES, FROM MY FAMILY TO HERE, HUNDREDS OF YEARS AWAY, ALL OF THEM LEADING TO NOTHING.
I'D HAVE TO KILL EVERY MAN I SEE. AND EVEN THEN...I'D NEVER KNOW.
I'M AN EXPLOSION HOPING TO BECOME A STAR.
BUT ALL I AM IS A LEFTOVER, SOME ANTIQUE.
WARNRRrHh--*

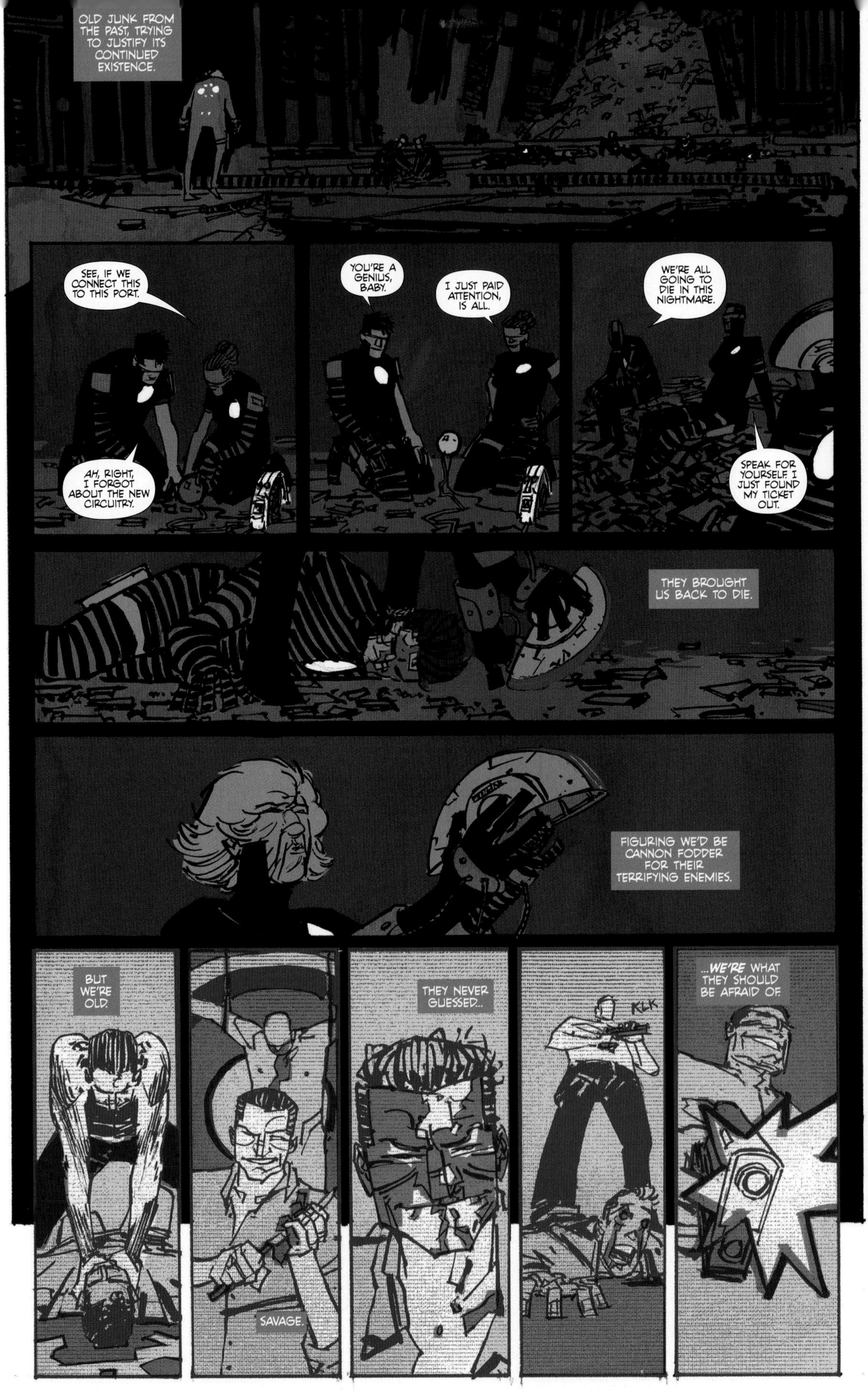
OLD JUNK FROM THE PAST, TRYING TO JUSTIFY ITS CONTINUED EXISTENCE.
SEE, IF WE CONNECT THIS TO THIS PORT.
AH, RIGHT, I FORGOT ABOUT THE NEW CIRCUITRY.
YOU'RE A GENIUS, BABY.
I JUST PAID ATTENTION, IS ALL.
WE'RE ALL GOING TO DIE IN THIS NIGHTMARE.
SPEAK FOR YOURSELF. I JUST FOUND MY TICKET OUT.
THEY BROUGHT US BACK TO DIE.
FIGURING WE'D BE CANNON FODDER FOR THEIR TERRIFYING ENEMIES.
BUT WE'RE OLD.
SAVAGE.
THEY NEVER GUESSED...
KLK
...WE'RE WHAT THEY SHOULD BE AFRAID OF.

3

KILLED IN ACTION

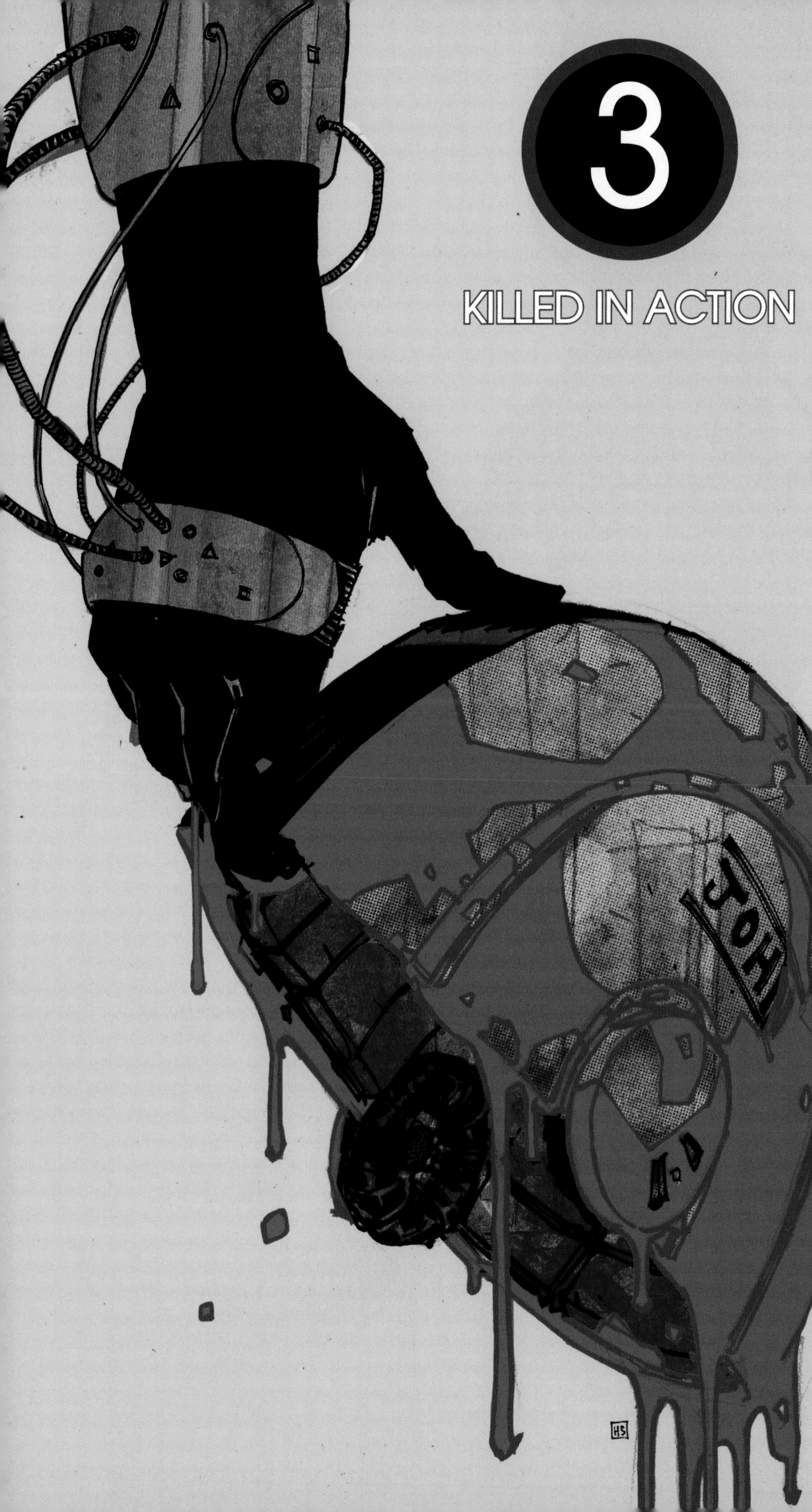
JOH

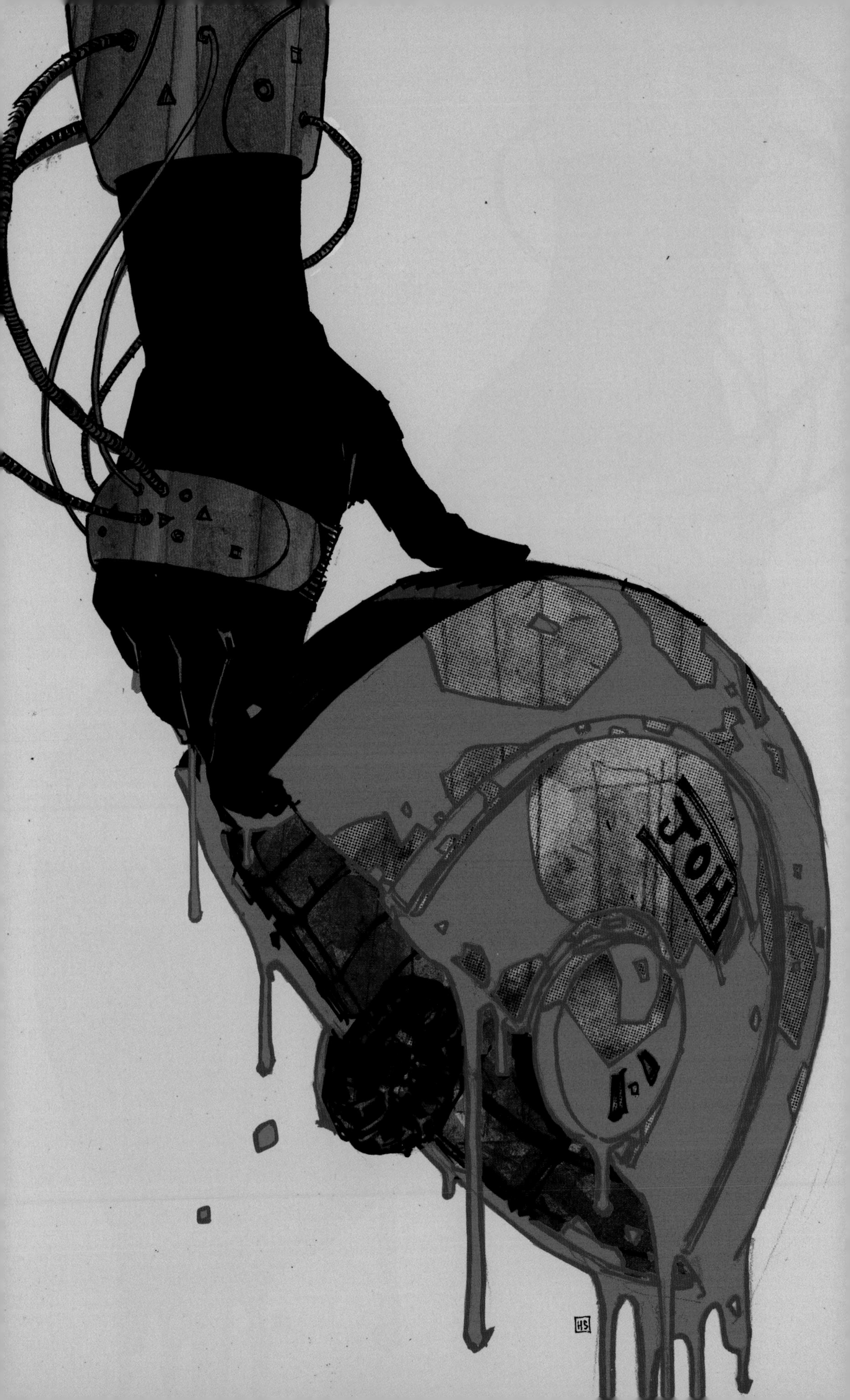
HOT

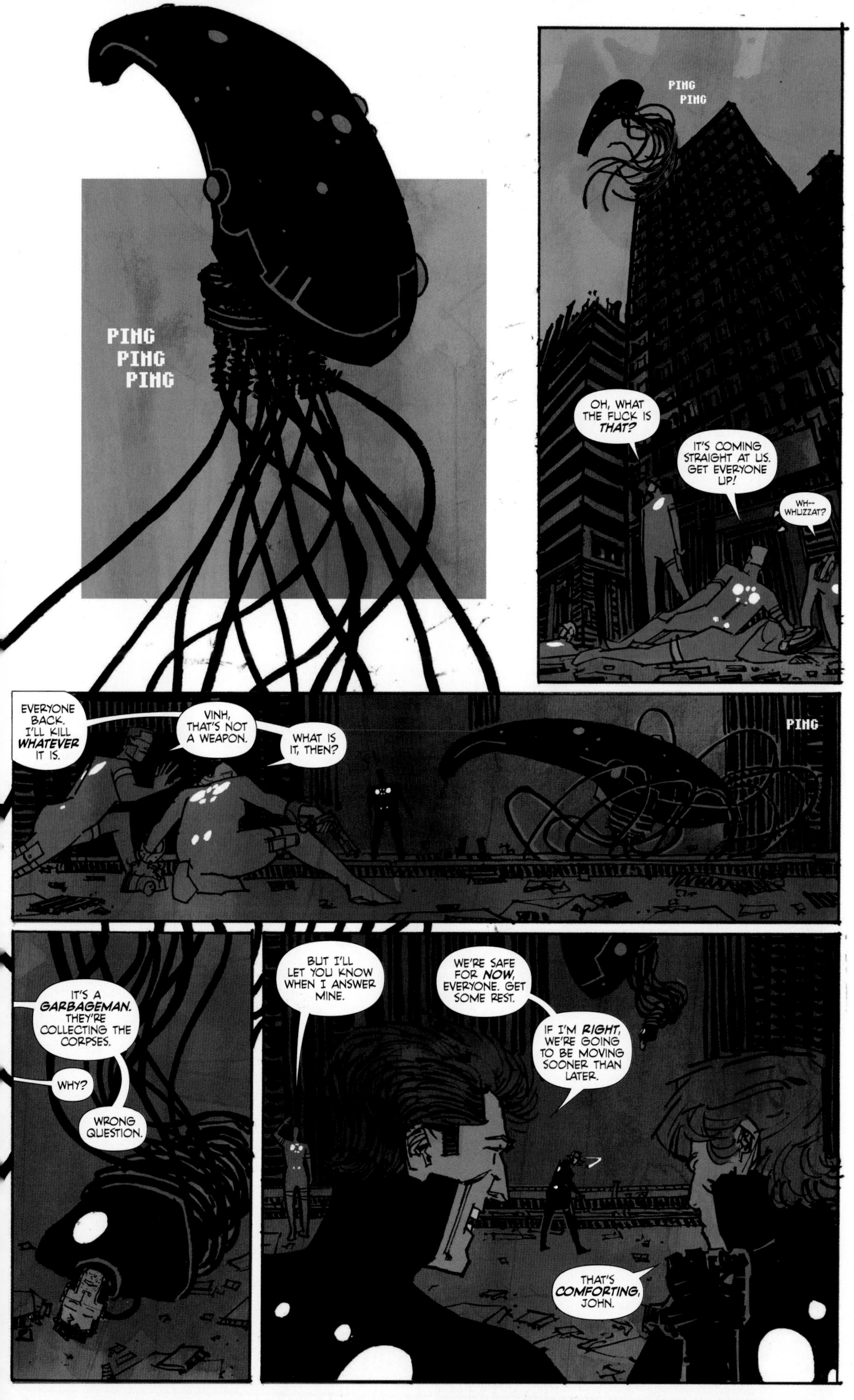

PING
PING
PING
PING
PING
OH, WHAT THE FUCK IS THAT?
IT'S COMING STRAIGHT AT US. GET EVERYONE UP!
WH-- WHUZZAT?
EVERYONE BACK. I'LL KILL WHATEVER IT IS.
VINH, THAT'S NOT A WEAPON.
WHAT IS IT, THEN?
PING
IT'S A GARBAGEMAN. THEY'RE COLLECTING THE CORPSES.
WHY?
WRONG QUESTION.
BUT I'LL LET YOU KNOW WHEN I ANSWER MINE.
WE'RE SAFE FOR NOW, EVERYONE. GET SOME REST.
IF I'M RIGHT, WE'RE GOING TO BE MOVING SOONER THAN LATER.
THAT'S COMFORTING, JOHN.

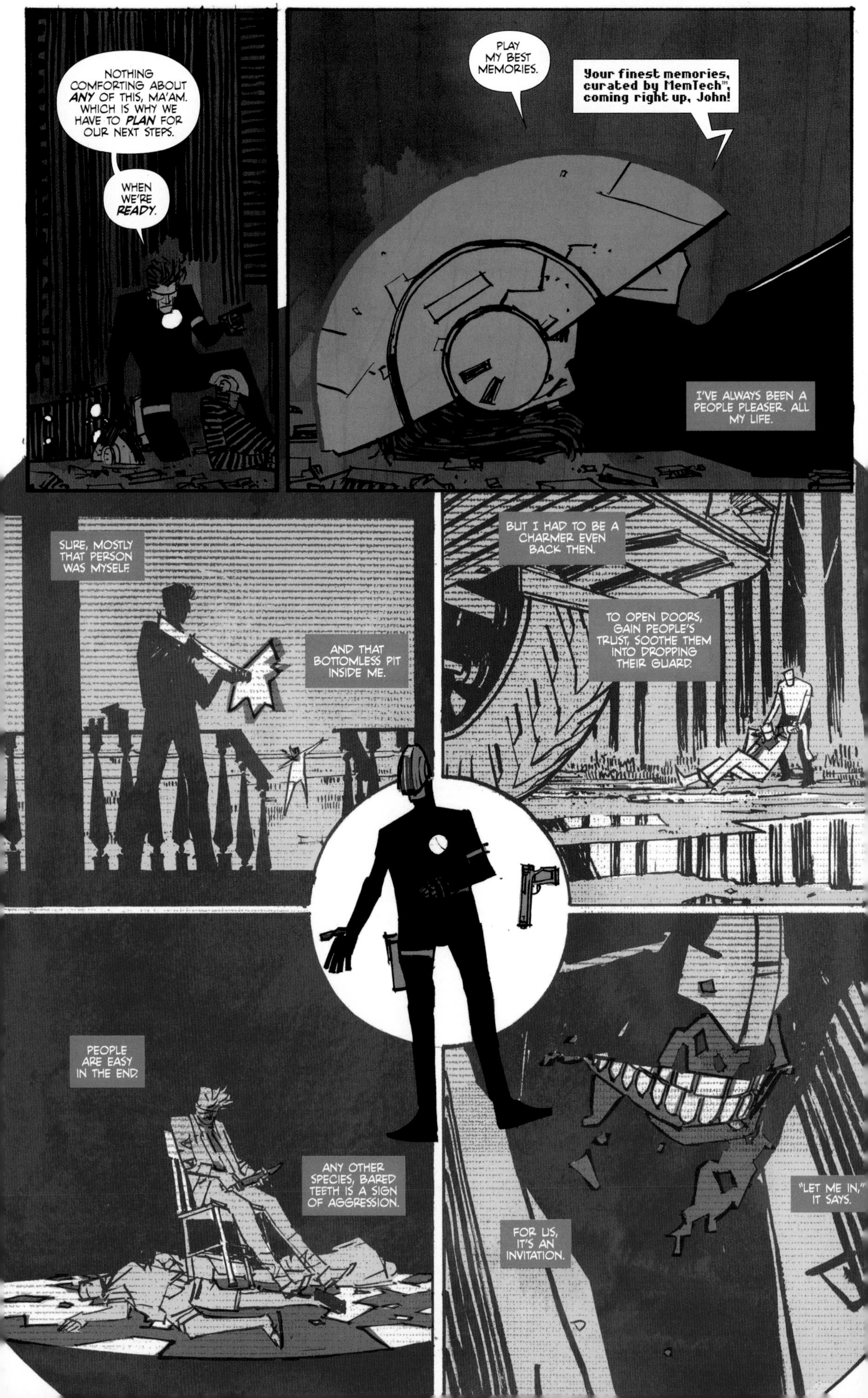
NOTHING COMFORTING ABOUT ANY OF THIS, MA'AM. WHICH IS WHY WE HAVE TO PLAN FOR OUR NEXT STEPS.
WHEN WE'RE READY.
PLAY MY BEST MEMORIES.
Your finest memories, curated by MemTech™, coming right up, John!
I'VE ALWAYS BEEN A PEOPLE PLEASER. ALL MY LIFE.
SURE, MOSTLY THAT PERSON WAS MYSELF.
AND THAT BOTTOMLESS PIT INSIDE ME.
BUT I HAD TO BE A CHARMER EVEN BACK THEN.
TO OPEN DOORS, GAIN PEOPLE'S TRUST, SOOTHE THEM INTO DROPPING THEIR GUARD.
PEOPLE ARE EASY IN THE END.
ANY OTHER SPECIES, BARED TEETH IS A SIGN OF AGGRESSION.
FOR US, IT'S AN INVITATION.
"LET ME IN," IT SAYS.

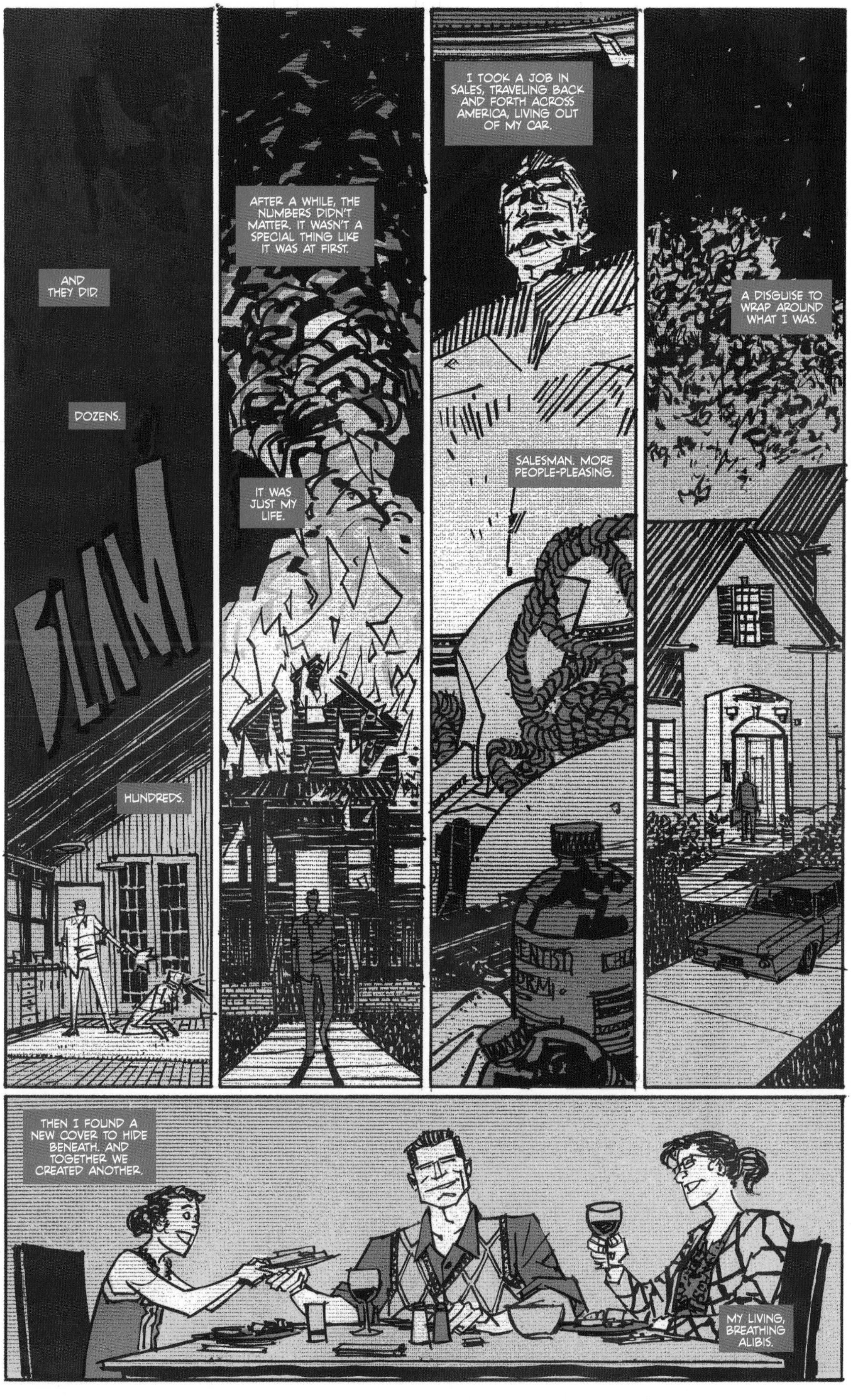
AND THEY DID.
DOZENS.
SLAM
HUNDREDS.
AFTER A WHILE, THE NUMBERS DIDN'T MATTER. IT WASN'T A SPECIAL THING LIKE IT WAS AT FIRST.
IT WAS JUST MY LIFE.
I TOOK A JOB IN SALES, TRAVELING BACK AND FORTH ACROSS AMERICA, LIVING OUT OF MY CAR.
SALESMAN. MORE PEOPLE-PLEASING.
A DISGUISE TO WRAP AROUND WHAT I WAS.
THEN I FOUND A NEW COVER TO HIDE BENEATH. AND TOGETHER WE CREATED ANOTHER.
MY LIVING, BREATHING ALIBIS.

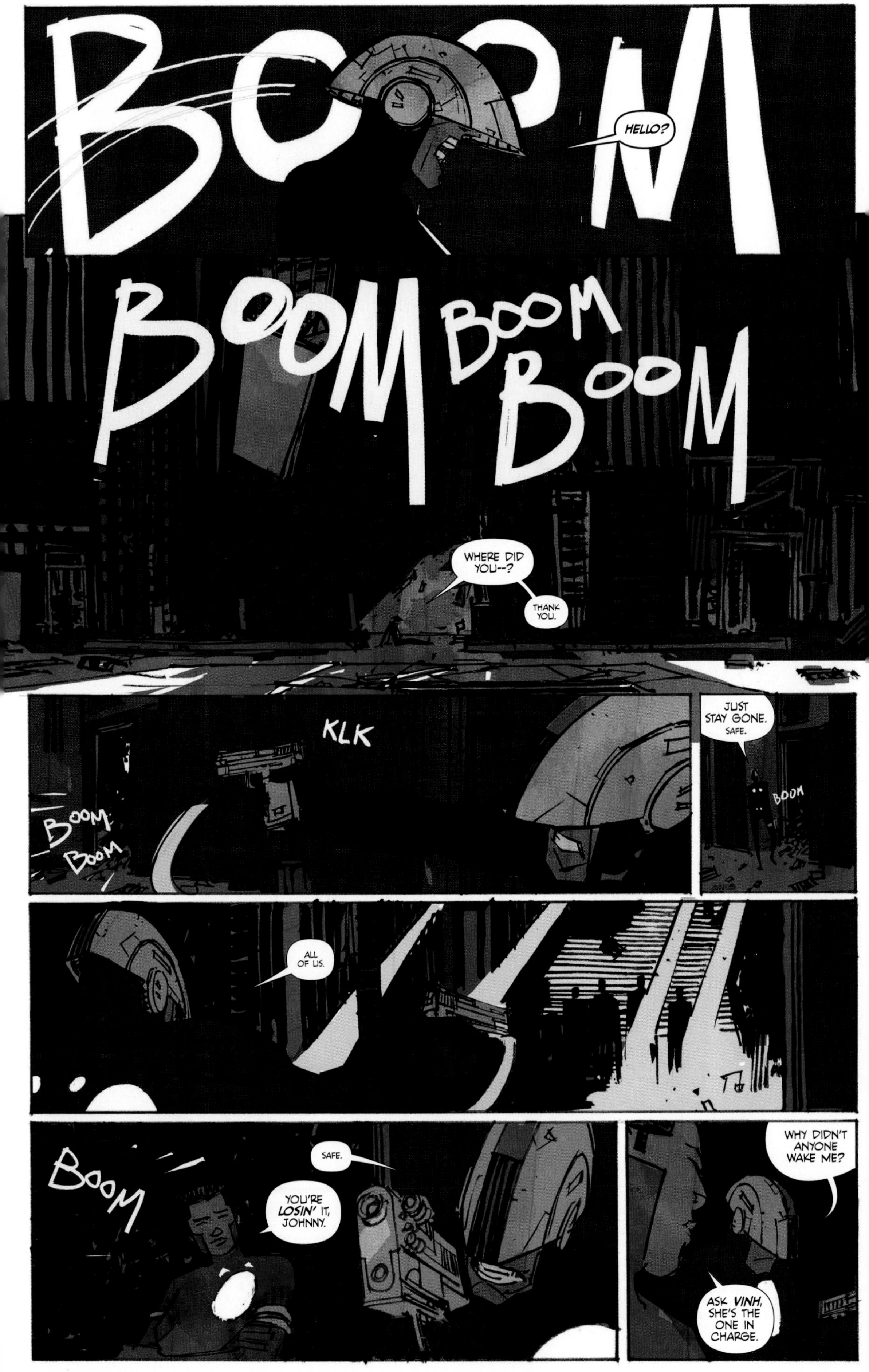
BOOM
HELLO?
BOOM BOOM BOOM
WHERE DID YOU--?
THANK YOU.
KLK
BOOM BOOM
JUST STAY GONE. SAFE.
BOOM
ALL OF US.
BOOM
SAFE.
YOU'RE *LOSIN'* IT, JOHNNY.
WHY DIDN'T ANYONE WAKE ME?
ASK *VINH*, SHE'S THE ONE IN CHARGE.

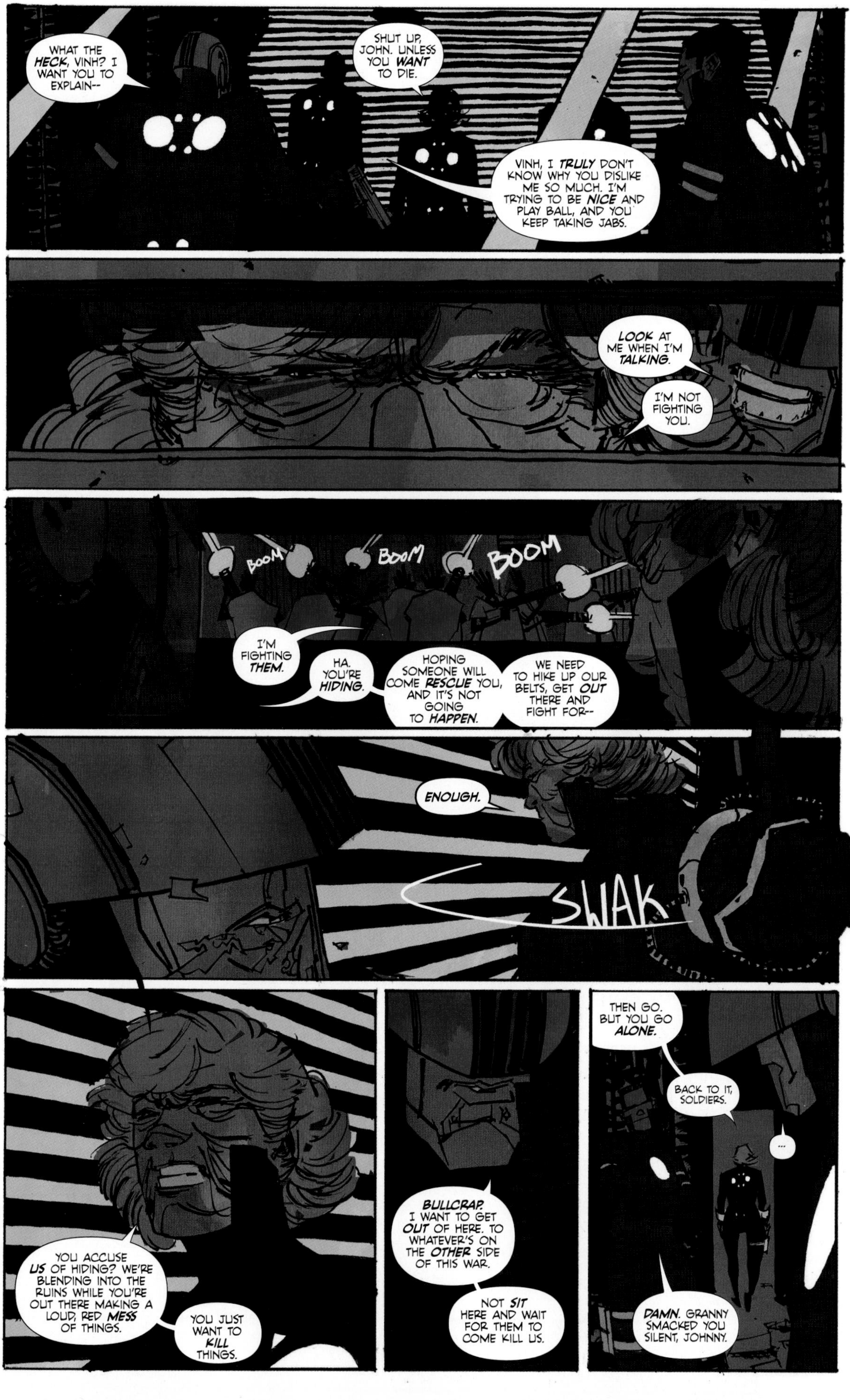
WHAT THE HECK, VINH? I WANT YOU TO EXPLAIN--
SHUT UP, JOHN. UNLESS YOU WANT TO DIE.
VINH, I TRULY DON'T KNOW WHY YOU DISLIKE ME SO MUCH. I'M TRYING TO BE NICE AND PLAY BALL, AND YOU KEEP TAKING JABS.
LOOK AT ME WHEN I'M TALKING.
I'M NOT FIGHTING YOU.
BOOM
BOOM
BOOM
I'M FIGHTING THEM.
HA. YOU'RE HIDING.
HOPING SOMEONE WILL COME RESCUE YOU, AND IT'S NOT GOING TO HAPPEN.
WE NEED TO HIKE UP OUR BELTS, GET OUT THERE AND FIGHT FOR--
ENOUGH.
SWAK
YOU ACCUSE US OF HIDING? WE'RE BLENDING INTO THE RUINS WHILE YOU'RE OUT THERE MAKING A LOUD, RED MESS OF THINGS.
YOU JUST WANT TO KILL THINGS.
BULLCRAP. I WANT TO GET OUT OF HERE. TO WHATEVER'S ON THE OTHER SIDE OF THIS WAR.
NOT SIT HERE AND WAIT FOR THEM TO COME KILL US.
THEN GO. BUT YOU GO ALONE.
BACK TO IT, SOLDIERS.
...
DAMN. GRANNY SMACKED YOU SILENT, JOHNNY.

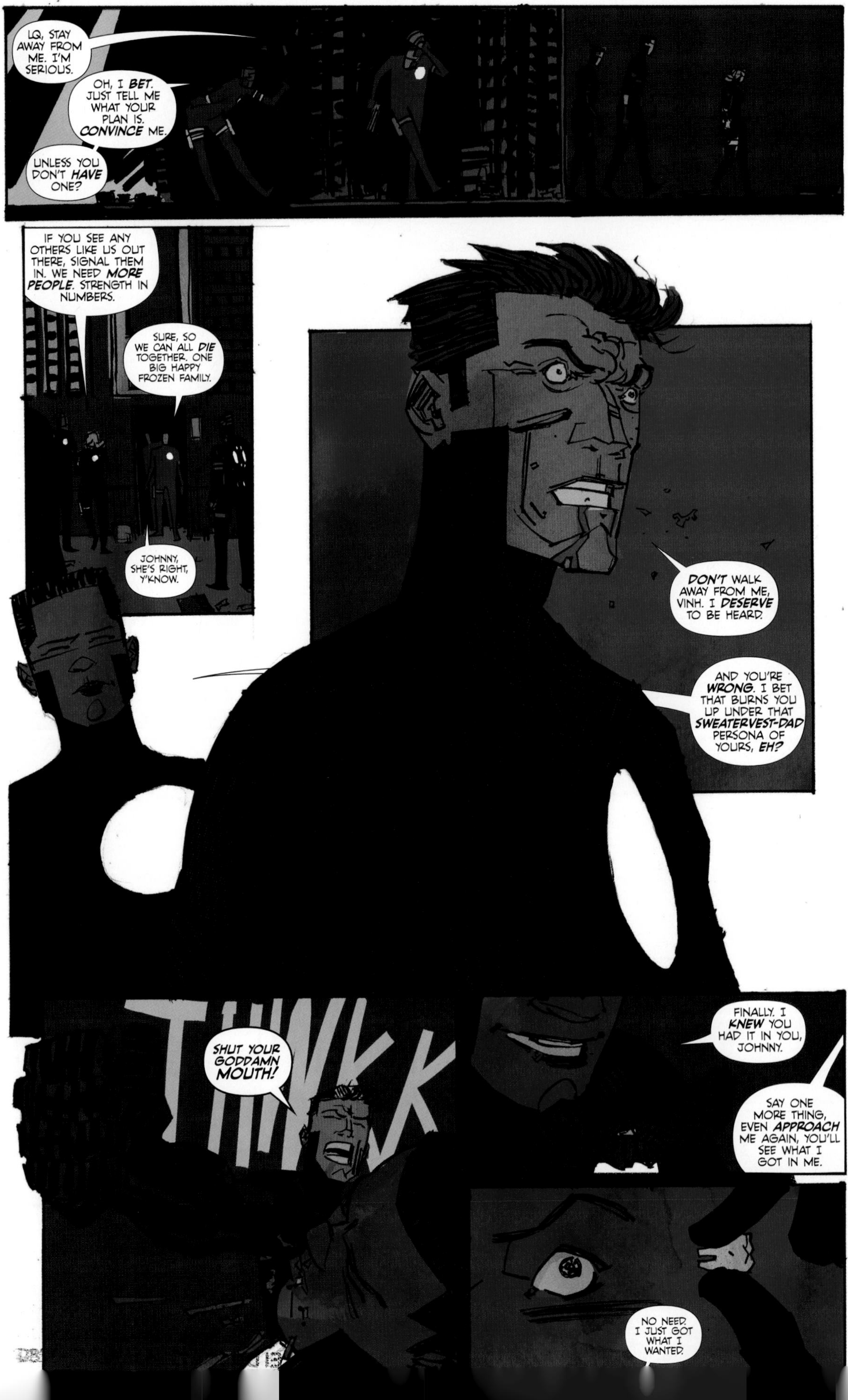
LQ, STAY AWAY FROM ME. I'M SERIOUS.
OH, I BET. JUST TELL ME WHAT YOUR PLAN IS. CONVINCE ME.
UNLESS YOU DON'T HAVE ONE?
IF YOU SEE ANY OTHERS LIKE US OUT THERE, SIGNAL THEM IN. WE NEED MORE PEOPLE. STRENGTH IN NUMBERS.
SURE, SO WE CAN ALL DIE TOGETHER. ONE BIG HAPPY FROZEN FAMILY.
JOHNNY, SHE'S RIGHT, Y'KNOW.
DON'T WALK AWAY FROM ME, VINH. I DESERVE TO BE HEARD.
AND YOU'RE WRONG. I BET THAT BURNS YOU UP UNDER THAT SWEATERVEST-DAD PERSONA OF YOURS, EH?
THWKK
SHUT YOUR GODDAMN MOUTH!
FINALLY. I KNEW YOU HAD IT IN YOU, JOHNNY.
SAY ONE MORE THING, EVEN APPROACH ME AGAIN, YOU'LL SEE WHAT I GOT IN ME.
NO NEED. I JUST GOT WHAT I WANTED.

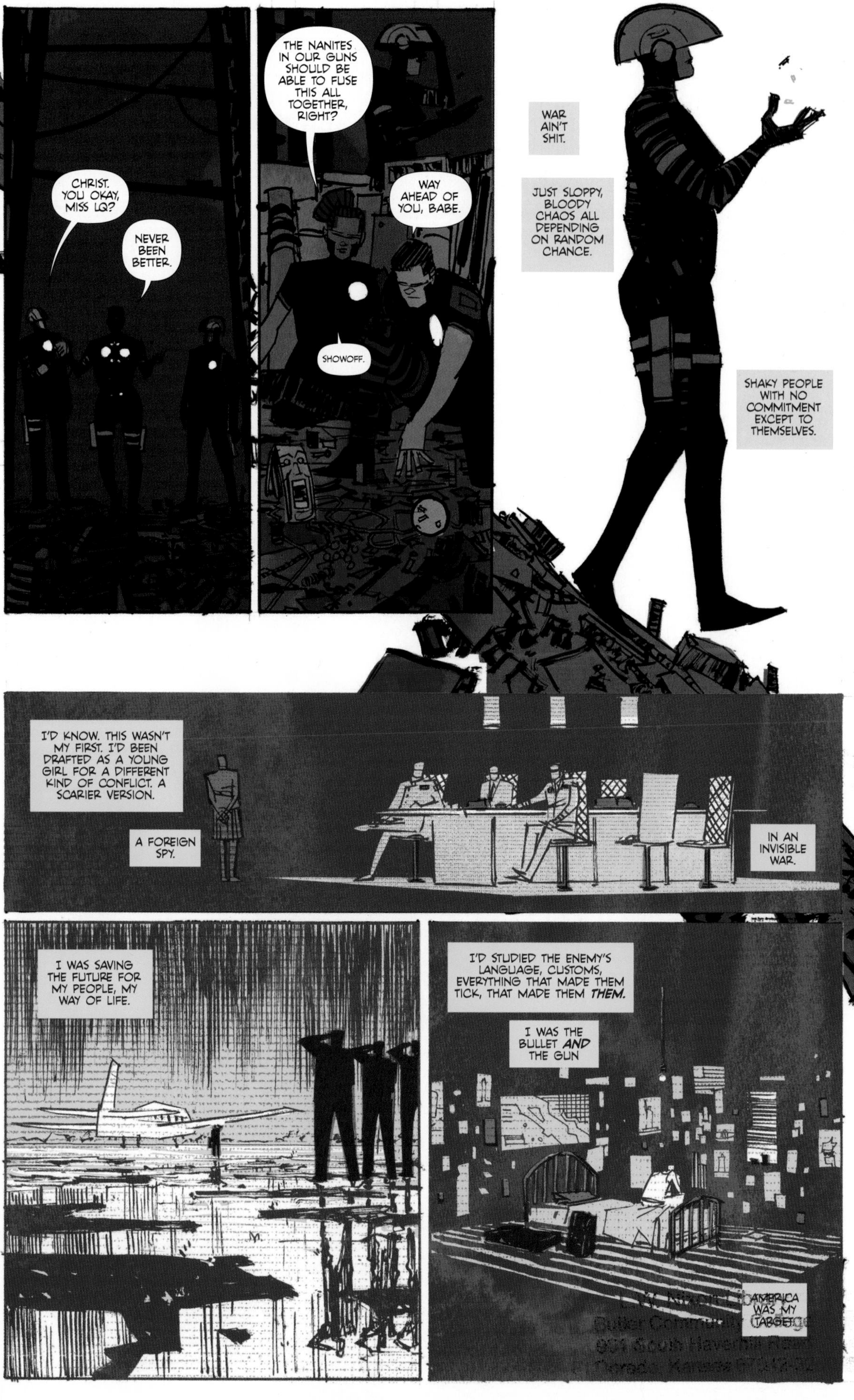
CHRIST. YOU OKAY, MISS LQ?
NEVER BEEN BETTER.
THE NANITES IN OUR GUNS SHOULD BE ABLE TO FUSE THIS ALL TOGETHER, RIGHT?
WAY AHEAD OF YOU, BABE.
SHOWOFF.
WAR AIN'T SHIT.
JUST SLOPPY, BLOODY CHAOS ALL DEPENDING ON RANDOM CHANCE.
SHAKY PEOPLE WITH NO COMMITMENT EXCEPT TO THEMSELVES.
I'D KNOW. THIS WASN'T MY FIRST. I'D BEEN DRAFTED AS A YOUNG GIRL FOR A DIFFERENT KIND OF CONFLICT. A SCARIER VERSION.
A FOREIGN SPY.
IN AN INVISIBLE WAR.
I WAS SAVING THE FUTURE FOR MY PEOPLE, MY WAY OF LIFE.
I'D STUDIED THE ENEMY'S LANGUAGE, CUSTOMS, EVERYTHING THAT MADE THEM TICK, THAT MADE THEM *THEM.*
I WAS THE BULLET *AND* THE GUN
AMERICA WAS MY TARGET.

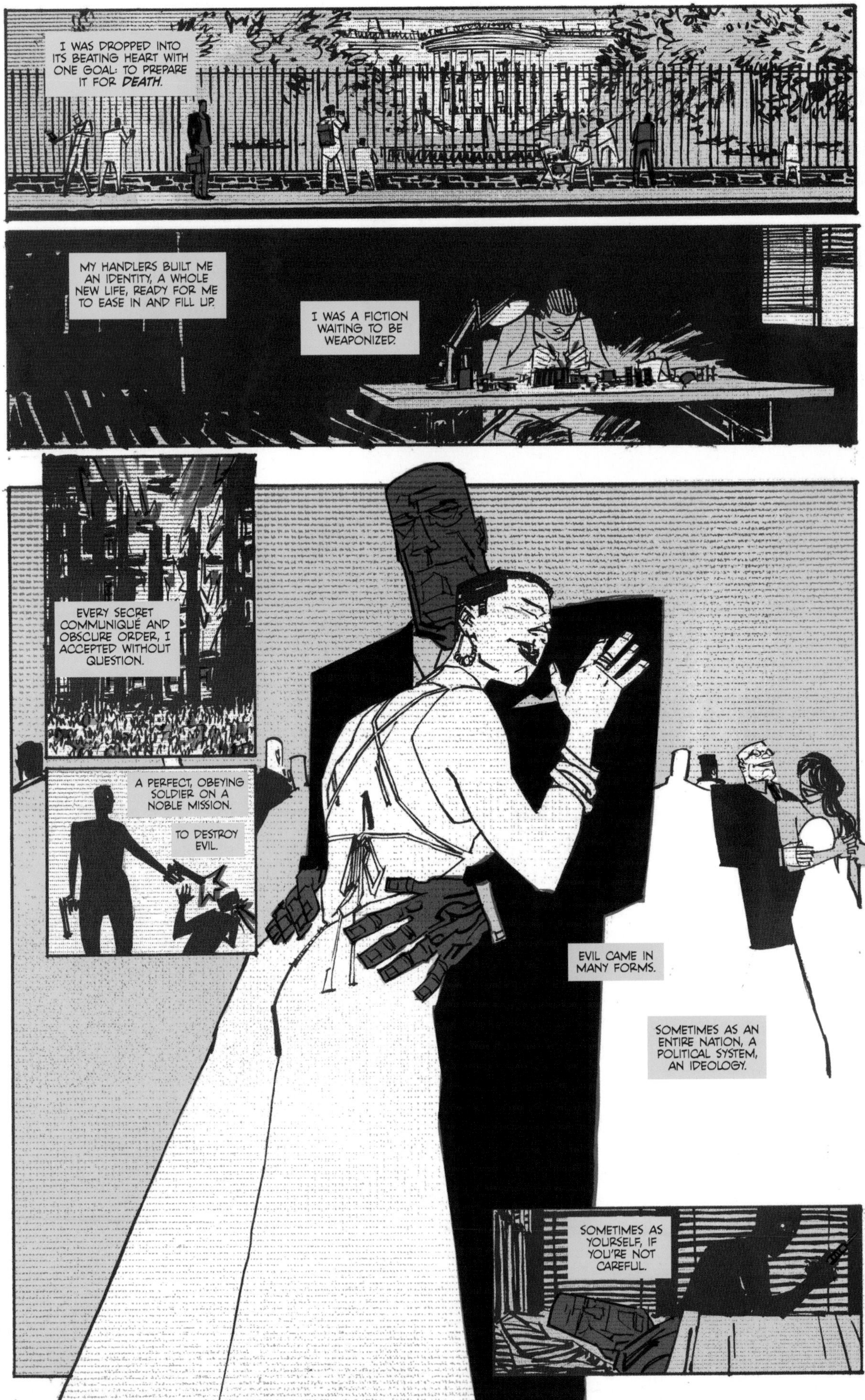
I WAS DROPPED INTO ITS BEATING HEART WITH ONE GOAL: TO PREPARE IT FOR *DEATH*.
MY HANDLERS BUILT ME AN IDENTITY, A WHOLE NEW LIFE, READY FOR ME TO EASE IN AND FILL UP.
I WAS A FICTION WAITING TO BE WEAPONIZED.
EVERY SECRET COMMUNIQUÉ AND OBSCURE ORDER, I ACCEPTED WITHOUT QUESTION.
A PERFECT, OBEYING SOLDIER ON A NOBLE MISSION.
TO DESTROY EVIL.
EVIL CAME IN MANY FORMS.
SOMETIMES AS AN ENTIRE NATION, A POLITICAL SYSTEM, AN IDEOLOGY.
SOMETIMES AS YOURSELF, IF YOU'RE NOT CAREFUL.

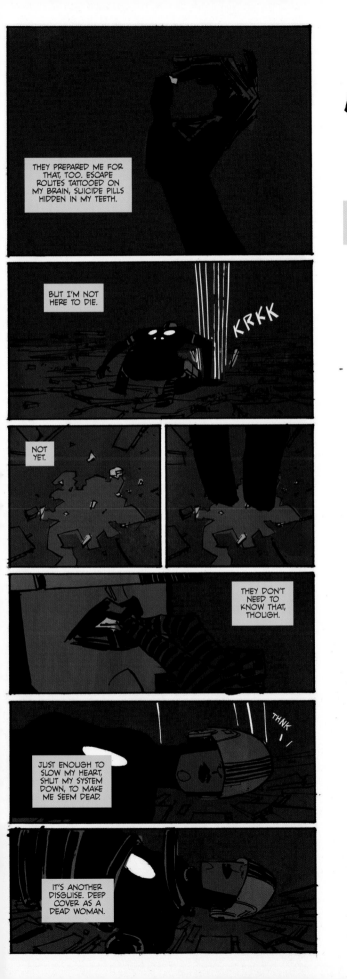

THEY PREPARED ME FOR THAT, TOO. ESCAPE ROUTES TATTOOED ON MY BRAIN, SUICIDE PILLS HIDDEN IN MY TEETH.

BUT I'M NOT HERE TO DIE.

KRKK

NOT YET.

THEY DON'T NEED TO KNOW THAT, THOUGH.

THAK

JUST ENOUGH TO SLOW MY HEART, SHUT MY SYSTEM DOWN, TO MAKE ME SEEM DEAD.

IT'S ANOTHER DISGUISE. DEEP COVER AS A DEAD WOMAN.

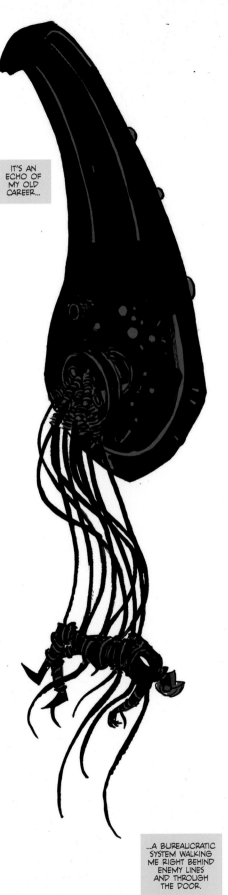

IT'S AN ECHO OF MY OLD CAREER...

...A BUREAUCRATIC SYSTEM WALKING ME RIGHT BEHIND ENEMY LINES AND THROUGH THE DOOR.

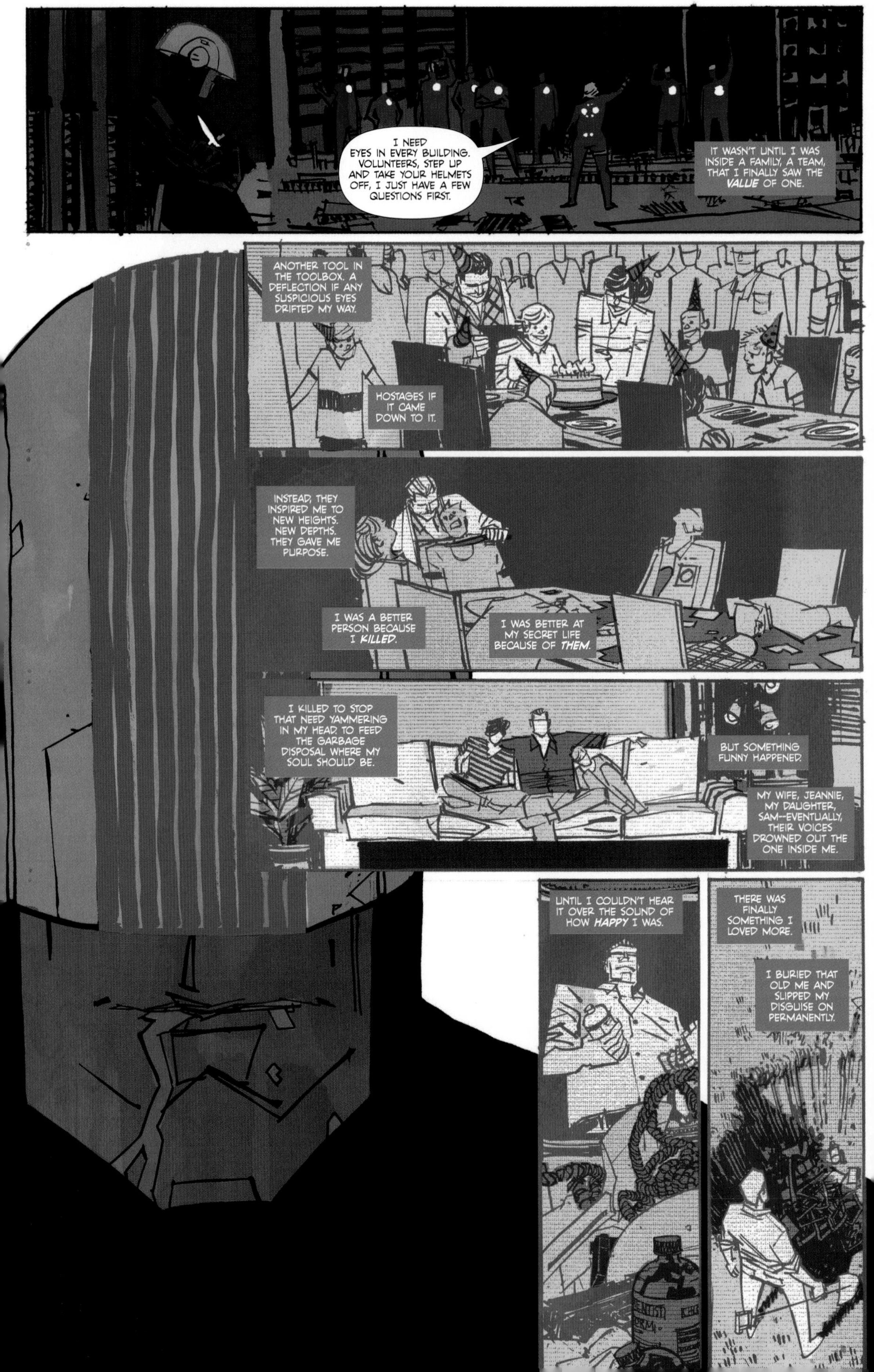
I NEED EYES IN EVERY BUILDING. VOLUNTEERS, STEP UP AND TAKE YOUR HELMETS OFF, I JUST HAVE A FEW QUESTIONS FIRST.
IT WASN'T UNTIL I WAS INSIDE A FAMILY, A TEAM, THAT I FINALLY SAW THE *VALUE* OF ONE.
ANOTHER TOOL IN THE TOOLBOX. A DEFLECTION IF ANY SUSPICIOUS EYES DRIFTED MY WAY.
HOSTAGES IF IT CAME DOWN TO IT.
INSTEAD, THEY INSPIRED ME TO NEW HEIGHTS. NEW DEPTHS. THEY GAVE ME PURPOSE.
I WAS A BETTER PERSON BECAUSE I *KILLED*.
I WAS BETTER AT MY SECRET LIFE BECAUSE OF *THEM*.
I KILLED TO STOP THAT NEED YAMMERING IN MY HEAD. TO FEED THE GARBAGE DISPOSAL WHERE MY SOUL SHOULD BE.
BUT SOMETHING FUNNY HAPPENED.
MY WIFE, JEANNIE, MY DAUGHTER, SAM--EVENTUALLY, THEIR VOICES DROWNED OUT THE ONE INSIDE ME.
UNTIL I COULDN'T HEAR IT OVER THE SOUND OF HOW *HAPPY* I WAS.
THERE WAS FINALLY SOMETHING I LOVED MORE.
I BURIED THAT OLD ME AND SLIPPED MY DISGUISE ON PERMANENTLY.

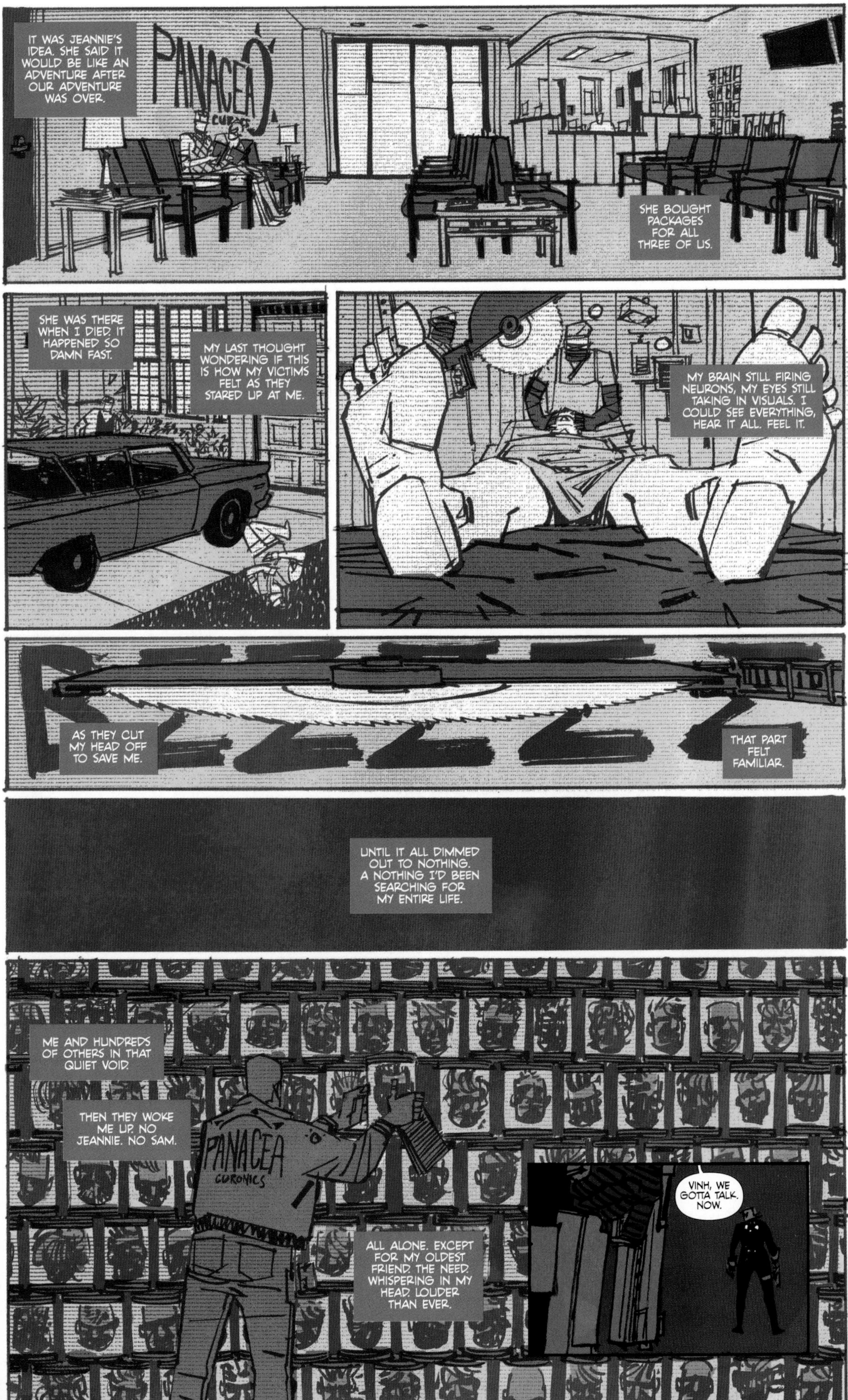
IT WAS JEANNIE'S IDEA. SHE SAID IT WOULD BE LIKE AN ADVENTURE AFTER OUR ADVENTURE WAS OVER.
PANACEA
SHE BOUGHT PACKAGES FOR ALL THREE OF US.
SHE WAS THERE WHEN I DIED. IT HAPPENED SO DAMN FAST.
MY LAST THOUGHT WONDERING IF THIS IS HOW MY VICTIMS FELT AS THEY STARED UP AT ME.
MY BRAIN STILL FIRING NEURONS, MY EYES STILL TAKING IN VISUALS. I COULD SEE EVERYTHING, HEAR IT ALL. FEEL IT.
AS THEY CUT MY HEAD OFF TO SAVE ME.
THAT PART FELT FAMILIAR.
UNTIL IT ALL DIMMED OUT TO NOTHING. A NOTHING I'D BEEN SEARCHING FOR MY ENTIRE LIFE.
ME AND HUNDREDS OF OTHERS IN THAT QUIET VOID.
THEN THEY WOKE ME UP. NO JEANNIE. NO SAM.
PANACEA CURONICS
ALL ALONE. EXCEPT FOR MY OLDEST FRIEND. THE NEED. WHISPERING IN MY HEAD. LOUDER THAN EVER.
VINH, WE GOTTA TALK. NOW.

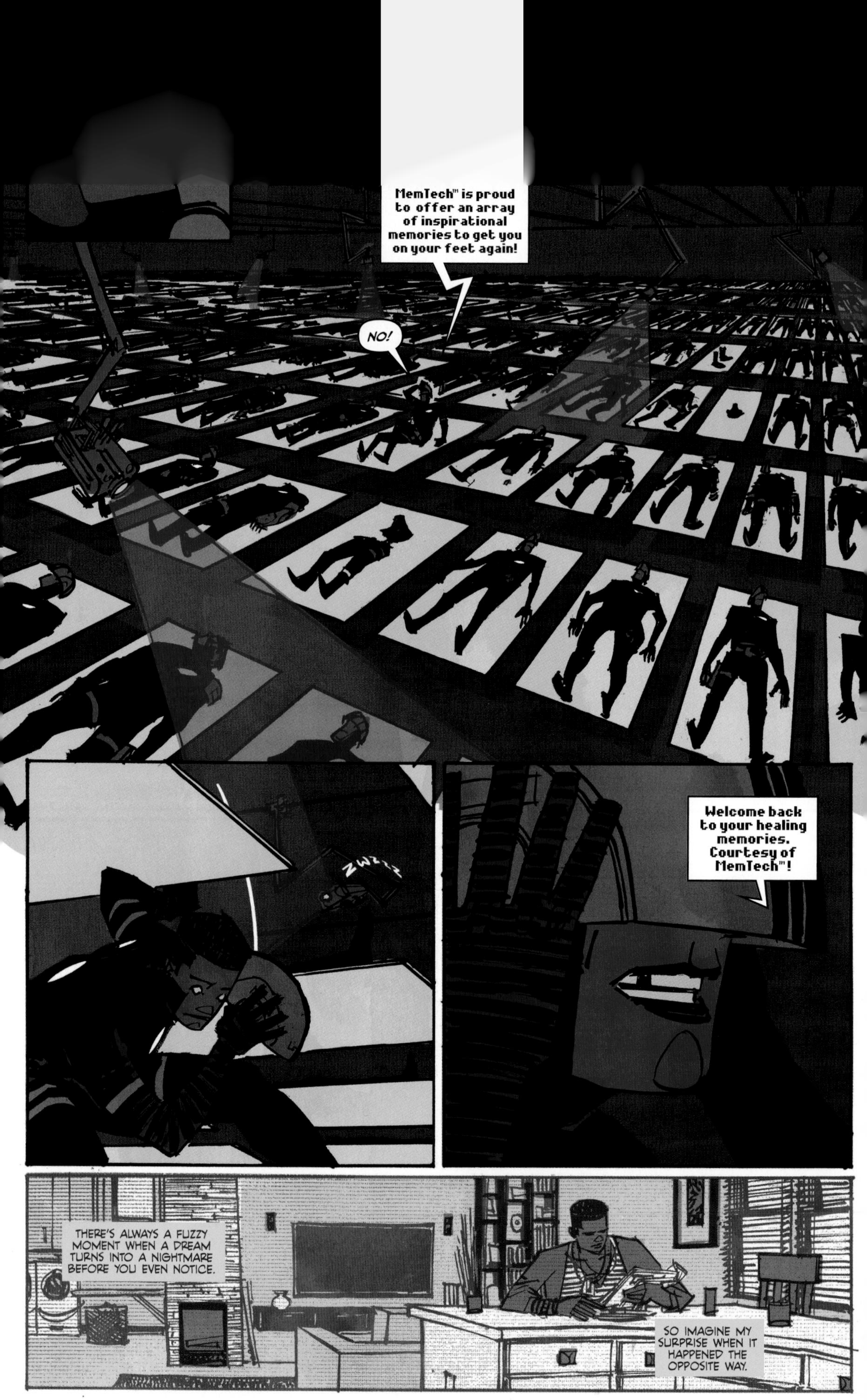
MemTech™ is proud to offer an array of inspirational memories to get you on your feet again!
NO!
ZWZZZ
Welcome back to your healing memories. Courtesy of MemTech™!
THERE'S ALWAYS A FUZZY MOMENT WHEN A DREAM TURNS INTO A NIGHTMARE BEFORE YOU EVEN NOTICE.
SO IMAGINE MY SURPRISE WHEN IT HAPPENED THE OPPOSITE WAY.

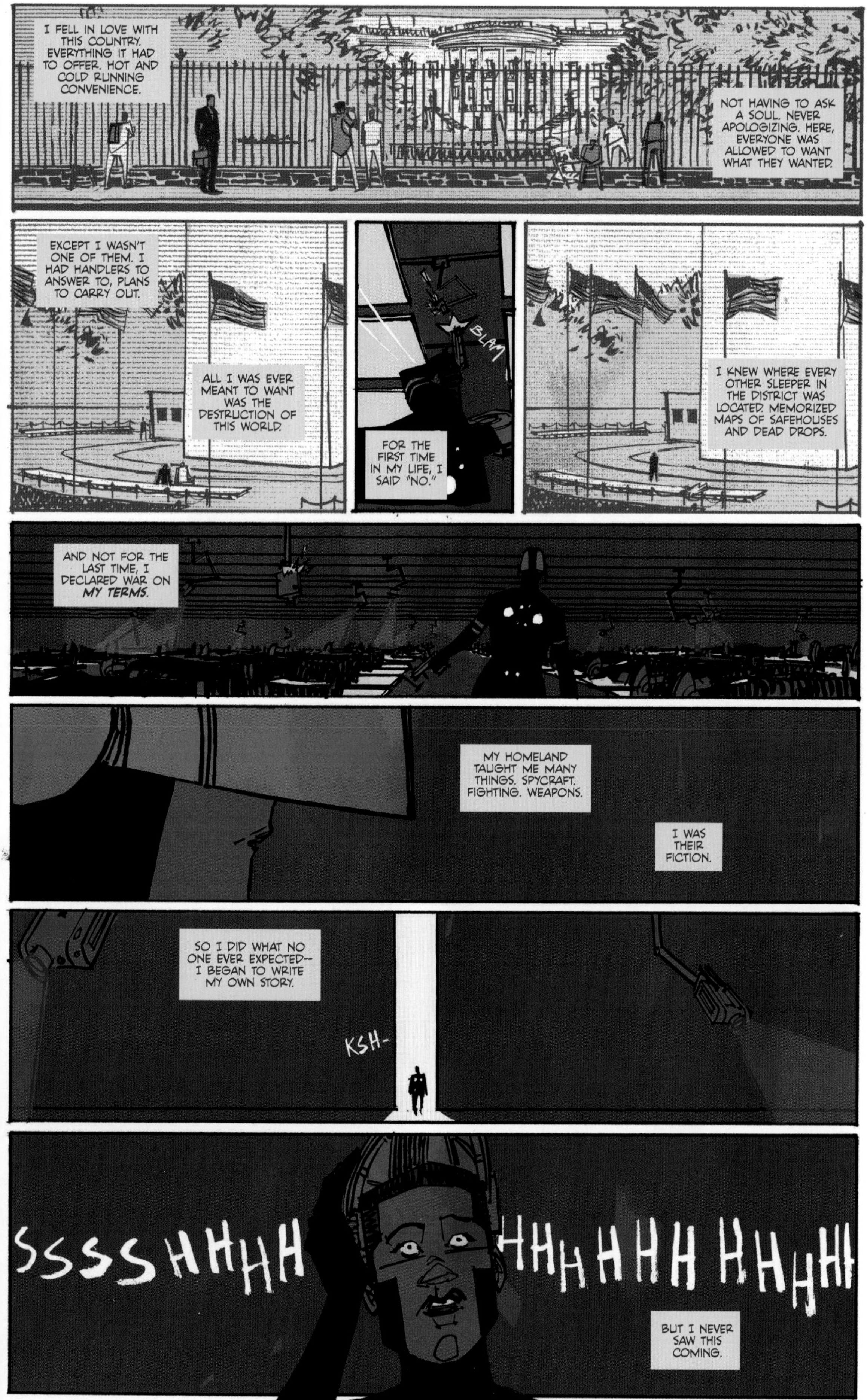

I FELL IN LOVE WITH THIS COUNTRY. EVERYTHING IT HAD TO OFFER. HOT AND COLD RUNNING CONVENIENCE.
NOT HAVING TO ASK A SOUL. NEVER APOLOGIZING. HERE, EVERYONE WAS ALLOWED TO WANT WHAT THEY WANTED.
EXCEPT I WASN'T ONE OF THEM. I HAD HANDLERS TO ANSWER TO, PLANS TO CARRY OUT.
ALL I WAS EVER MEANT TO WANT WAS THE DESTRUCTION OF THIS WORLD.
BLAM
FOR THE FIRST TIME IN MY LIFE, I SAID "NO."
I KNEW WHERE EVERY OTHER SLEEPER IN THE DISTRICT WAS LOCATED. MEMORIZED MAPS OF SAFEHOUSES AND DEAD DROPS.
AND NOT FOR THE LAST TIME, I DECLARED WAR ON *MY TERMS*.
MY HOMELAND TAUGHT ME MANY THINGS. SPYCRAFT. FIGHTING. WEAPONS.
I WAS THEIR FICTION.
SO I DID WHAT NO ONE EVER EXPECTED-- I BEGAN TO WRITE MY OWN STORY.
KSH-
SSSSHHHH
HHHHHHHHHHHH
BUT I NEVER SAW THIS COMING.

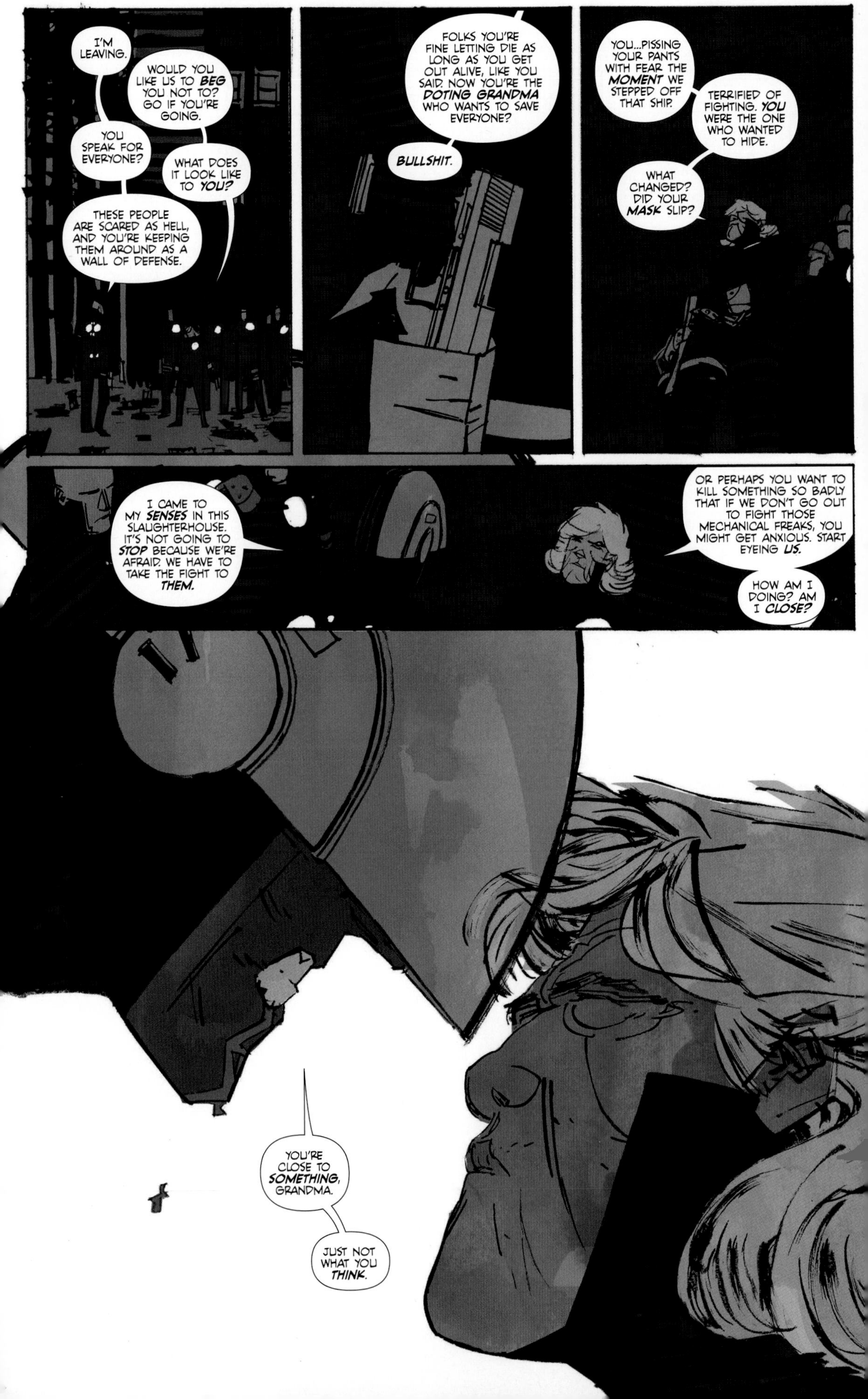
I'M LEAVING.
WOULD YOU LIKE US TO **BEG** YOU NOT TO? GO IF YOU'RE GOING.
YOU SPEAK FOR EVERYONE?
WHAT DOES IT LOOK LIKE TO **YOU?**
THESE PEOPLE ARE SCARED AS HELL, AND YOU'RE KEEPING THEM AROUND AS A WALL OF DEFENSE.
FOLKS YOU'RE FINE LETTING DIE AS LONG AS YOU GET OUT ALIVE, LIKE YOU SAID. NOW YOU'RE THE **DOTING GRANDMA** WHO WANTS TO SAVE EVERYONE?
BULLSHIT.
YOU...PISSING YOUR PANTS WITH FEAR THE **MOMENT** WE STEPPED OFF THAT SHIP.
TERRIFIED OF FIGHTING. **YOU** WERE THE ONE WHO WANTED TO HIDE.
WHAT CHANGED? DID YOUR **MASK** SLIP?
I CAME TO MY **SENSES** IN THIS SLAUGHTERHOUSE. IT'S NOT GOING TO **STOP** BECAUSE WE'RE AFRAID. WE HAVE TO TAKE THE FIGHT TO **THEM.**
OR PERHAPS YOU WANT TO KILL SOMETHING SO BADLY THAT IF WE DON'T GO OUT TO FIGHT THOSE MECHANICAL FREAKS, YOU MIGHT GET ANXIOUS. START EYEING **US.**
HOW AM I DOING? AM I **CLOSE?**
YOU'RE CLOSE TO **SOMETHING,** GRANDMA.
JUST NOT WHAT YOU **THINK.**

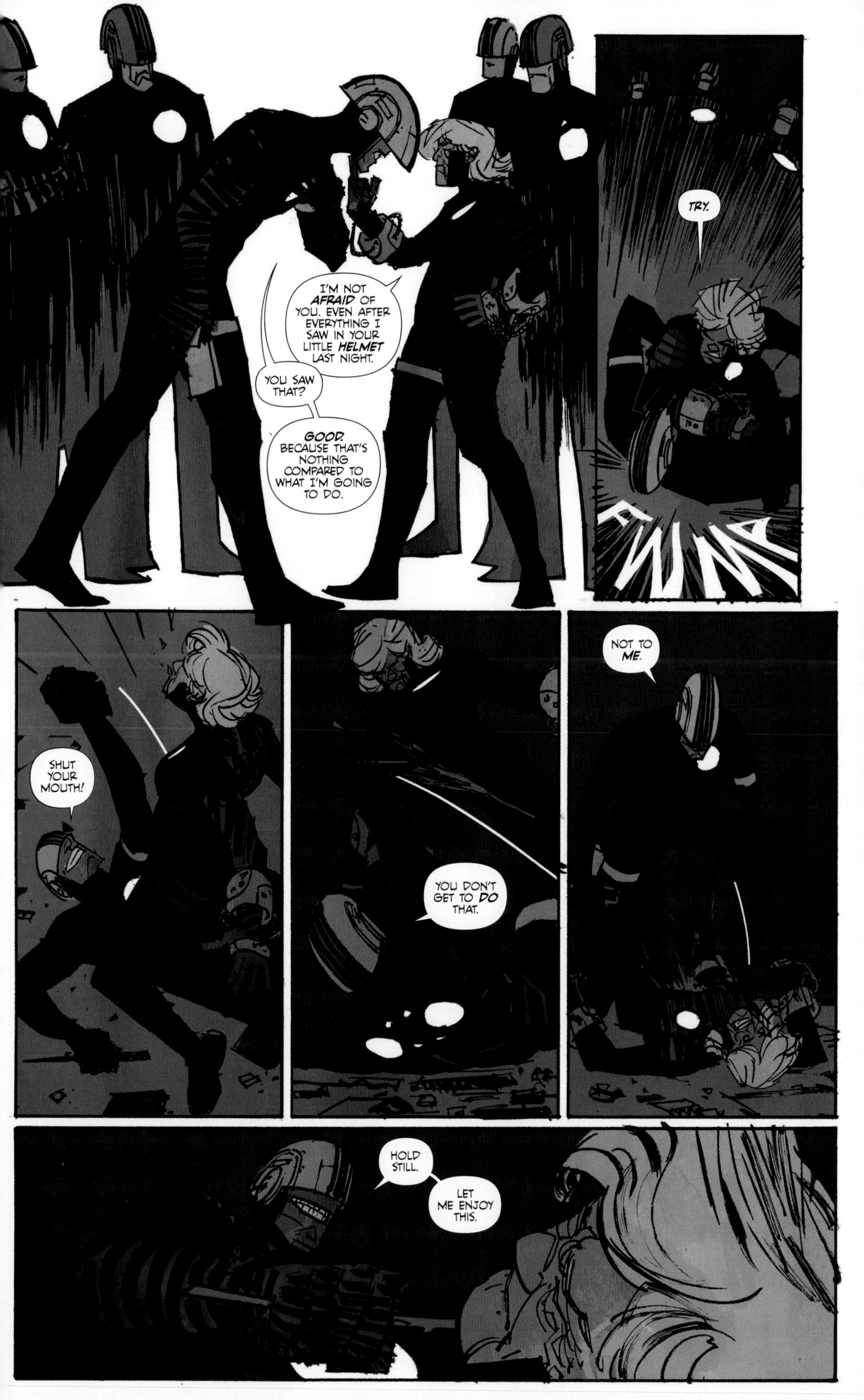

I'M NOT AFRAID OF YOU. EVEN AFTER EVERYTHING I SAW IN YOUR LITTLE HELMET LAST NIGHT.
YOU SAW THAT?
GOOD. BECAUSE THAT'S NOTHING COMPARED TO WHAT I'M GOING TO DO.
TRY.
FWAP
SHUT YOUR MOUTH!
YOU DON'T GET TO DO THAT.
NOT TO ME.
HOLD STILL.
LET ME ENJOY THIS.

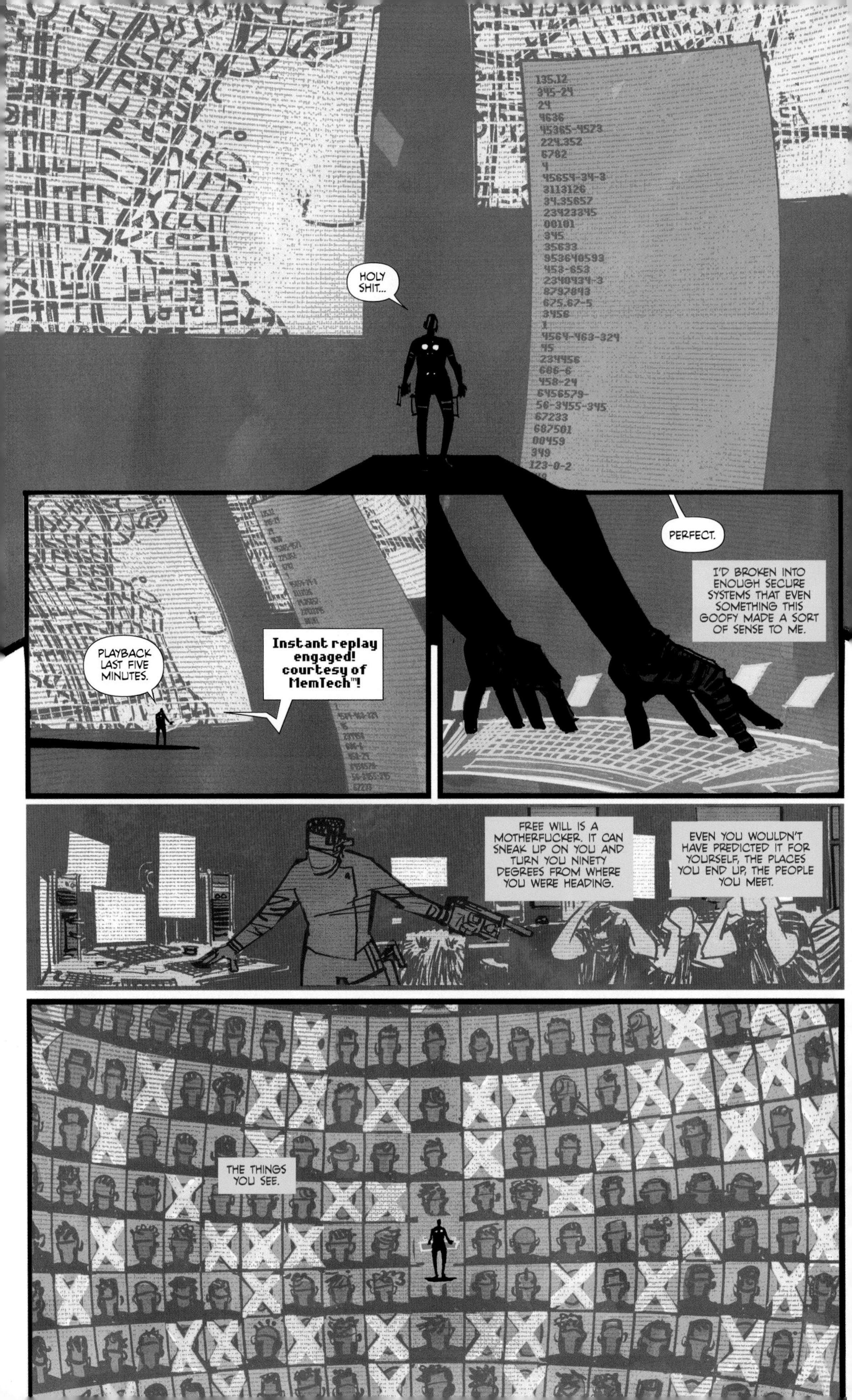
135.12
345-24
24
4636
45365-4523
224.352
6782
4
45654-34-3
3113126
34.35657
23423345
00101
345
35633
953640593
453-653
2340434-3
8797843
625.67-5
3456
1
4564-463-324
45
234456
606-6
458-24
6456579-
56-3455-345
67233
687501
00459
349
123-0-2
HOLY SHIT...
PLAYBACK LAST FIVE MINUTES.
Instant replay engaged! courtesy of MemTech™!
PERFECT.
I'D BROKEN INTO ENOUGH SECURE SYSTEMS THAT EVEN SOMETHING THIS GOOFY MADE A SORT OF SENSE TO ME.
FREE WILL IS A MOTHERFUCKER. IT CAN SNEAK UP ON YOU AND TURN YOU NINETY DEGREES FROM WHERE YOU WERE HEADING.
EVEN YOU WOULDN'T HAVE PREDICTED IT FOR YOURSELF, THE PLACES YOU END UP, THE PEOPLE YOU MEET.
THE THINGS YOU SEE.

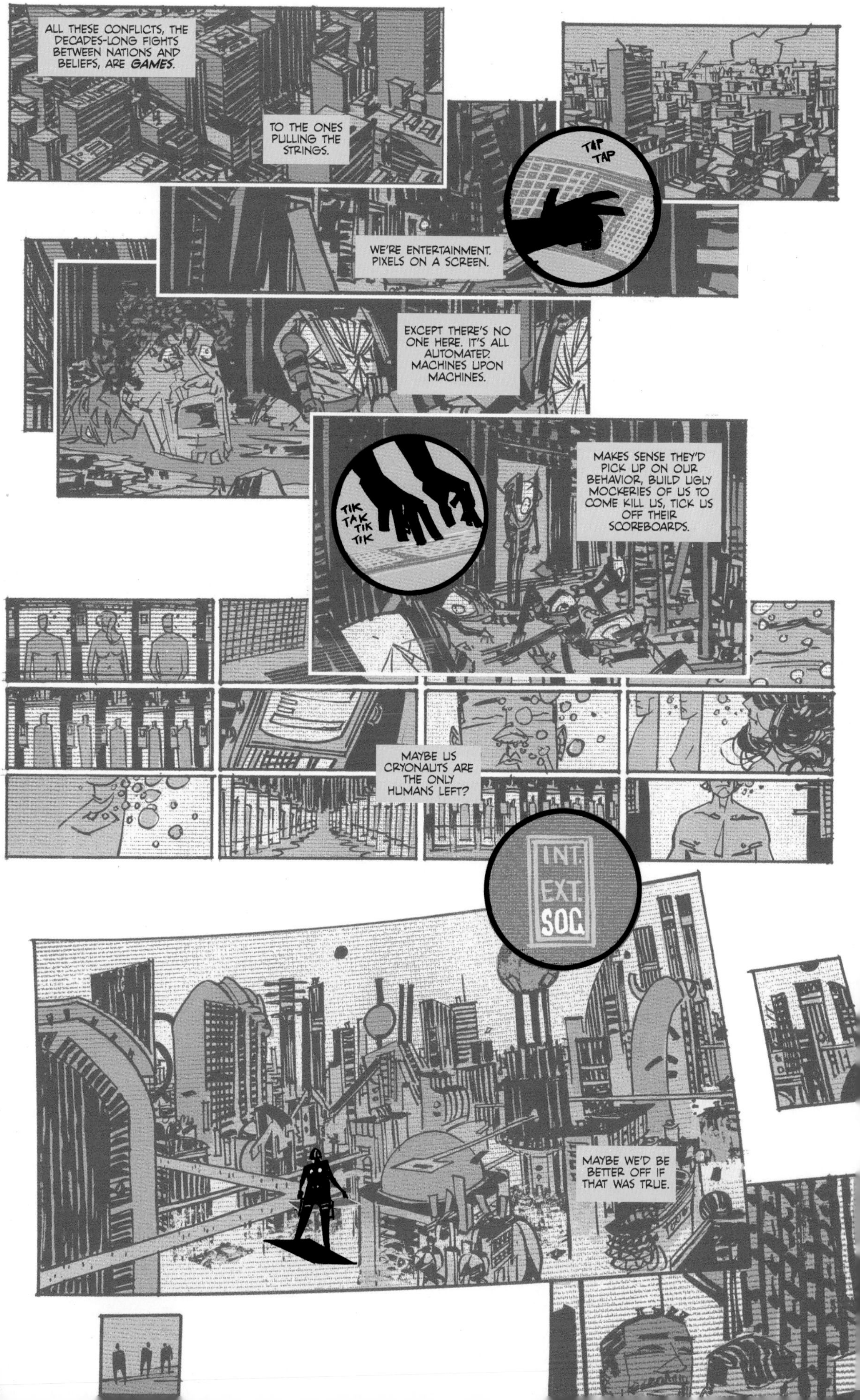
ALL THESE CONFLICTS, THE DECADES-LONG FIGHTS BETWEEN NATIONS AND BELIEFS, ARE *GAMES*.
TO THE ONES PULLING THE STRINGS.
TAP TAP
WE'RE ENTERTAINMENT. PIXELS ON A SCREEN.
EXCEPT THERE'S NO ONE HERE. IT'S ALL AUTOMATED. MACHINES UPON MACHINES.
TIK TAK TIK TIK
MAKES SENSE THEY'D PICK UP ON OUR BEHAVIOR, BUILD UGLY MOCKERIES OF US TO COME KILL US, TICK US OFF THEIR SCOREBOARDS.
MAYBE US CRYONAUTS ARE THE ONLY HUMANS LEFT?
INT.
EXT.
SOC.
MAYBE WE'D BE BETTER OFF IF THAT WAS TRUE.

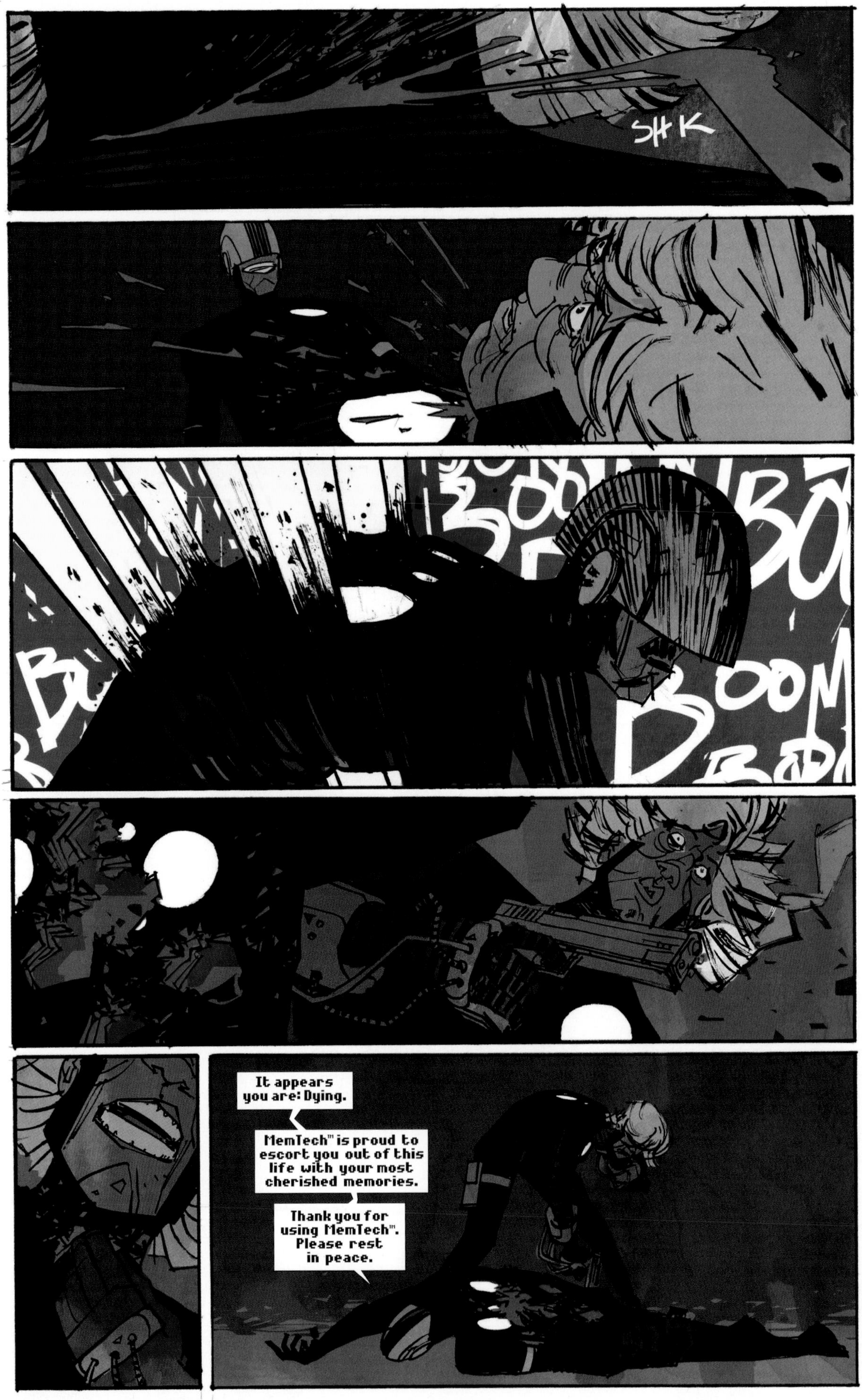
SHK
BOOM
It appears you are: Dying.
MemTech™ is proud to escort you out of this life with your most cherished memories.
Thank you for using MemTech™. Please rest in peace.

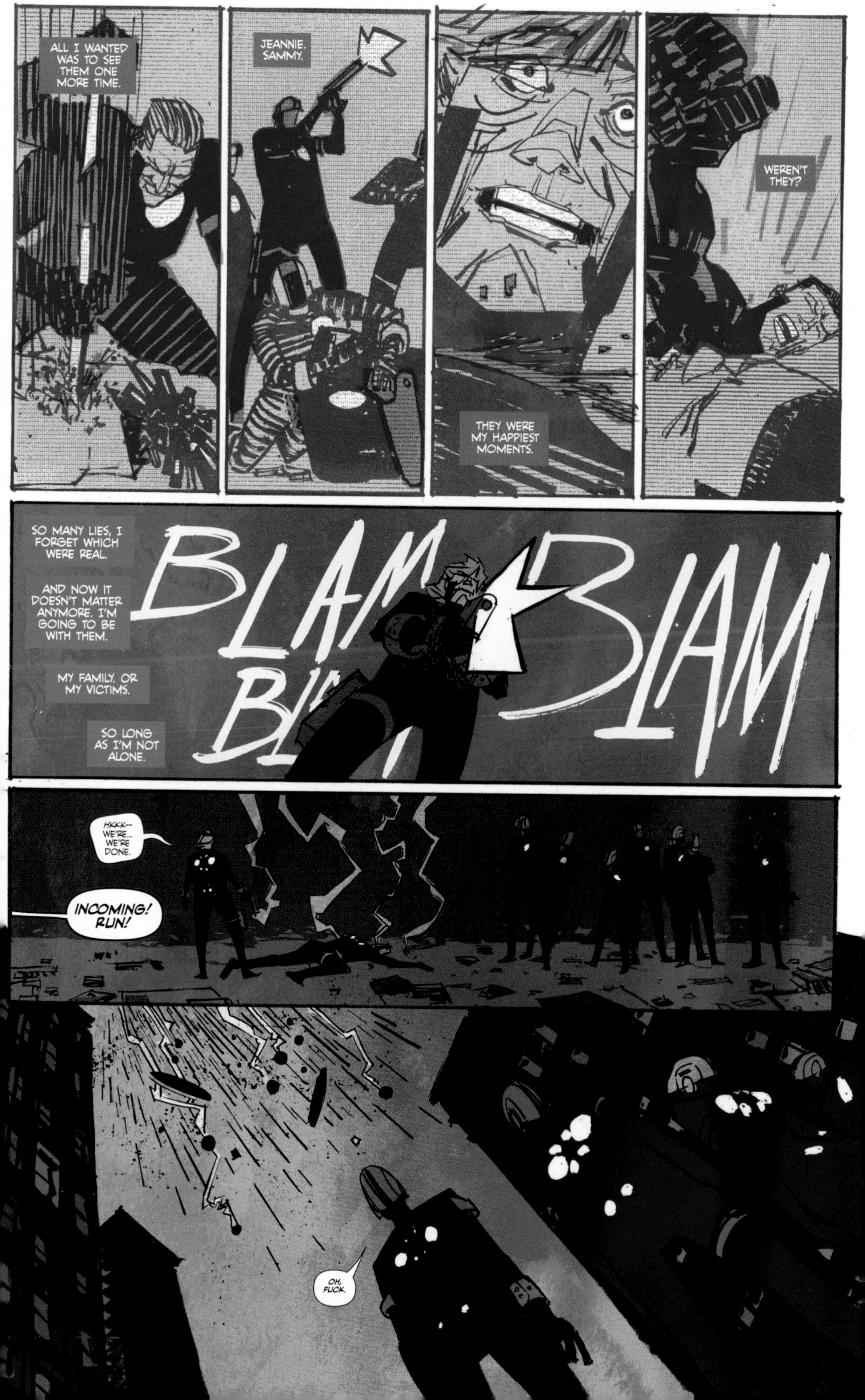
ALL I WANTED WAS TO SEE THEM ONE MORE TIME.
JEANNIE. SAMMY.
THEY WERE MY HAPPIEST MOMENTS.
WEREN'T THEY?
SO MANY LIES, I FORGET WHICH WERE REAL.
AND NOW IT DOESN'T MATTER ANYMORE. I'M GOING TO BE WITH THEM.
MY FAMILY. OR MY VICTIMS.
SO LONG AS I'M NOT ALONE.
BLAM
BLAM
HKKK-- WE'RE... WE'RE DONE.
INCOMING! RUN!
OH, FUCK.

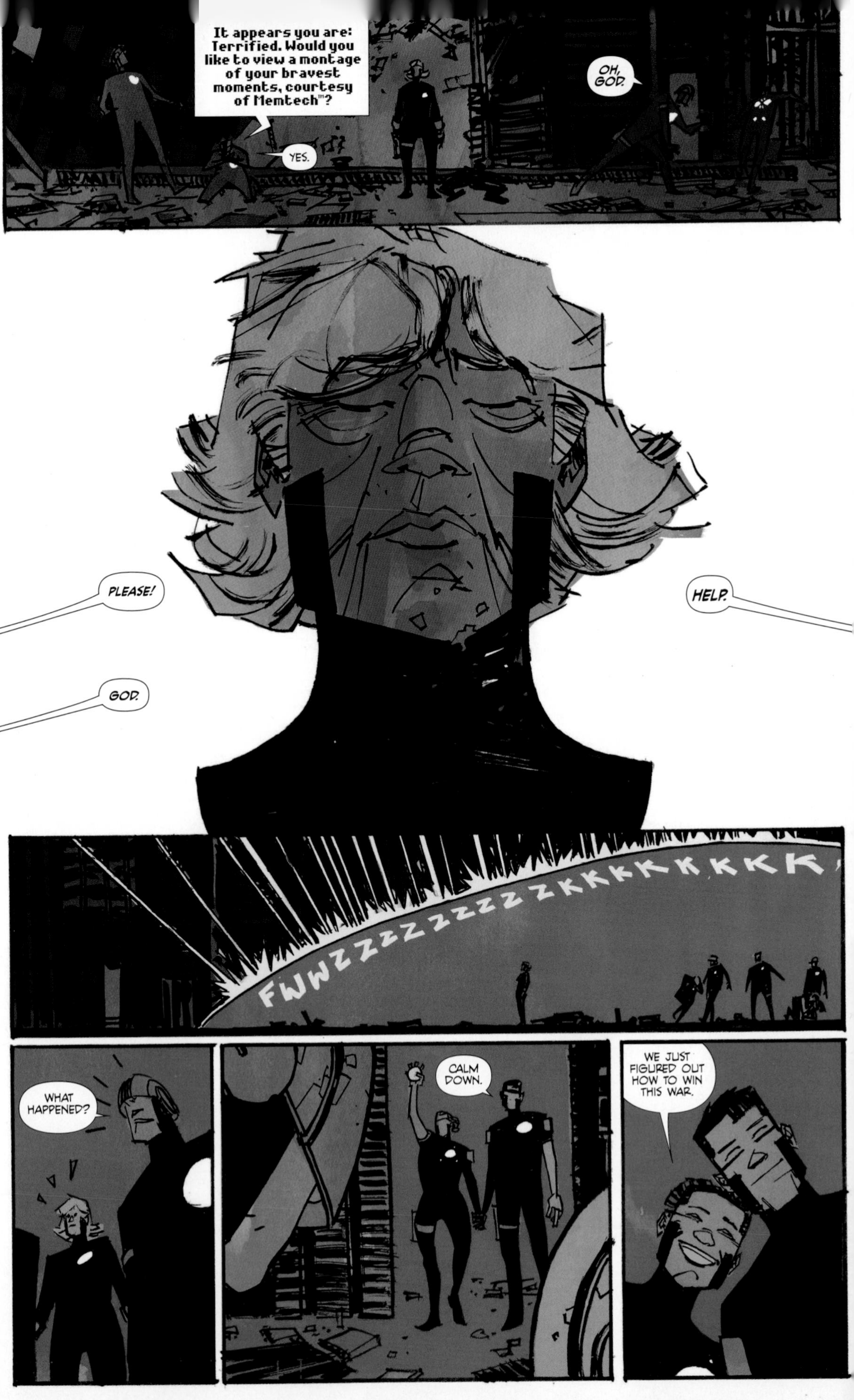
It appears you are: Terrified. Would you like to view a montage of your bravest moments, courtesy of Memtech™?
YES.
OH, GOD.
PLEASE!
HELP.
GOD.
FWWZZZZZZZZZKKKKKKKK
WHAT HAPPENED?
CALM DOWN.
WE JUST FIGURED OUT HOW TO WIN THIS WAR.

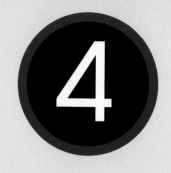

4

FIVE-SIDED PUZZLE

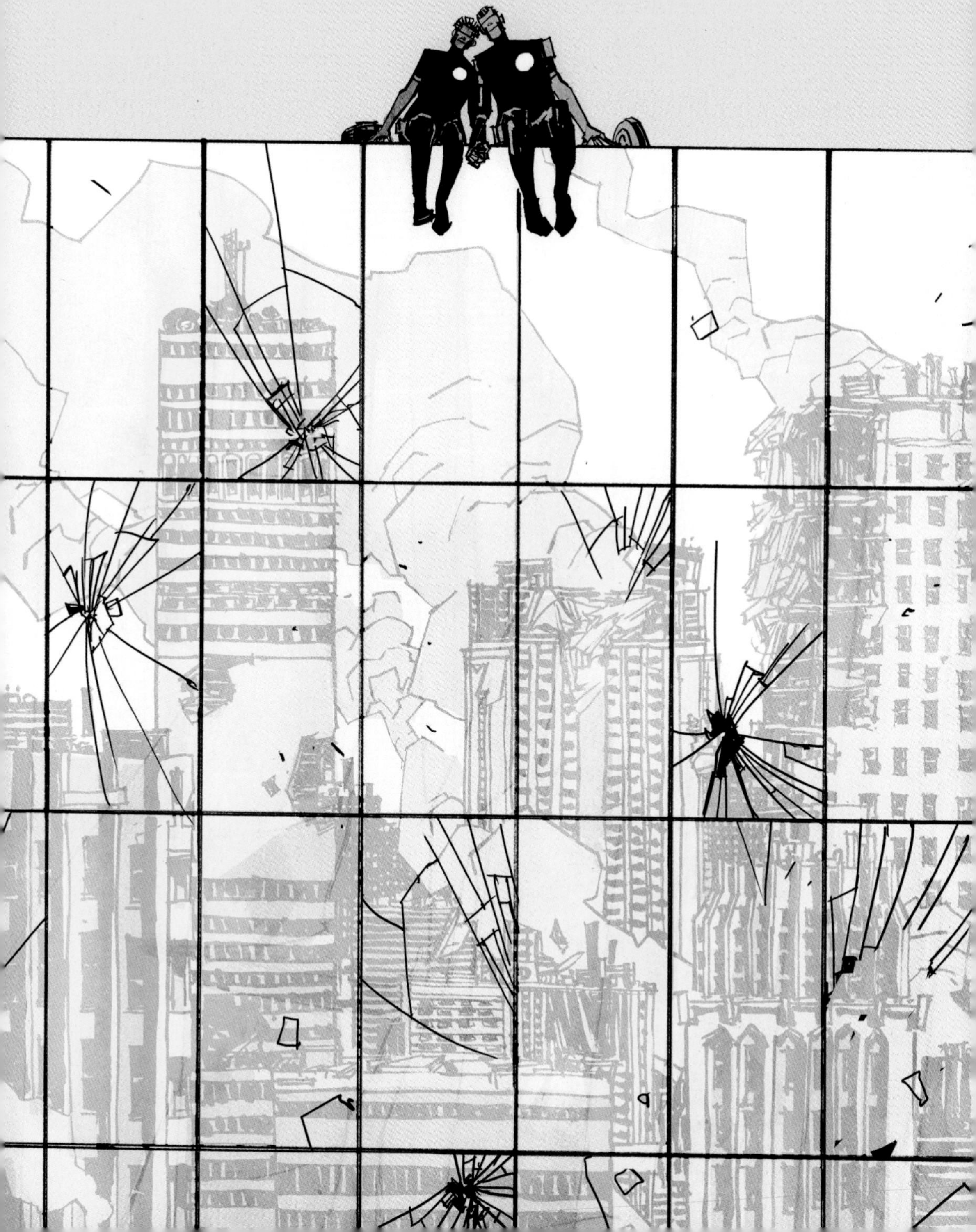

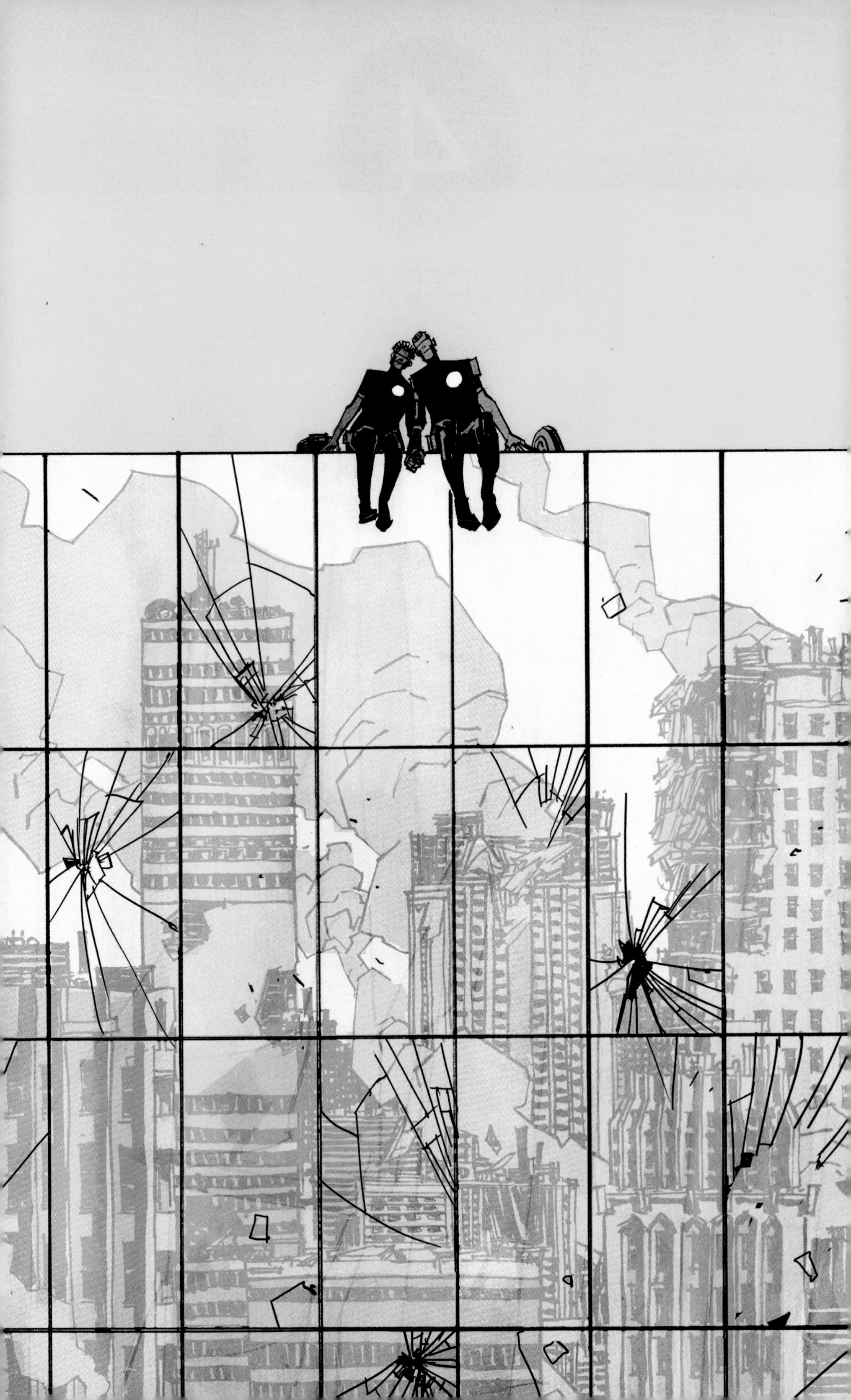

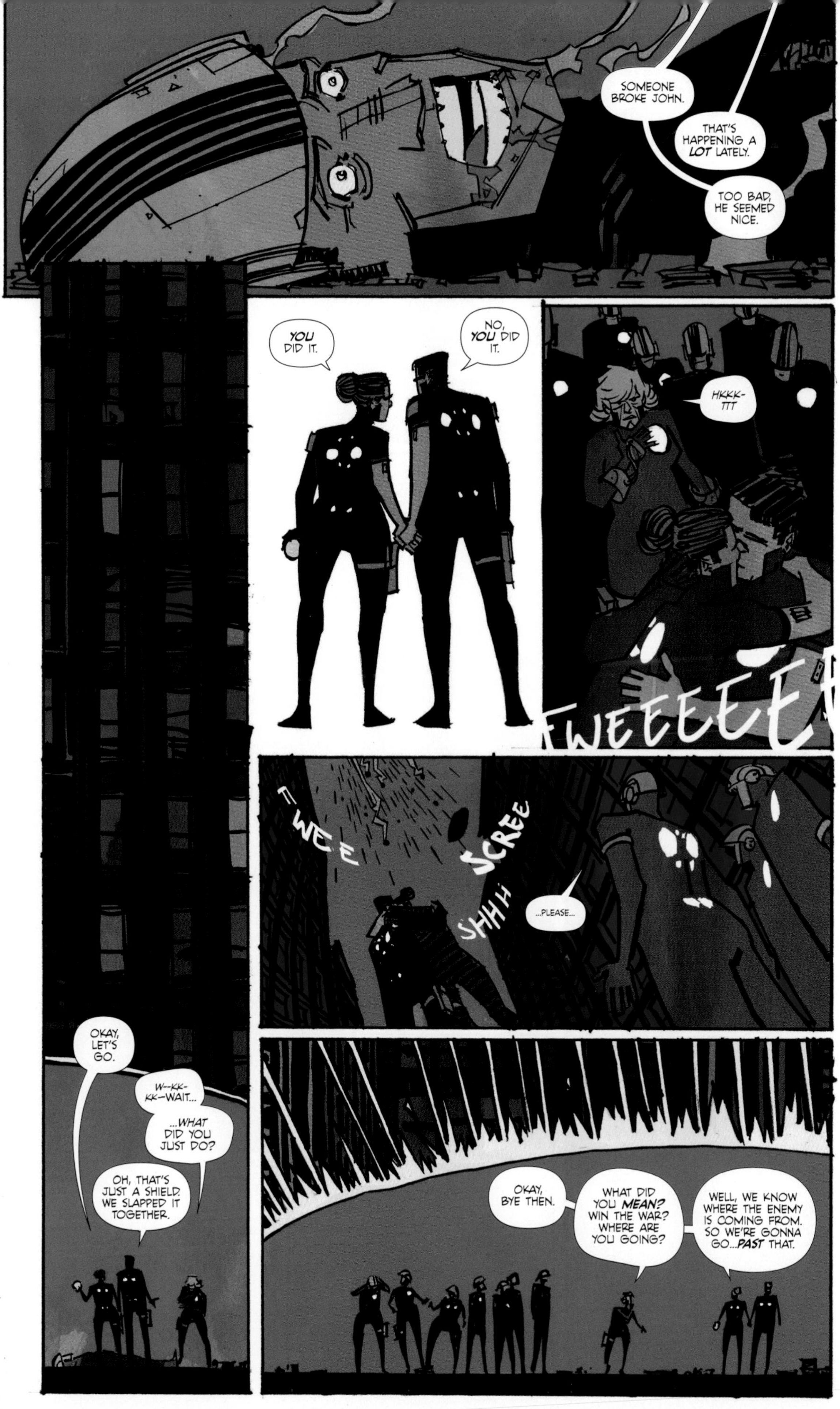
SOMEONE BROKE JOHN.
THAT'S HAPPENING A LOT LATELY.
TOO BAD, HE SEEMED NICE.
OKAY, LET'S GO.
W--KK-KK--WAIT...
...WHAT DID YOU JUST DO?
OH, THAT'S JUST A SHIELD. WE SLAPPED IT TOGETHER.
YOU DID IT.
NO, YOU DID IT.
HKKK-TTT
FWEEEEEE
FWEE
SCREE
SHHH
...PLEASE...
OKAY, BYE THEN.
WHAT DID YOU MEAN? WIN THE WAR? WHERE ARE YOU GOING?
WELL, WE KNOW WHERE THE ENEMY IS COMING FROM. SO WE'RE GONNA GO...PAST THAT.

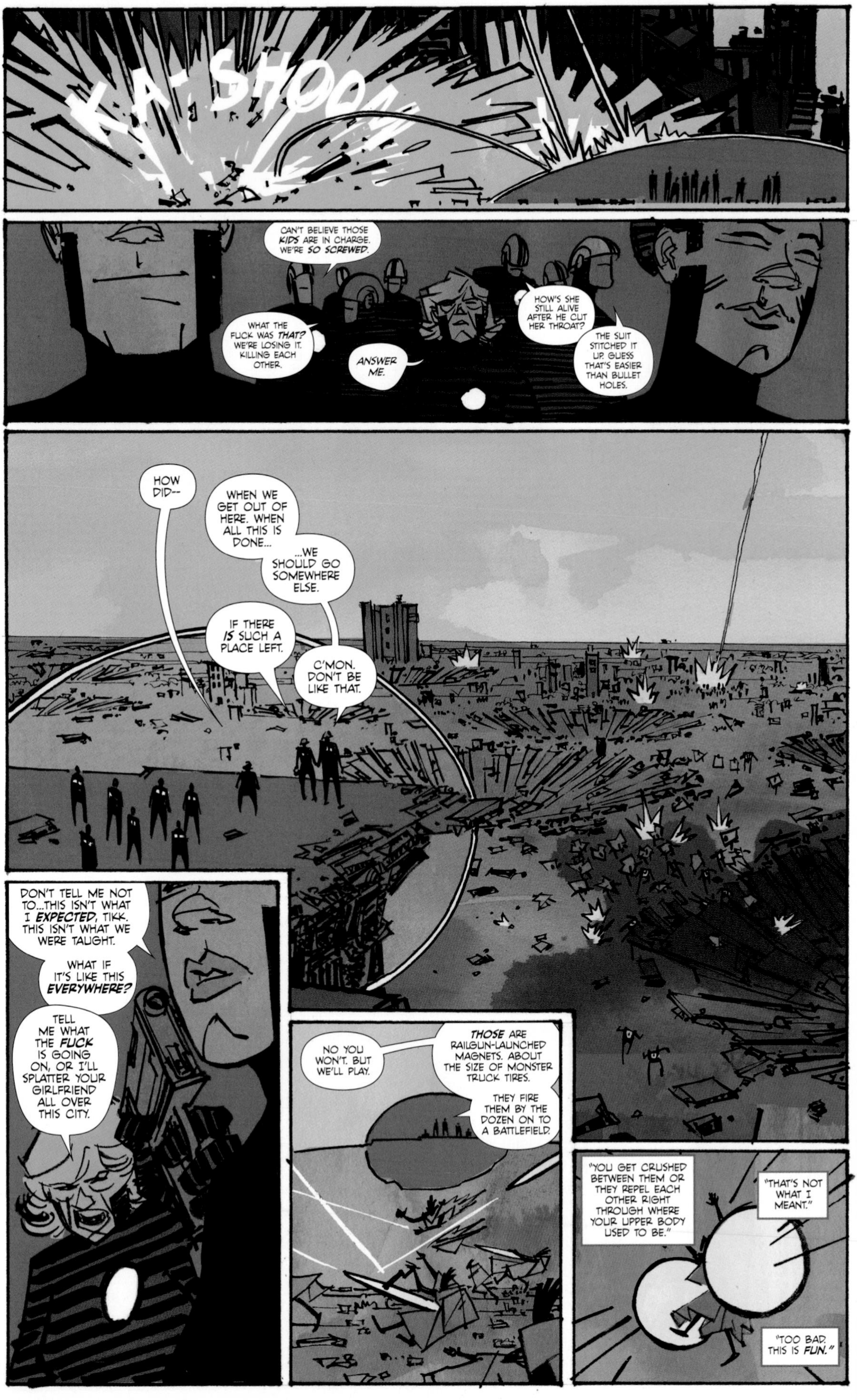
KA-SHOOM
CAN'T BELIEVE THOSE *KIDS* ARE IN CHARGE. WE'RE *SO SCREWED*.
WHAT THE FUCK WAS *THAT?* WE'RE LOSING IT. KILLING EACH OTHER.
ANSWER ME.
HOW'S SHE STILL ALIVE AFTER HE CUT HER THROAT?
THE SUIT STITCHED IT UP. GUESS THAT'S EASIER THAN BULLET HOLES.
HOW DID--
WHEN WE GET OUT OF HERE. WHEN ALL THIS IS DONE...
...WE SHOULD GO SOMEWHERE ELSE.
IF THERE *IS* SUCH A PLACE LEFT.
C'MON. DON'T BE LIKE THAT.
DON'T TELL ME NOT TO...THIS ISN'T WHAT I ***EXPECTED***, TIKK. THIS ISN'T WHAT WE WERE TAUGHT.
WHAT IF IT'S LIKE THIS ***EVERYWHERE?***
TELL ME WHAT THE ***FUCK*** IS GOING ON, OR I'LL SPLATTER YOUR GIRLFRIEND ALL OVER THIS CITY.
NO YOU WON'T. BUT WE'LL PLAY.
THOSE ARE RAILGUN-LAUNCHED MAGNETS. ABOUT THE SIZE OF MONSTER TRUCK TIRES.
THEY FIRE THEM BY THE DOZEN ON TO A BATTLEFIELD.
"YOU GET CRUSHED BETWEEN THEM OR THEY REPEL EACH OTHER RIGHT THROUGH WHERE YOUR UPPER BODY USED TO BE."
"THAT'S NOT WHAT I MEANT."
"TOO BAD. THIS IS ***FUN.***"

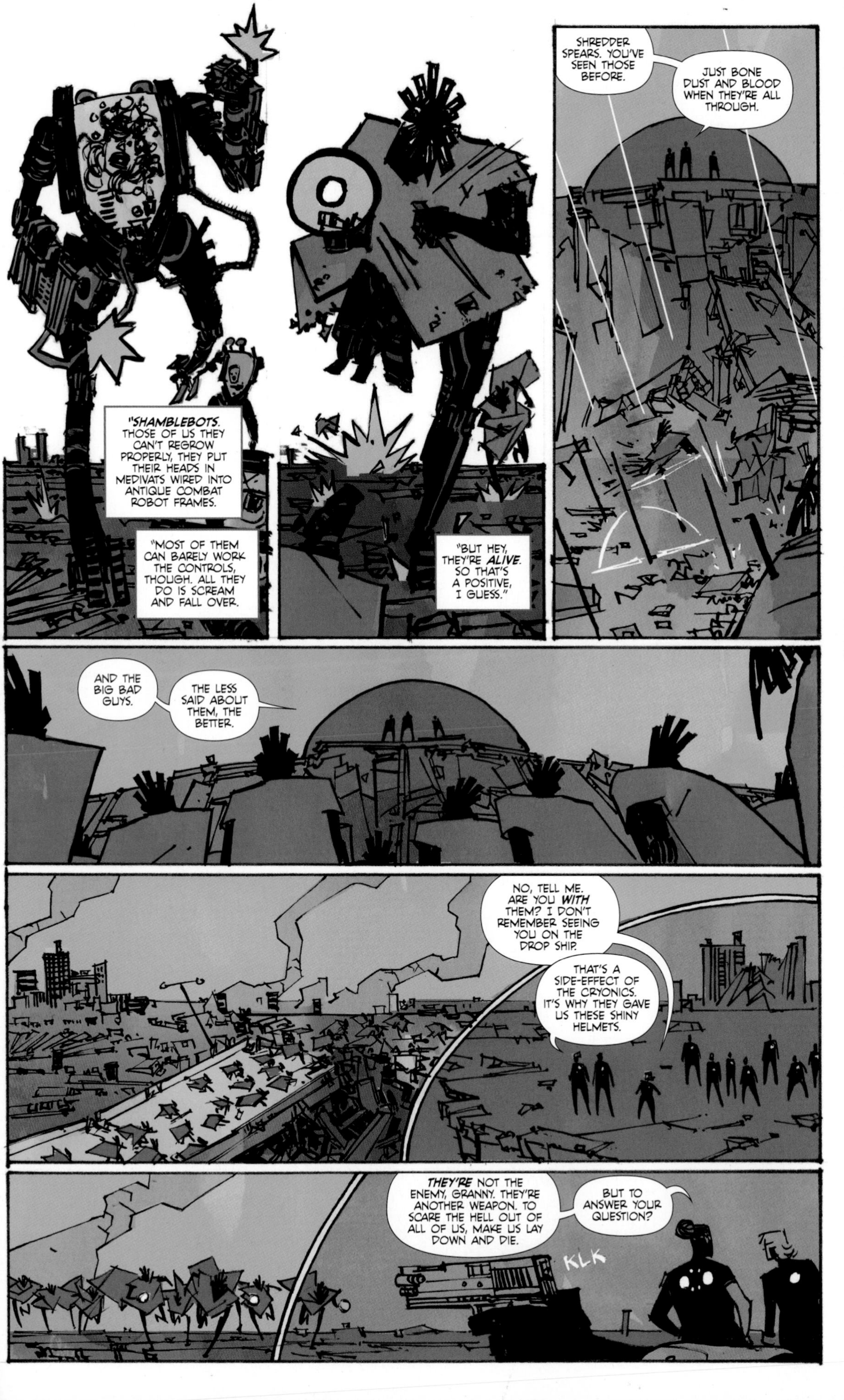
"SHAMBLEBOTS. THOSE OF US THEY CAN'T REGROW PROPERLY, THEY PUT THEIR HEADS IN MEDIVATS WIRED INTO ANTIQUE COMBAT ROBOT FRAMES.
"MOST OF THEM CAN BARELY WORK THE CONTROLS, THOUGH. ALL THEY DO IS SCREAM AND FALL OVER.
"BUT HEY, THEY'RE ALIVE. SO THAT'S A POSITIVE, I GUESS."
SHREDDER SPEARS. YOU'VE SEEN THOSE BEFORE.
JUST BONE DUST AND BLOOD WHEN THEY'RE ALL THROUGH.
AND THE BIG BAD GUYS.
THE LESS SAID ABOUT THEM, THE BETTER.
NO, TELL ME. ARE YOU WITH THEM? I DON'T REMEMBER SEEING YOU ON THE DROP SHIP.
THAT'S A SIDE-EFFECT OF THE CRYONICS. IT'S WHY THEY GAVE US THESE SHINY HELMETS.
THEY'RE NOT THE ENEMY, GRANNY. THEY'RE ANOTHER WEAPON. TO SCARE THE HELL OUT OF ALL OF US, MAKE US LAY DOWN AND DIE.
BUT TO ANSWER YOUR QUESTION?
KLK

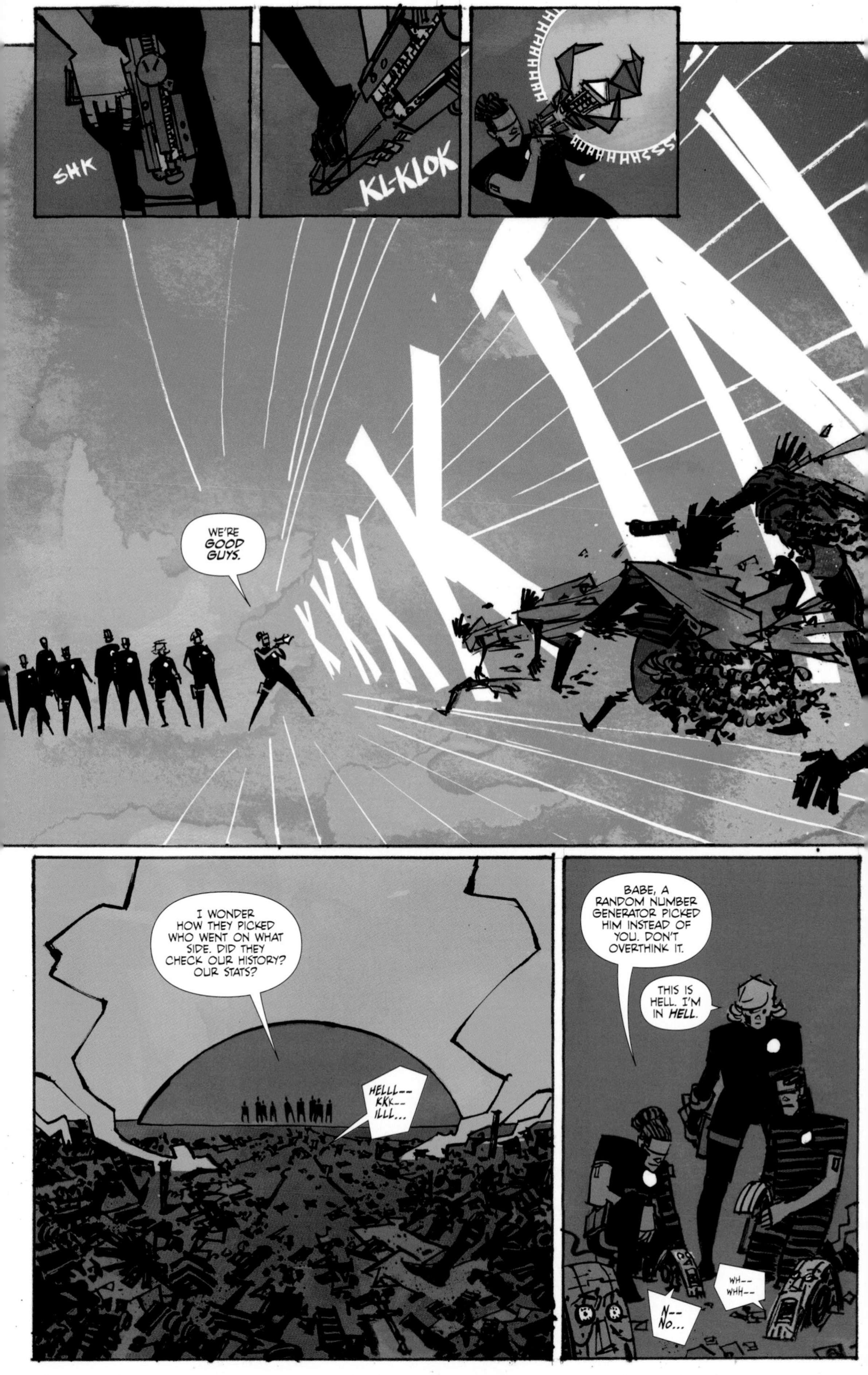
SHK
KL-KLOK
HHHHHHHHH
HHHHHHHHSSS
WE'RE GOOD GUYS.
KKKTAT
I WONDER HOW THEY PICKED WHO WENT ON WHAT SIDE. DID THEY CHECK OUR HISTORY? OUR STATS?
HELLL-- KKK-- ILLL...
BABE, A RANDOM NUMBER GENERATOR PICKED HIM INSTEAD OF YOU. DON'T OVERTHINK IT.
THIS IS HELL. I'M IN HELL.
N-- NO...
WH-- WHH--

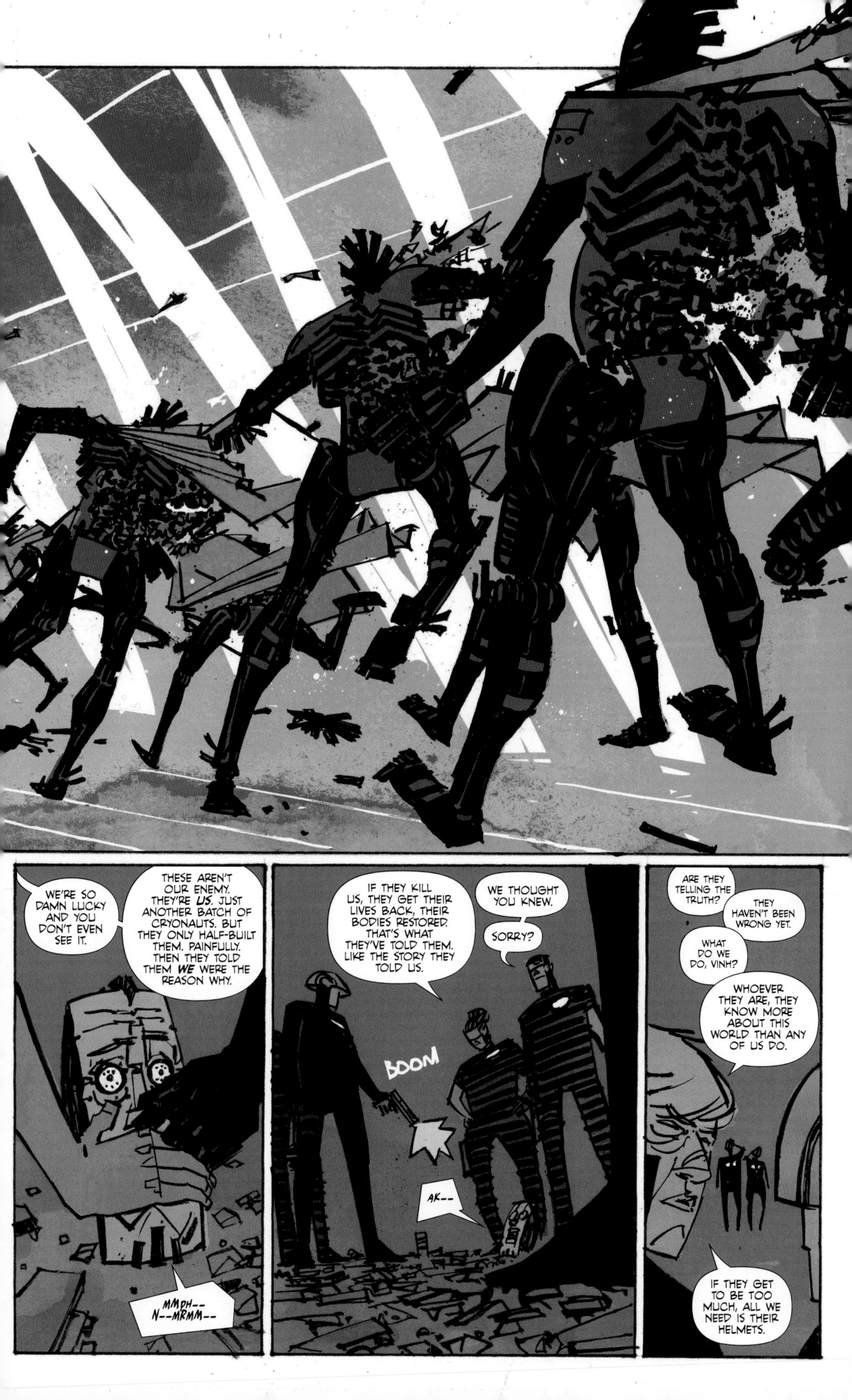
WE'RE SO DAMN LUCKY AND YOU DON'T EVEN SEE IT.
THESE AREN'T OUR ENEMY. THEY'RE US. JUST ANOTHER BATCH OF CRYONAUTS. BUT THEY ONLY HALF-BUILT THEM. PAINFULLY. THEN THEY TOLD THEM WE WERE THE REASON WHY.
MMPH-- N--MRMM--
IF THEY KILL US, THEY GET THEIR LIVES BACK, THEIR BODIES RESTORED. THAT'S WHAT THEY'VE TOLD THEM. LIKE THE STORY THEY TOLD US.
WE THOUGHT YOU KNEW.
SORRY?
BOOM
AK--
ARE THEY TELLING THE TRUTH?
THEY HAVEN'T BEEN WRONG YET.
WHAT DO WE DO, VINH?
WHOEVER THEY ARE, THEY KNOW MORE ABOUT THIS WORLD THAN ANY OF US DO.
IF THEY GET TO BE TOO MUCH, ALL WE NEED IS THEIR HELMETS.

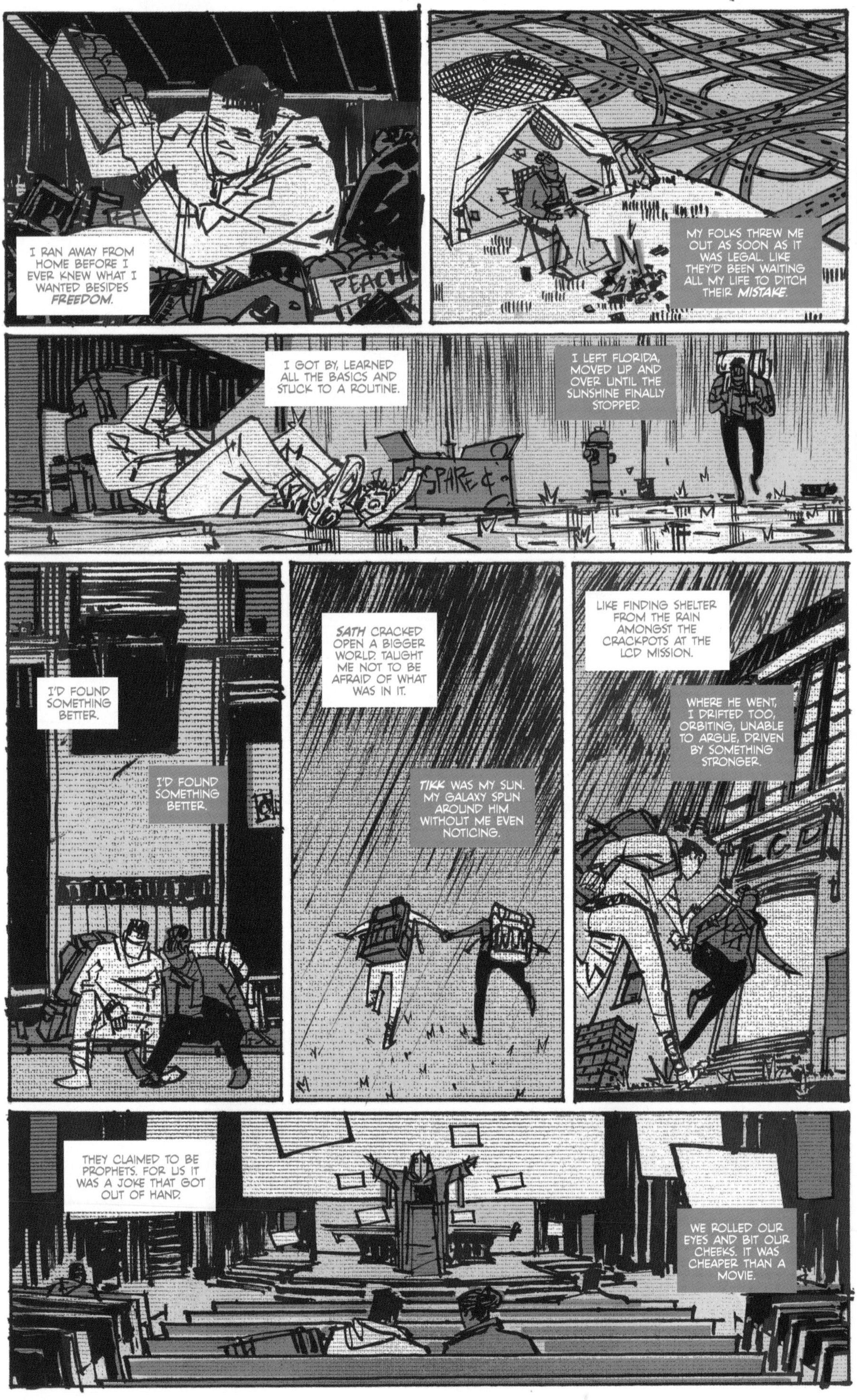
I RAN AWAY FROM HOME BEFORE I EVER KNEW WHAT I WANTED BESIDES *FREEDOM*.
PEACH
MY FOLKS THREW ME OUT AS SOON AS IT WAS LEGAL. LIKE THEY'D BEEN WAITING ALL MY LIFE TO DITCH THEIR *MISTAKE*.
I GOT BY, LEARNED ALL THE BASICS AND STUCK TO A ROUTINE.
SPARE ¢
I LEFT FLORIDA, MOVED UP AND OVER UNTIL THE SUNSHINE FINALLY STOPPED.
I'D FOUND SOMETHING BETTER.
I'D FOUND SOMETHING BETTER.
SATH CRACKED OPEN A BIGGER WORLD. TAUGHT ME NOT TO BE AFRAID OF WHAT WAS IN IT.
TIKK WAS MY SUN. MY GALAXY SPUN AROUND HIM WITHOUT ME EVEN NOTICING.
LIKE FINDING SHELTER FROM THE RAIN AMONGST THE CRACKPOTS AT THE LCD MISSION.
WHERE HE WENT, I DRIFTED TOO, ORBITING, UNABLE TO ARGUE, DRIVEN BY SOMETHING STRONGER.
LCD
THEY CLAIMED TO BE PROPHETS. FOR US IT WAS A JOKE THAT GOT OUT OF HAND.
WE ROLLED OUR EYES AND BIT OUR CHEEKS. IT WAS CHEAPER THAN A MOVIE.

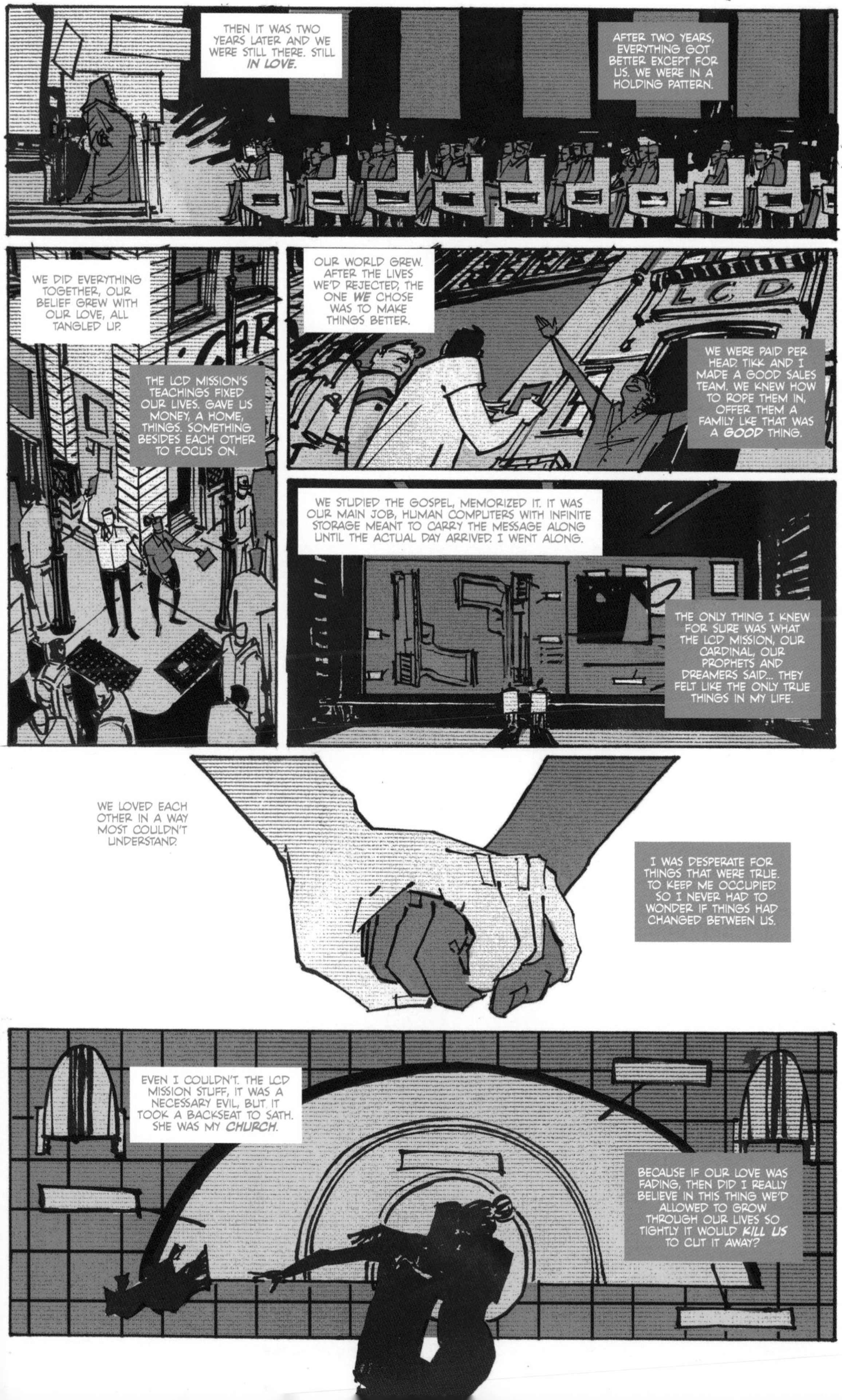
THEN IT WAS TWO YEARS LATER AND WE WERE STILL THERE. STILL *IN LOVE.*
AFTER TWO YEARS, EVERYTHING GOT BETTER EXCEPT FOR US. WE WERE IN A HOLDING PATTERN.
WE DID EVERYTHING TOGETHER, OUR BELIEF GREW WITH OUR LOVE, ALL TANGLED UP.
THE LCD MISSION'S TEACHINGS FIXED OUR LIVES. GAVE US MONEY, A HOME, THINGS. SOMETHING BESIDES EACH OTHER TO FOCUS ON.
OUR WORLD GREW. AFTER THE LIVES WE'D REJECTED, THE ONE *WE* CHOSE WAS TO MAKE THINGS BETTER.
LCD
WE WERE PAID PER HEAD. TIKK AND I MADE A GOOD SALES TEAM. WE KNEW HOW TO ROPE THEM IN, OFFER THEM A FAMILY LKE THAT WAS A *GOOD* THING.
WE STUDIED THE GOSPEL, MEMORIZED IT. IT WAS OUR MAIN JOB, HUMAN COMPUTERS WITH INFINITE STORAGE MEANT TO CARRY THE MESSAGE ALONG UNTIL THE ACTUAL DAY ARRIVED. I WENT ALONG.
THE ONLY THING I KNEW FOR SURE WAS WHAT THE LCD MISSION, OUR CARDINAL, OUR PROPHETS AND DREAMERS SAID... THEY FELT LIKE THE ONLY TRUE THINGS IN MY LIFE.
WE LOVED EACH OTHER IN A WAY MOST COULDN'T UNDERSTAND.
I WAS DESPERATE FOR THINGS THAT WERE TRUE. TO KEEP ME OCCUPIED SO I NEVER HAD TO WONDER IF THINGS HAD CHANGED BETWEEN US.
EVEN I COULDN'T. THE LCD MISSION STUFF, IT WAS A NECESSARY EVIL, BUT, IT TOOK A BACKSEAT TO SATH. SHE WAS MY *CHURCH*.
BECAUSE IF OUR LOVE WAS FADING, THEN DID I REALLY BELIEVE IN THIS THING WE'D ALLOWED TO GROW THROUGH OUR LIVES SO TIGHTLY IT WOULD *KILL US* TO CUT IT AWAY?

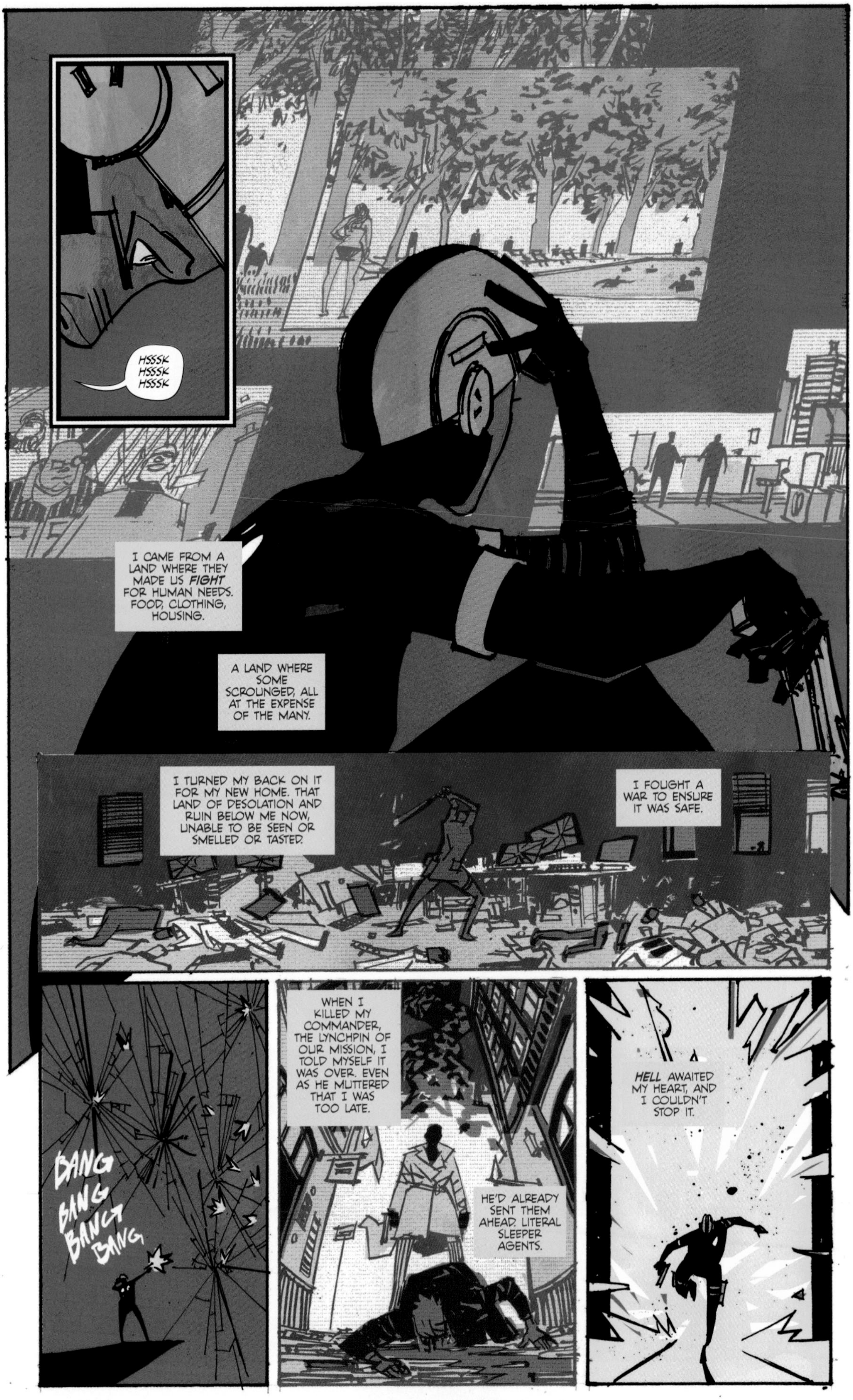
HSSSK HSSSK HSSSK
I CAME FROM A LAND WHERE THEY MADE US FIGHT FOR HUMAN NEEDS. FOOD, CLOTHING, HOUSING.
A LAND WHERE SOME SCROUNGED, ALL AT THE EXPENSE OF THE MANY.
I TURNED MY BACK ON IT FOR MY NEW HOME. THAT LAND OF DESOLATION AND RUIN BELOW ME NOW, UNABLE TO BE SEEN OR SMELLED OR TASTED.
I FOUGHT A WAR TO ENSURE IT WAS SAFE.
BANG BANG BANG BANG
WHEN I KILLED MY COMMANDER, THE LYNCHPIN OF OUR MISSION, I TOLD MYSELF IT WAS OVER. EVEN AS HE MUTTERED THAT I WAS TOO LATE.
HE'D ALREADY SENT THEM AHEAD. LITERAL SLEEPER AGENTS.
HELL AWAITED MY HEART, AND I COULDN'T STOP IT.

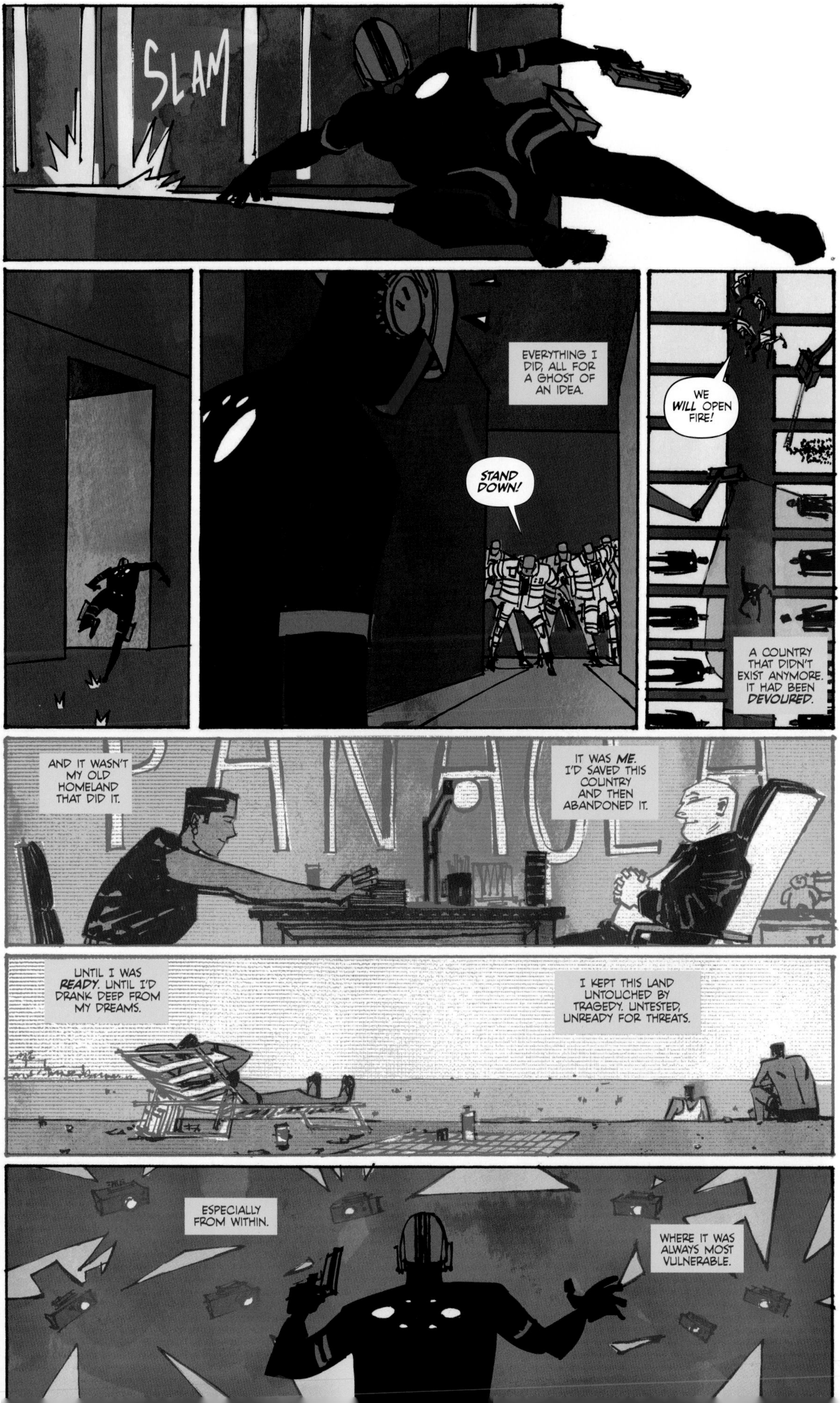
SLAM
EVERYTHING I DID, ALL FOR A GHOST OF AN IDEA.
STAND DOWN!
WE WILL OPEN FIRE!
A COUNTRY THAT DIDN'T EXIST ANYMORE. IT HAD BEEN DEVOURED.
AND IT WASN'T MY OLD HOMELAND THAT DID IT.
IT WAS ME. I'D SAVED THIS COUNTRY AND THEN ABANDONED IT.
UNTIL I WAS READY. UNTIL I'D DRANK DEEP FROM MY DREAMS.
I KEPT THIS LAND UNTOUCHED BY TRAGEDY. UNTESTED, UNREADY FOR THREATS.
ESPECIALLY FROM WITHIN.
WHERE IT WAS ALWAYS MOST VULNERABLE.

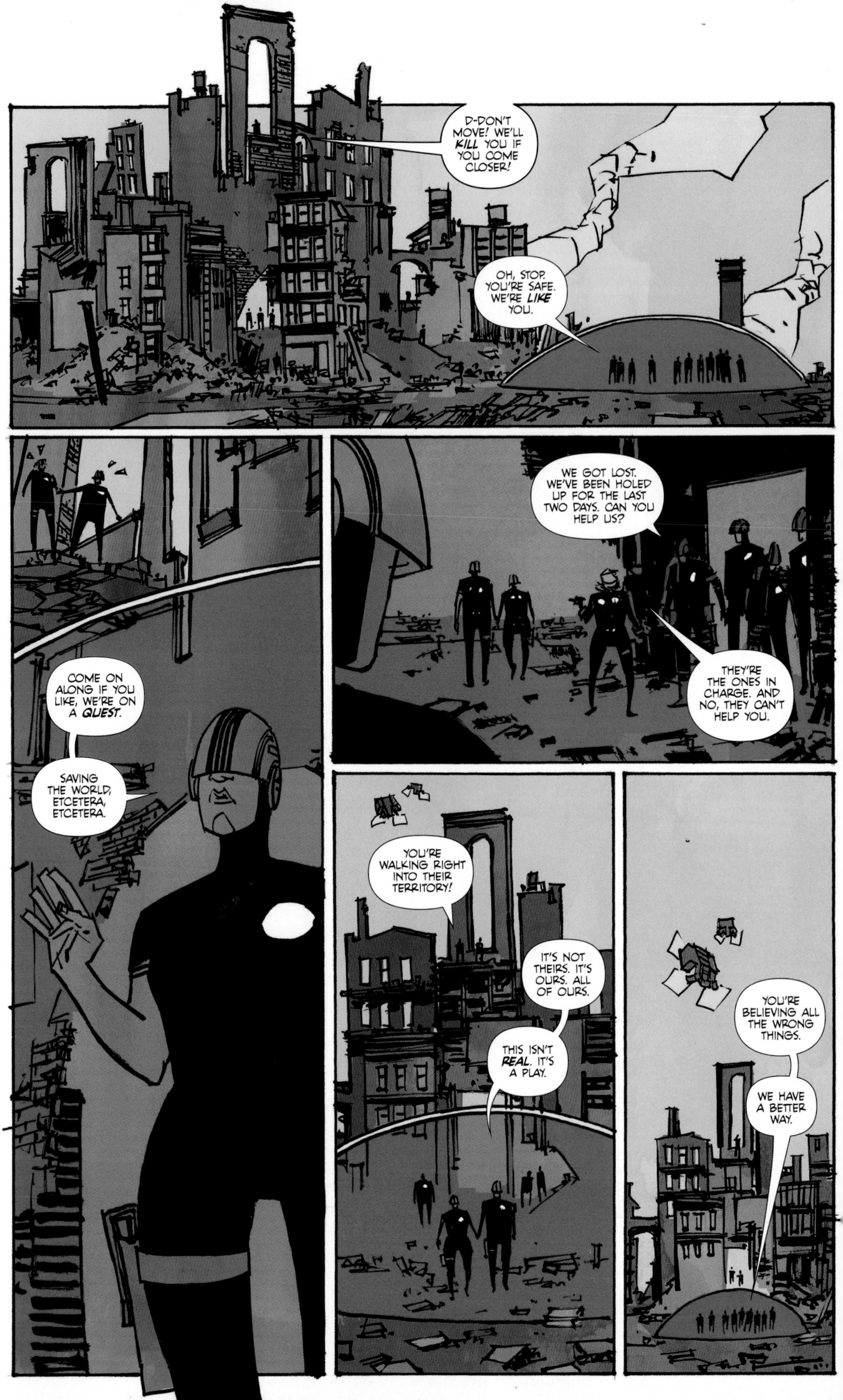
D-DON'T MOVE! WE'LL KILL YOU IF YOU COME CLOSER!
OH, STOP. YOU'RE SAFE. WE'RE LIKE YOU.
COME ON ALONG IF YOU LIKE, WE'RE ON A QUEST.
SAVING THE WORLD, ETCETERA, ETCETERA.
WE GOT LOST. WE'VE BEEN HOLED UP FOR THE LAST TWO DAYS. CAN YOU HELP US?
THEY'RE THE ONES IN CHARGE. AND NO, THEY CAN'T HELP YOU.
YOU'RE WALKING RIGHT INTO THEIR TERRITORY!
IT'S NOT THEIRS. IT'S OURS. ALL OF OURS.
THIS ISN'T REAL. IT'S A PLAY.
YOU'RE BELIEVING ALL THE WRONG THINGS.
WE HAVE A BETTER WAY.

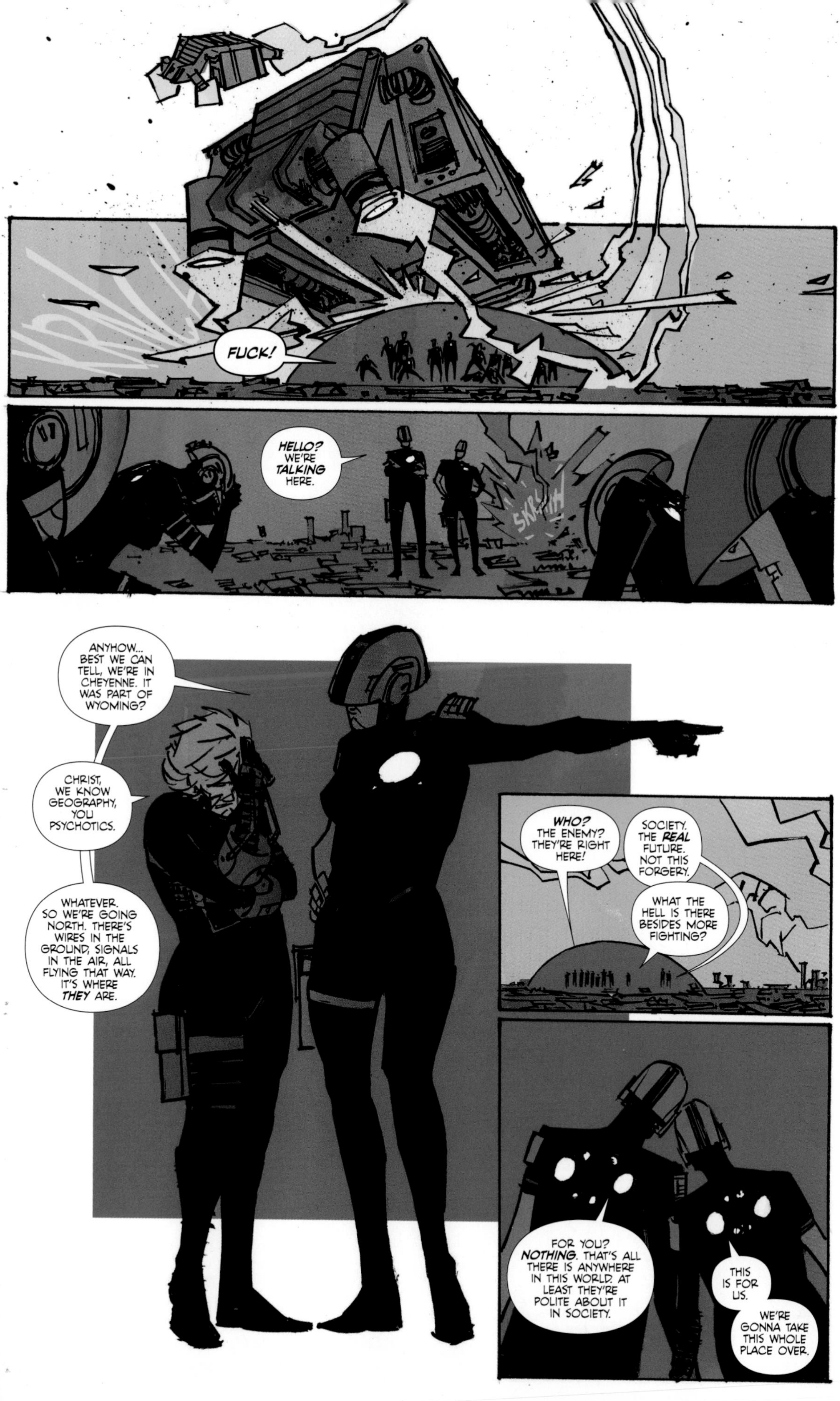
FUCK!
HELLO? WE'RE TALKING HERE.
SKRAAH
ANYHOW... BEST WE CAN TELL, WE'RE IN CHEYENNE. IT WAS PART OF WYOMING?
CHRIST, WE KNOW GEOGRAPHY, YOU PSYCHOTICS.
WHATEVER. SO WE'RE GOING NORTH. THERE'S WIRES IN THE GROUND, SIGNALS IN THE AIR, ALL FLYING THAT WAY. IT'S WHERE THEY ARE.
WHO? THE ENEMY? THEY'RE RIGHT HERE!
SOCIETY. THE REAL FUTURE. NOT THIS FORGERY.
WHAT THE HELL IS THERE BESIDES MORE FIGHTING?
FOR YOU? NOTHING. THAT'S ALL THERE IS ANYWHERE IN THIS WORLD. AT LEAST THEY'RE POLITE ABOUT IT IN SOCIETY.
THIS IS FOR US.
WE'RE GONNA TAKE THIS WHOLE PLACE OVER.

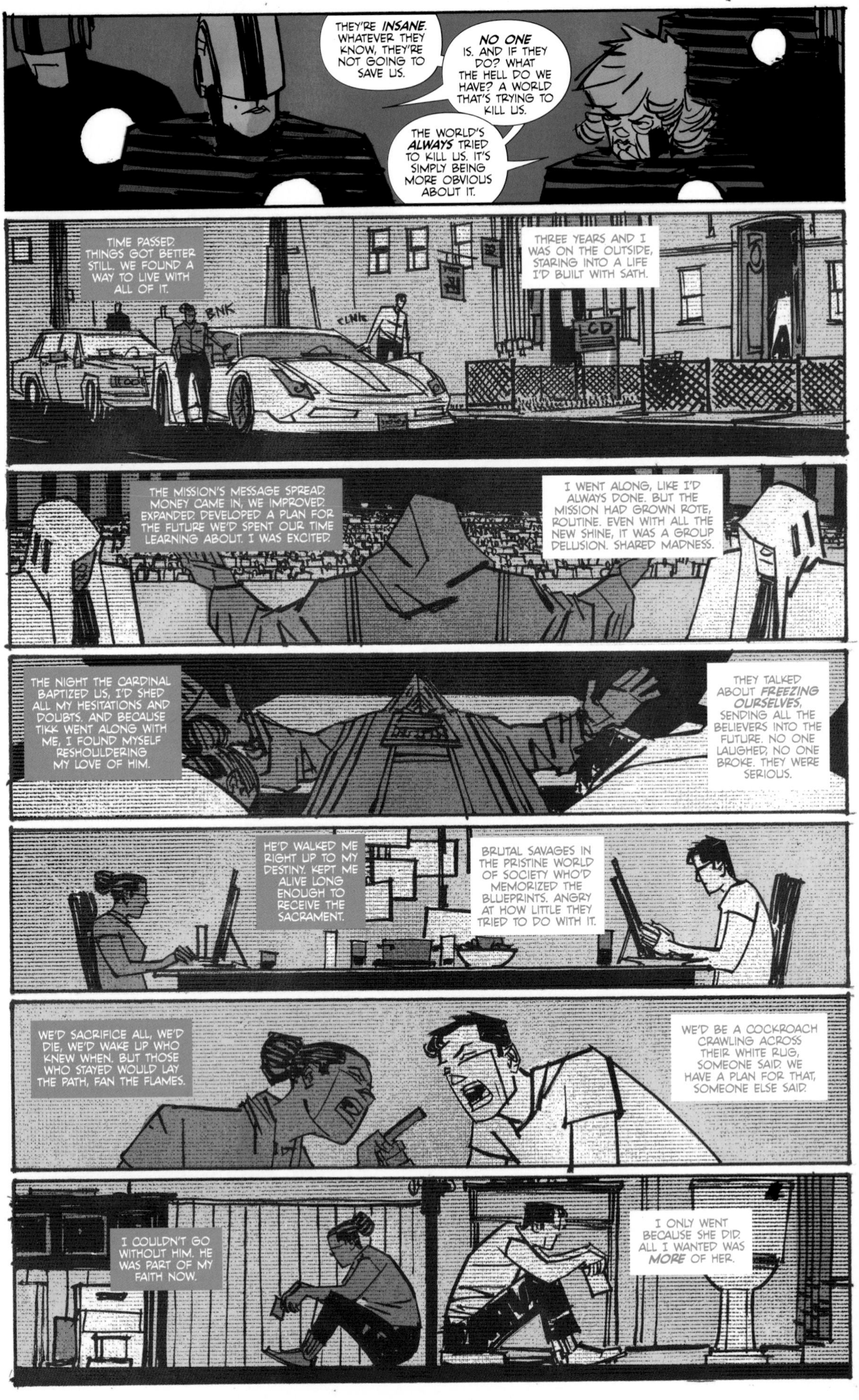
THEY'RE INSANE. WHATEVER THEY KNOW, THEY'RE NOT GOING TO SAVE US.
NO ONE IS. AND IF THEY DO? WHAT THE HELL DO WE HAVE? A WORLD THAT'S TRYING TO KILL US.
THE WORLD'S ALWAYS TRIED TO KILL US. IT'S SIMPLY BEING MORE OBVIOUS ABOUT IT.
TIME PASSED. THINGS GOT BETTER STILL. WE FOUND A WAY TO LIVE WITH ALL OF IT.
BNK
CLNK
THREE YEARS AND I WAS ON THE OUTSIDE, STARING INTO A LIFE I'D BUILT WITH SATH.
LCD
THE MISSION'S MESSAGE SPREAD. MONEY CAME IN, WE IMPROVED. EXPANDED. DEVELOPED A PLAN FOR THE FUTURE WE'D SPENT OUR TIME LEARNING ABOUT. I WAS EXCITED.
I WENT ALONG, LIKE I'D ALWAYS DONE. BUT THE MISSION HAD GROWN ROTE, ROUTINE. EVEN WITH ALL THE NEW SHINE, IT WAS A GROUP DELUSION. SHARED MADNESS.
THE NIGHT THE CARDINAL BAPTIZED US, I'D SHED ALL MY HESITATIONS AND DOUBTS. AND BECAUSE TIKK WENT ALONG WITH ME, I FOUND MYSELF RESHOULDERING MY LOVE OF HIM.
THEY TALKED ABOUT FREEZING OURSELVES, SENDING ALL THE BELIEVERS INTO THE FUTURE. NO ONE LAUGHED, NO ONE BROKE. THEY WERE SERIOUS.
HE'D WALKED ME RIGHT UP TO MY DESTINY. KEPT ME ALIVE LONG ENOUGH TO RECEIVE THE SACRAMENT.
BRUTAL SAVAGES IN THE PRISTINE WORLD OF SOCIETY WHO'D MEMORIZED THE BLUEPRINTS. ANGRY AT HOW LITTLE THEY TRIED TO DO WITH IT.
WE'D SACRIFICE ALL, WE'D DIE, WE'D WAKE UP WHO KNEW WHEN. BUT THOSE WHO STAYED WOULD LAY THE PATH, FAN THE FLAMES.
WE'D BE A COCKROACH CRAWLING ACROSS THEIR WHITE RUG, SOMEONE SAID. WE HAVE A PLAN FOR THAT, SOMEONE ELSE SAID.
I COULDN'T GO WITHOUT HIM. HE WAS PART OF MY FAITH NOW.
I ONLY WENT BECAUSE SHE DID. ALL I WANTED WAS MORE OF HER.

I DIDN'T WANT TO CHOOSE. WE'D BEEN PLAYING CHICKEN SO LONG, THROWING OURSELVES TOGETHER INTO ONE THING AFTER ANOTHER.

I HAD NOWHERE ELSE TO GO. NO ONE ELSE I WANTED TO BE WITH. SHE COULD HAVE ASKED ME TO LIE IN FRONT OF THE BUS AND I WOULD'VE.

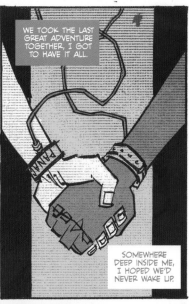

WE TOOK THE LAST GREAT ADVENTURE TOGETHER. I GOT TO HAVE IT ALL.

SOMEWHERE DEEP INSIDE ME, I HOPED WE'D NEVER WAKE UP.

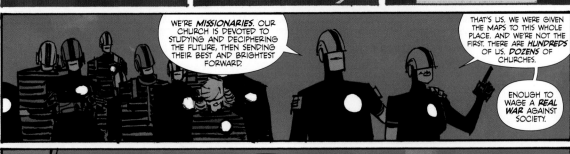

WE'RE **MISSIONARIES**. OUR CHURCH IS DEVOTED TO STUDYING AND DECIPHERING THE FUTURE, THEN SENDING THEIR BEST AND BRIGHTEST FORWARD.

THAT'S US. WE WERE GIVEN THE MAPS TO THIS WHOLE PLACE. AND WE'RE NOT THE FIRST. THERE ARE **HUNDREDS** OF US. **DOZENS** OF CHURCHES.

ENOUGH TO WAGE A **REAL WAR** AGAINST SOCIETY.

KLK

YOU TRULY ARE MAD. OR YOU'RE PLAYING GAMES WITH US.

KLK

KLK

EITHER WAY, WE'RE DONE CODDLING YOU.

KLK

KLK

KLK

KLK

KLK

DROP YOUR HANDS.

KLK

KLK

BROTHER, SISTER. I THOUGHT I RECOGNIZED YOU. I APOLOGIZE.

OH, IT'S FINE.

IT HAS BEEN A WHILE AND THERE ARE SO **MANY** OF US.

I CAME ALL THIS WAY TO KEEP PROTECTING MY ADOPTIVE HOME.

I THOUGHT IT WOULD ALWAYS BE HERE, THAT IT WAS AS CONSTANT AS THE OCEAN BENEATH THE PLANE THAT BROUGHT ME HERE.

WHEN I WOKE UP, I HAD TO COPE WITH ITS DEATH, BARELY ENOUGH TIME TO MOURN BEFORE THE GROUND FELL OUT FROM BENEATH ME.

AMERICA WASN'T DEAD. NO DEADER THAN WE WERE.

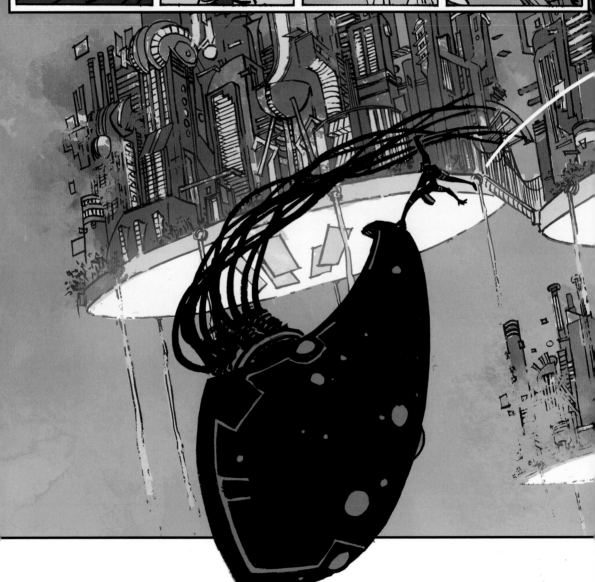

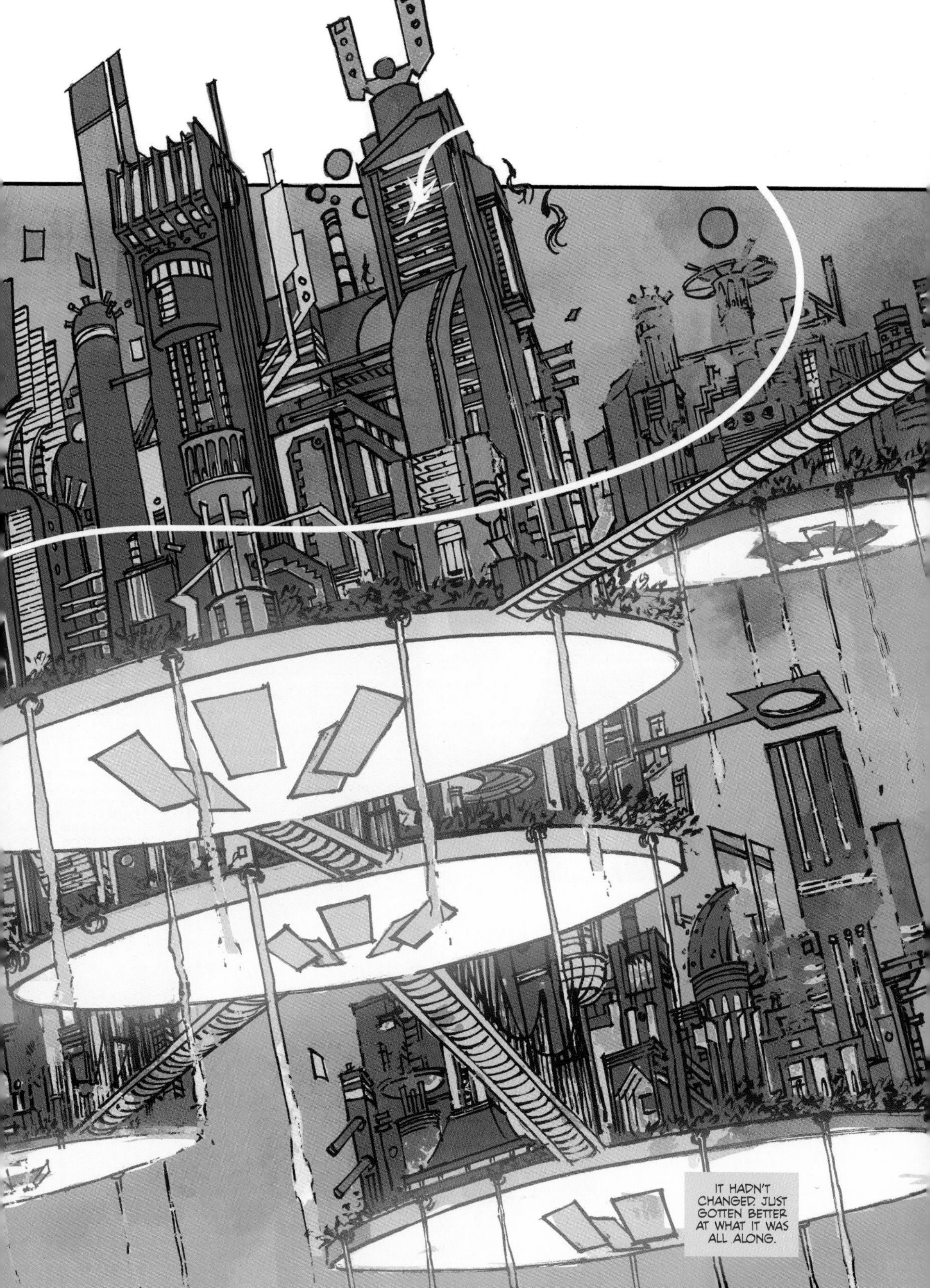
IT HADN'T CHANGED. JUST GOTTEN BETTER AT WHAT IT WAS ALL ALONG.

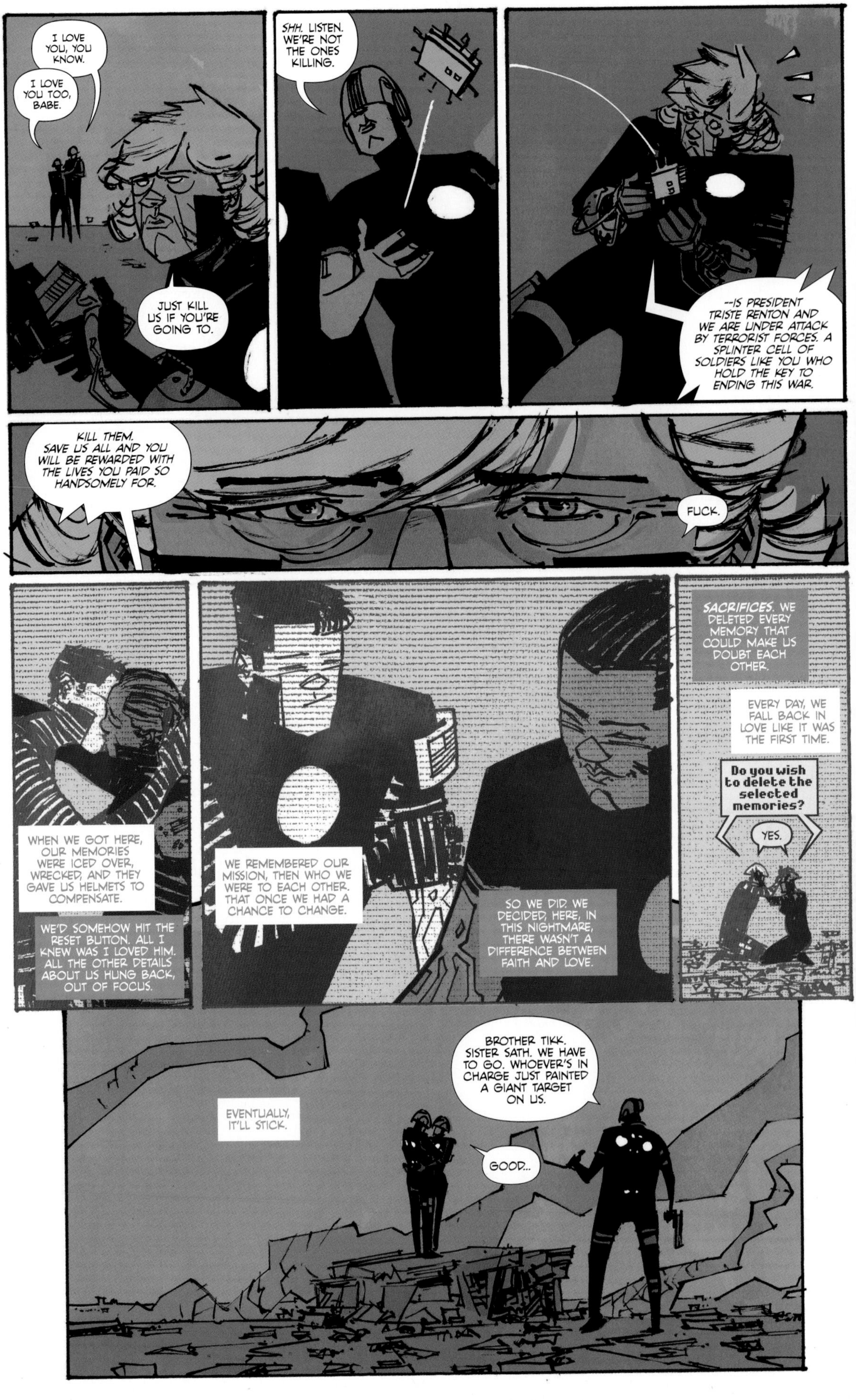
I LOVE YOU, YOU KNOW.
I LOVE YOU TOO, BABE.
JUST KILL US IF YOU'RE GOING TO.
SHH. LISTEN. WE'RE NOT THE ONES KILLING.
--IS PRESIDENT TRISTE RENTON AND WE ARE UNDER ATTACK BY TERRORIST FORCES. A SPLINTER CELL OF SOLDIERS LIKE YOU WHO HOLD THE KEY TO ENDING THIS WAR.
KILL THEM. SAVE US ALL AND YOU WILL BE REWARDED WITH THE LIVES YOU PAID SO HANDSOMELY FOR.
FUCK.
WHEN WE GOT HERE, OUR MEMORIES WERE ICED OVER, WRECKED, AND THEY GAVE US HELMETS TO COMPENSATE.
WE'D SOMEHOW HIT THE RESET BUTTON. ALL I KNEW WAS I LOVED HIM. ALL THE OTHER DETAILS ABOUT US HUNG BACK, OUT OF FOCUS.
WE REMEMBERED OUR MISSION, THEN WHO WE WERE TO EACH OTHER. THAT ONCE WE HAD A CHANCE TO CHANGE.
SO WE DID. WE DECIDED, HERE, IN THIS NIGHTMARE, THERE WASN'T A DIFFERENCE BETWEEN FAITH AND LOVE.
SACRIFICES. WE DELETED EVERY MEMORY THAT COULD MAKE US DOUBT EACH OTHER.
EVERY DAY, WE FALL BACK IN LOVE LIKE IT WAS THE FIRST TIME.
Do you wish to delete the selected memories?
YES.
EVENTUALLY, IT'LL STICK.
BROTHER TIKK. SISTER SATH. WE HAVE TO GO. WHOEVER'S IN CHARGE JUST PAINTED A GIANT TARGET ON US.
GOOD...

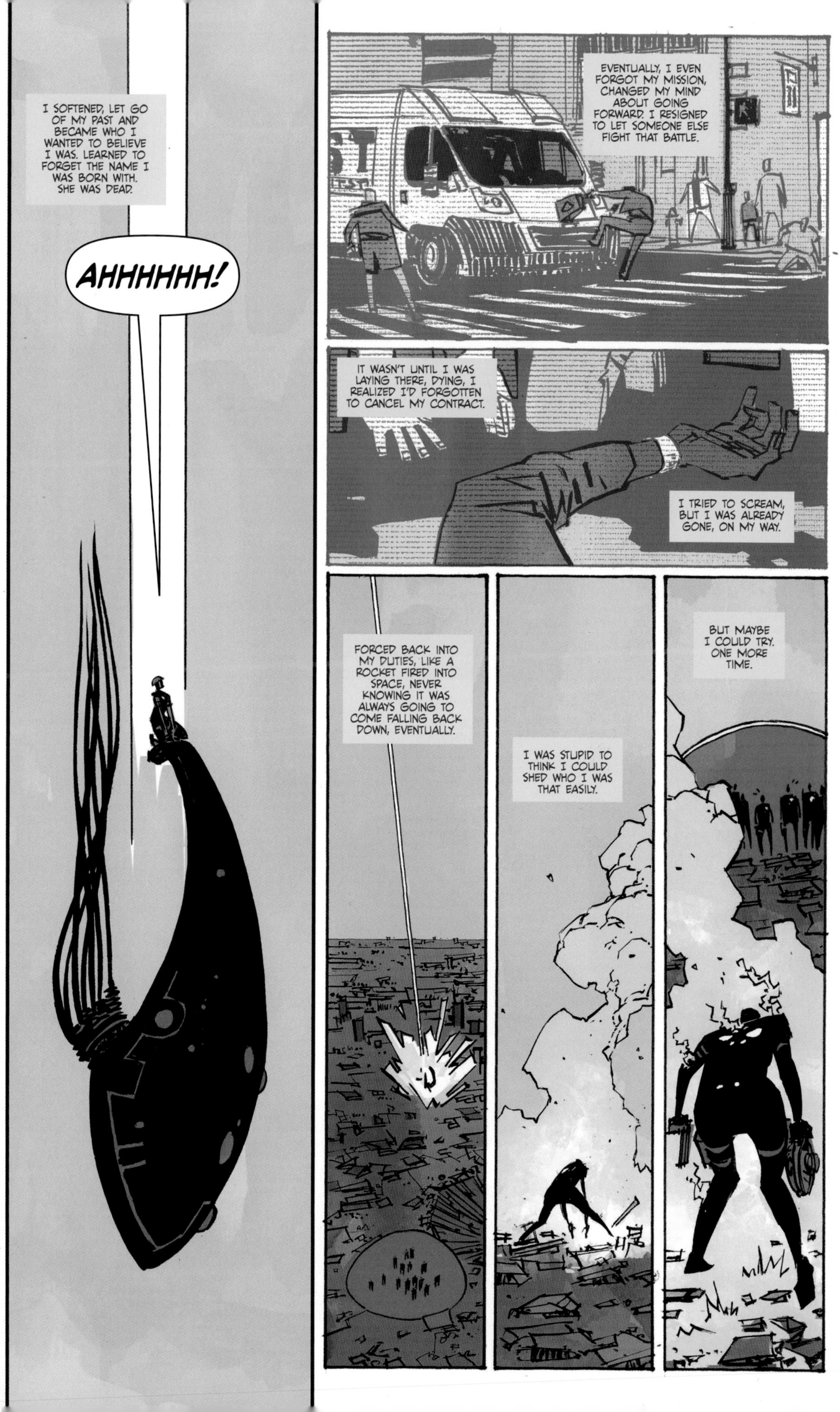
I SOFTENED, LET GO OF MY PAST AND BECAME WHO I WANTED TO BELIEVE I WAS. LEARNED TO FORGET THE NAME I WAS BORN WITH. SHE WAS DEAD.
AHHHHHH!
EVENTUALLY, I EVEN FORGOT MY MISSION, CHANGED MY MIND ABOUT GOING FORWARD. I RESIGNED TO LET SOMEONE ELSE FIGHT THAT BATTLE.
IT WASN'T UNTIL I WAS LAYING THERE, DYING, I REALIZED I'D FORGOTTEN TO CANCEL MY CONTRACT.
I TRIED TO SCREAM, BUT I WAS ALREADY GONE, ON MY WAY.
FORCED BACK INTO MY DUTIES, LIKE A ROCKET FIRED INTO SPACE, NEVER KNOWING IT WAS ALWAYS GOING TO COME FALLING BACK DOWN, EVENTUALLY.
I WAS STUPID TO THINK I COULD SHED WHO I WAS THAT EASILY.
BUT MAYBE I COULD TRY. ONE MORE TIME.

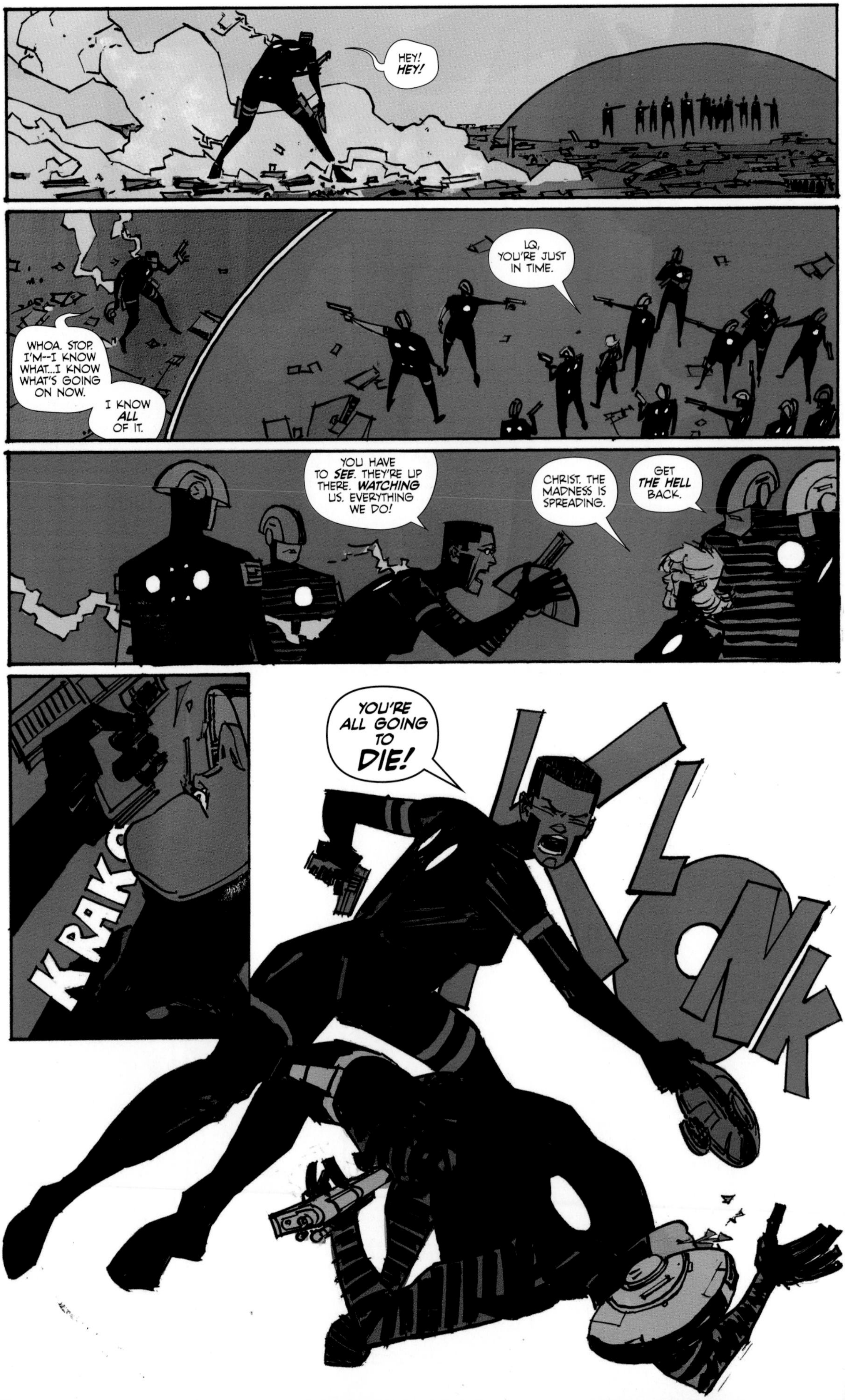
HEY! HEY!
LQ, YOU'RE JUST IN TIME.
WHOA. STOP. I'M--I KNOW WHAT...I KNOW WHAT'S GOING ON NOW.
I KNOW ALL OF IT.
YOU HAVE TO SEE. THEY'RE UP THERE. WATCHING US. EVERYTHING WE DO!
CHRIST. THE MADNESS IS SPREADING.
GET THE HELL BACK.
KRAK
YOU'RE ALL GOING TO DIE!
KLONK

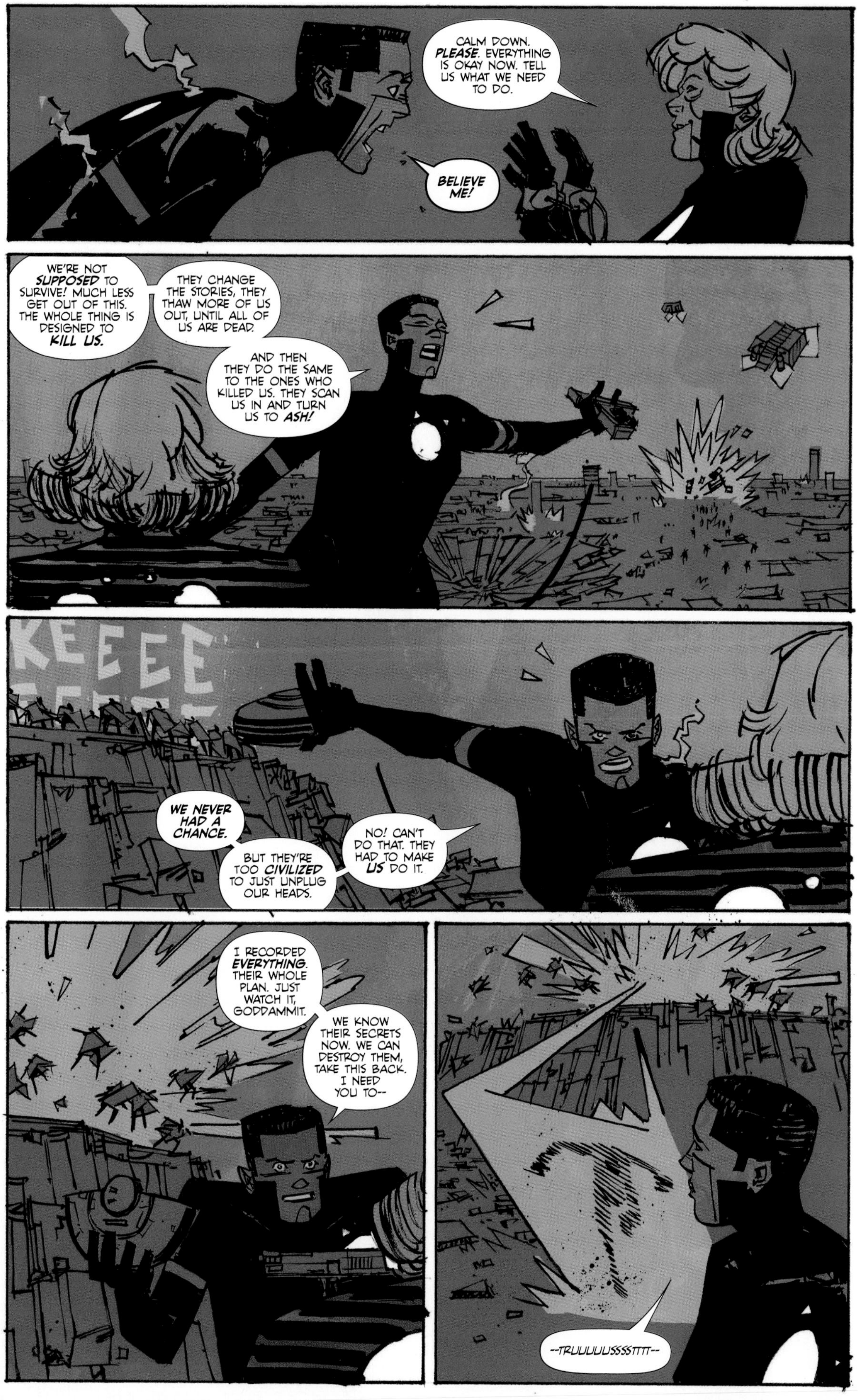
CALM DOWN. PLEASE. EVERYTHING IS OKAY NOW. TELL US WHAT WE NEED TO DO.
BELIEVE ME!
WE'RE NOT SUPPOSED TO SURVIVE! MUCH LESS GET OUT OF THIS. THE WHOLE THING IS DESIGNED TO KILL US.
THEY CHANGE THE STORIES, THEY THAW MORE OF US OUT, UNTIL ALL OF US ARE DEAD.
AND THEN THEY DO THE SAME TO THE ONES WHO KILLED US. THEY SCAN US IN AND TURN US TO ASH!
KEEEE
WE NEVER HAD A CHANCE.
BUT THEY'RE TOO CIVILIZED TO JUST UNPLUG OUR HEADS.
NO! CAN'T DO THAT. THEY HAD TO MAKE US DO IT.
I RECORDED EVERYTHING. THEIR WHOLE PLAN. JUST WATCH IT, GODDAMMIT.
WE KNOW THEIR SECRETS NOW. WE CAN DESTROY THEM, TAKE THIS BACK. I NEED YOU TO--
--TRUUUUUSSSSTTTT--

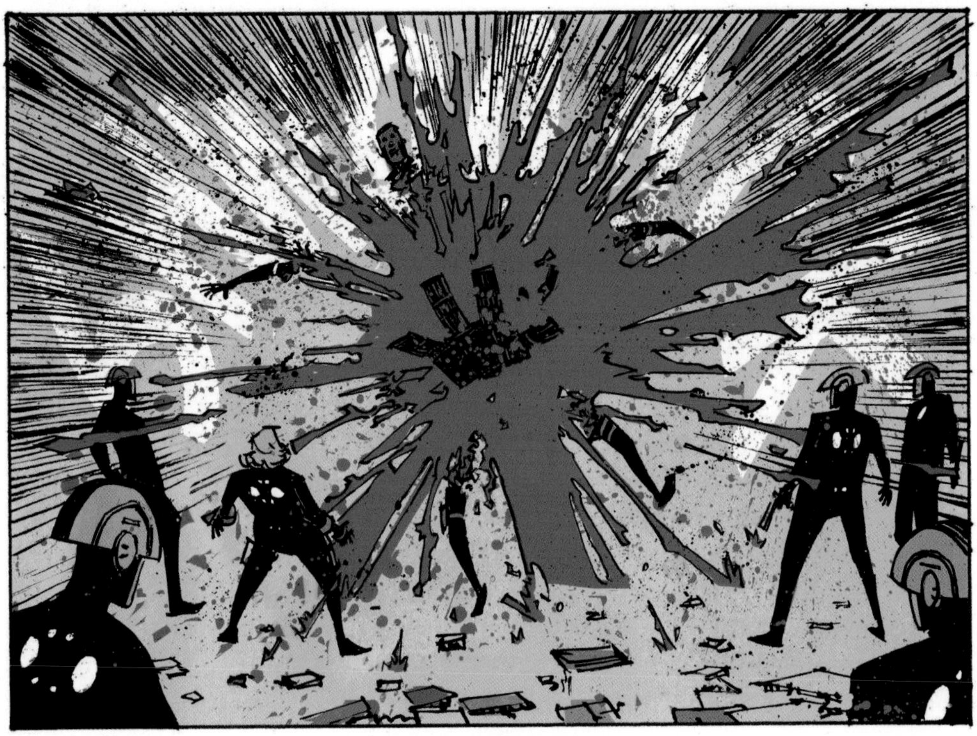

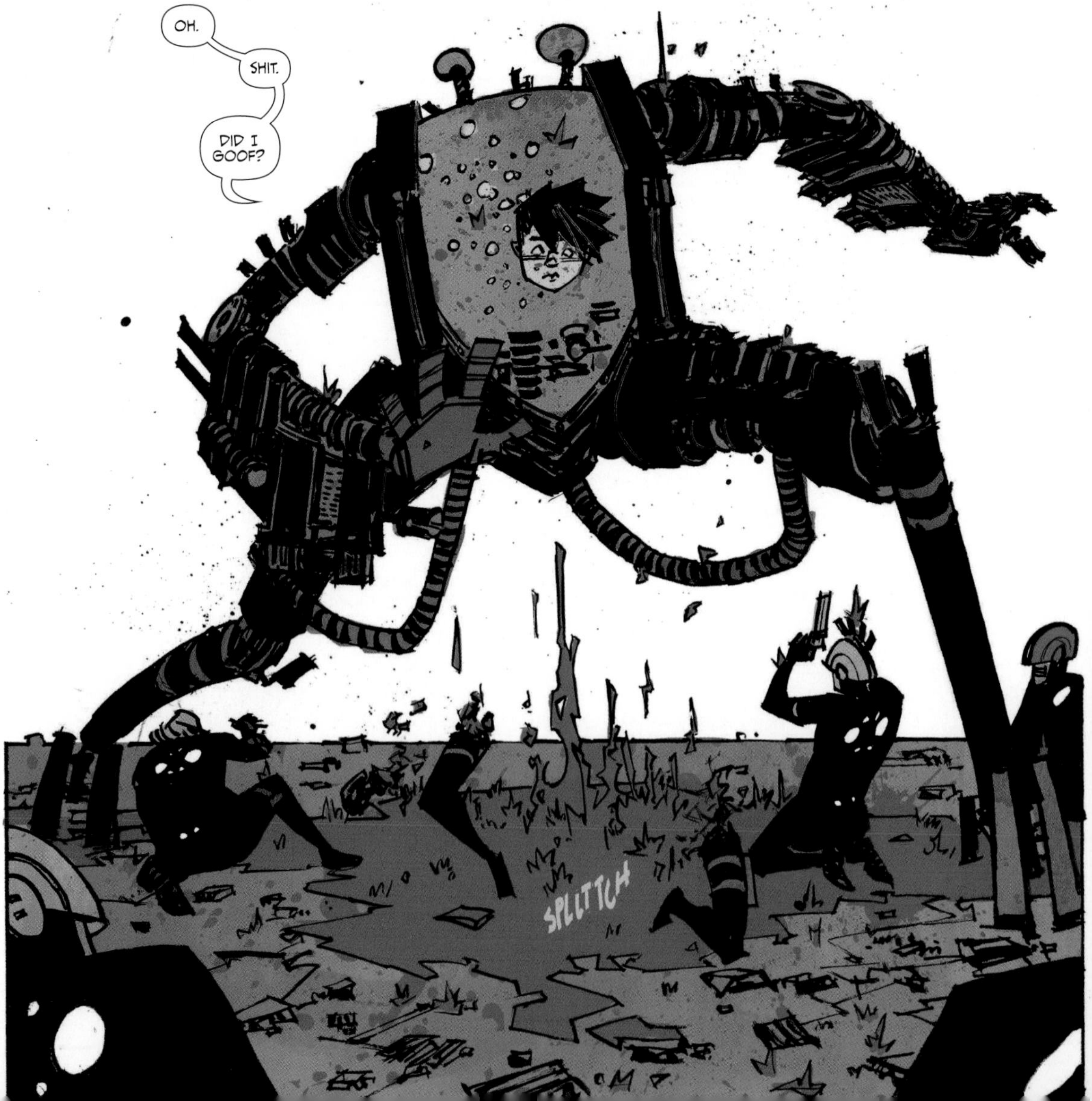
OH.
SHIT.
DID I GOOF?
SPLLTTCH

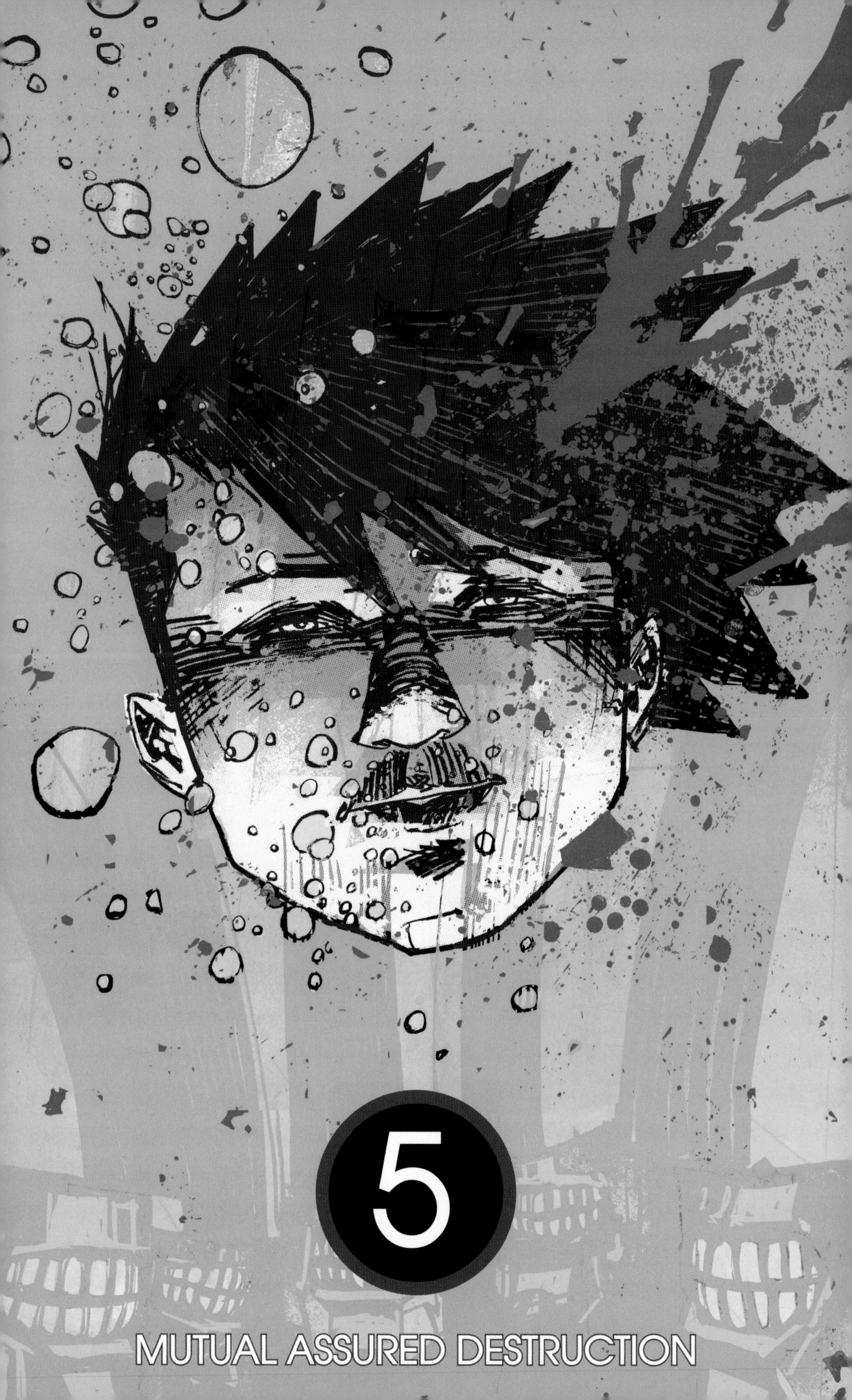
5
MUTUAL ASSURED DESTRUCTION

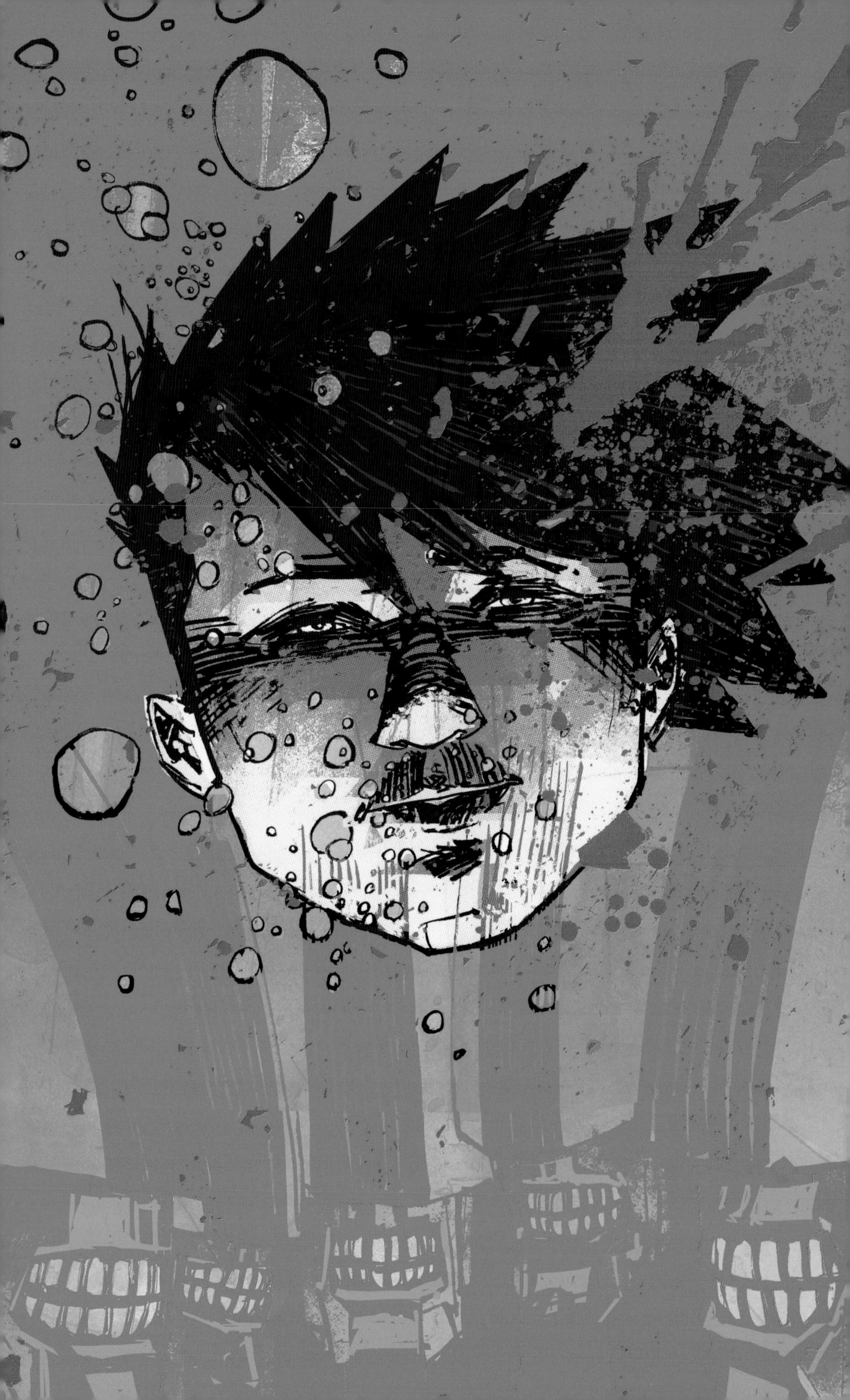

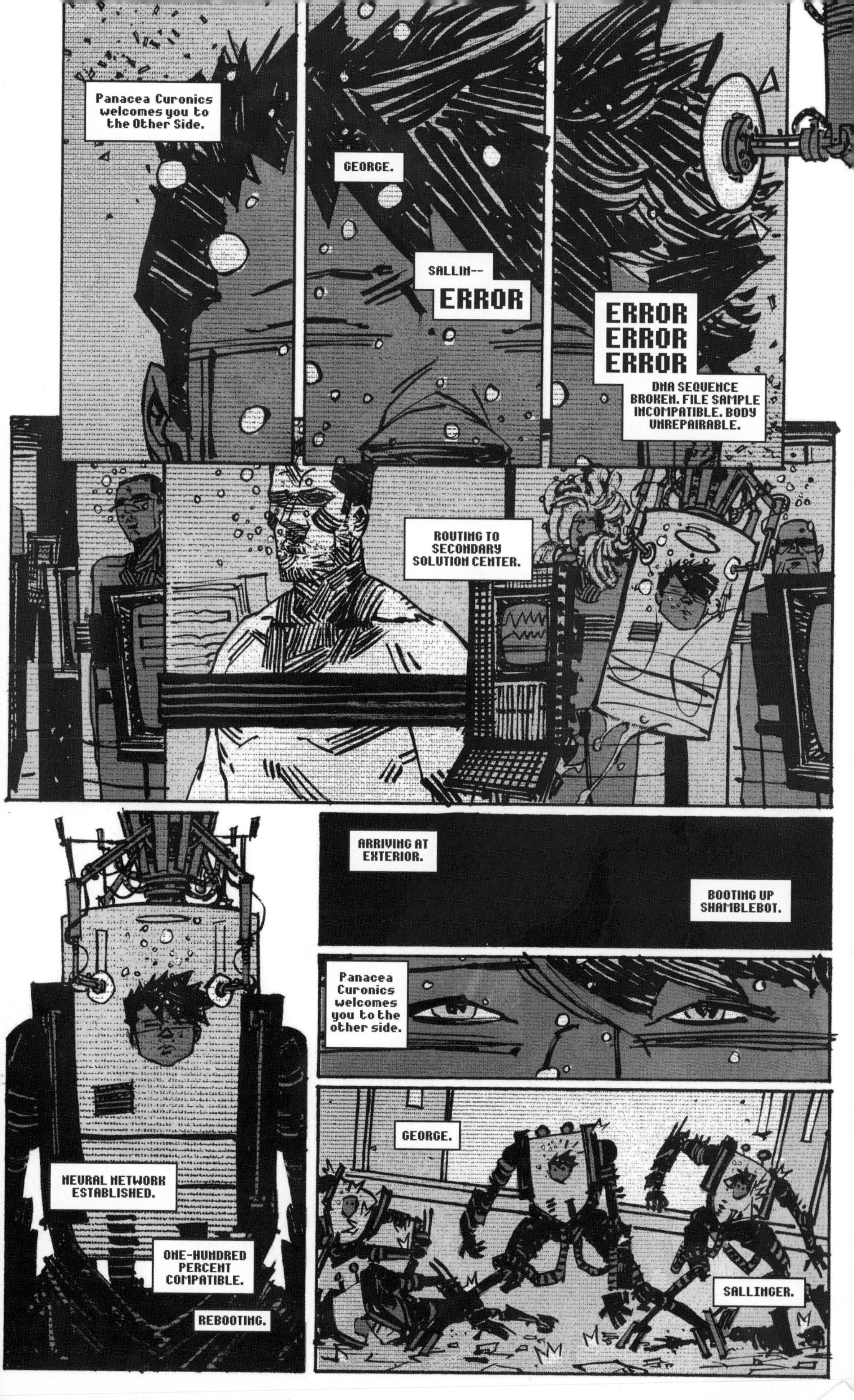
Panacea Curonics welcomes you to the Other Side.
GEORGE.
SALLIN--
ERROR
ERROR ERROR ERROR
DNA SEQUENCE BROKEN. FILE SAMPLE INCOMPATIBLE. BODY UNREPAIRABLE.
ROUTING TO SECONDARY SOLUTION CENTER.
NEURAL NETWORK ESTABLISHED.
ONE-HUNDRED PERCENT COMPATIBLE.
REBOOTING.
ARRIVING AT EXTERIOR.
BOOTING UP SHAMBLEBOT.
Panacea Curonics welcomes you to the other side.
GEORGE.
SALLINGER.

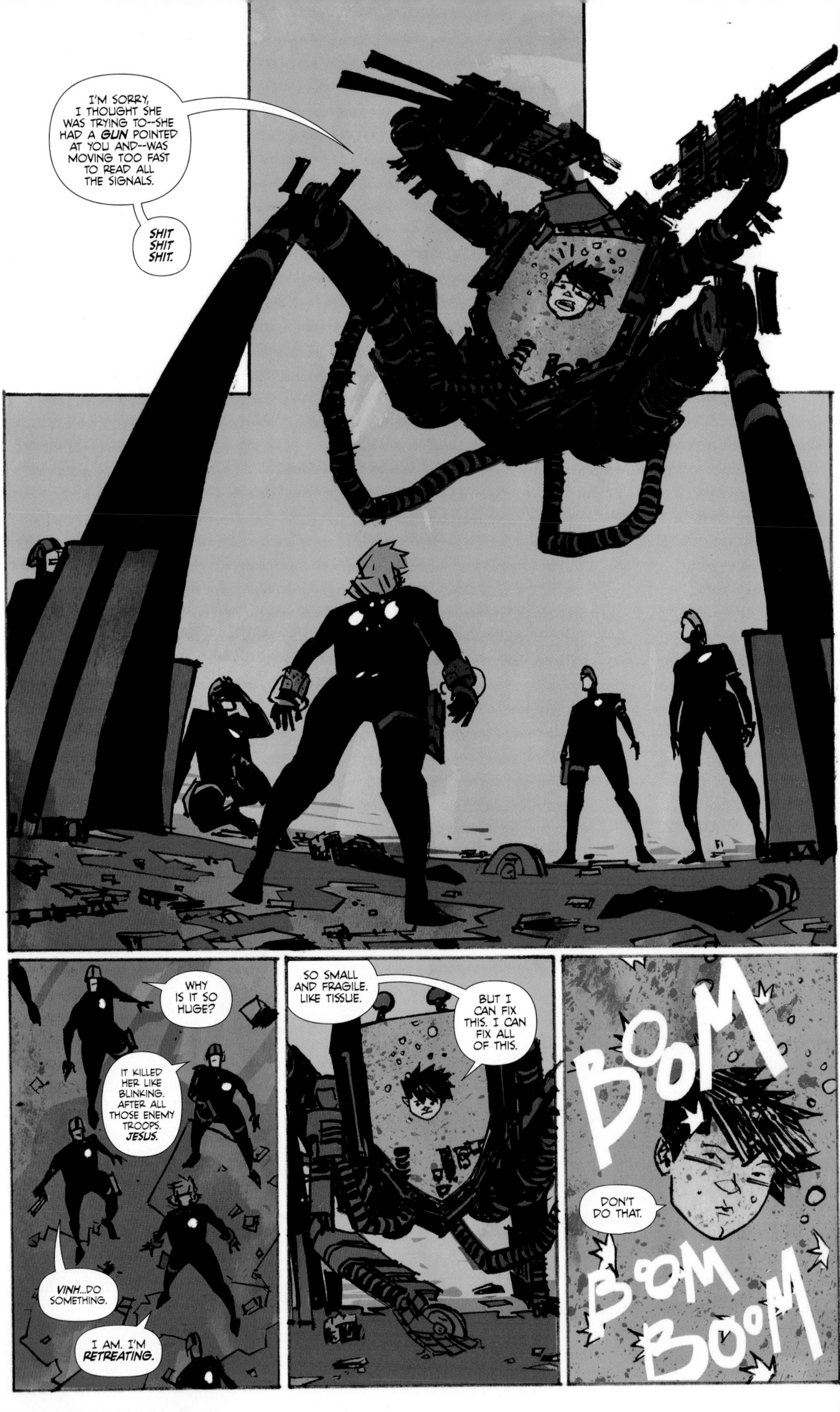
I'M SORRY, I THOUGHT SHE WAS TRYING TO--SHE HAD A **GUN** POINTED AT YOU AND--WAS MOVING TOO FAST TO READ ALL THE SIGNALS.
SHIT SHIT SHIT.
WHY IS IT SO HUGE?
IT KILLED HER LIKE BLINKING. AFTER ALL THOSE ENEMY TROOPS. ***JESUS.***
VINH...DO SOMETHING.
I AM. I'M ***RETREATING.***
SO SMALL AND FRAGILE. LIKE TISSUE.
BUT I CAN FIX THIS. I CAN FIX ALL OF THIS.
BOOM
DON'T DO THAT.
BOOM
BOOM

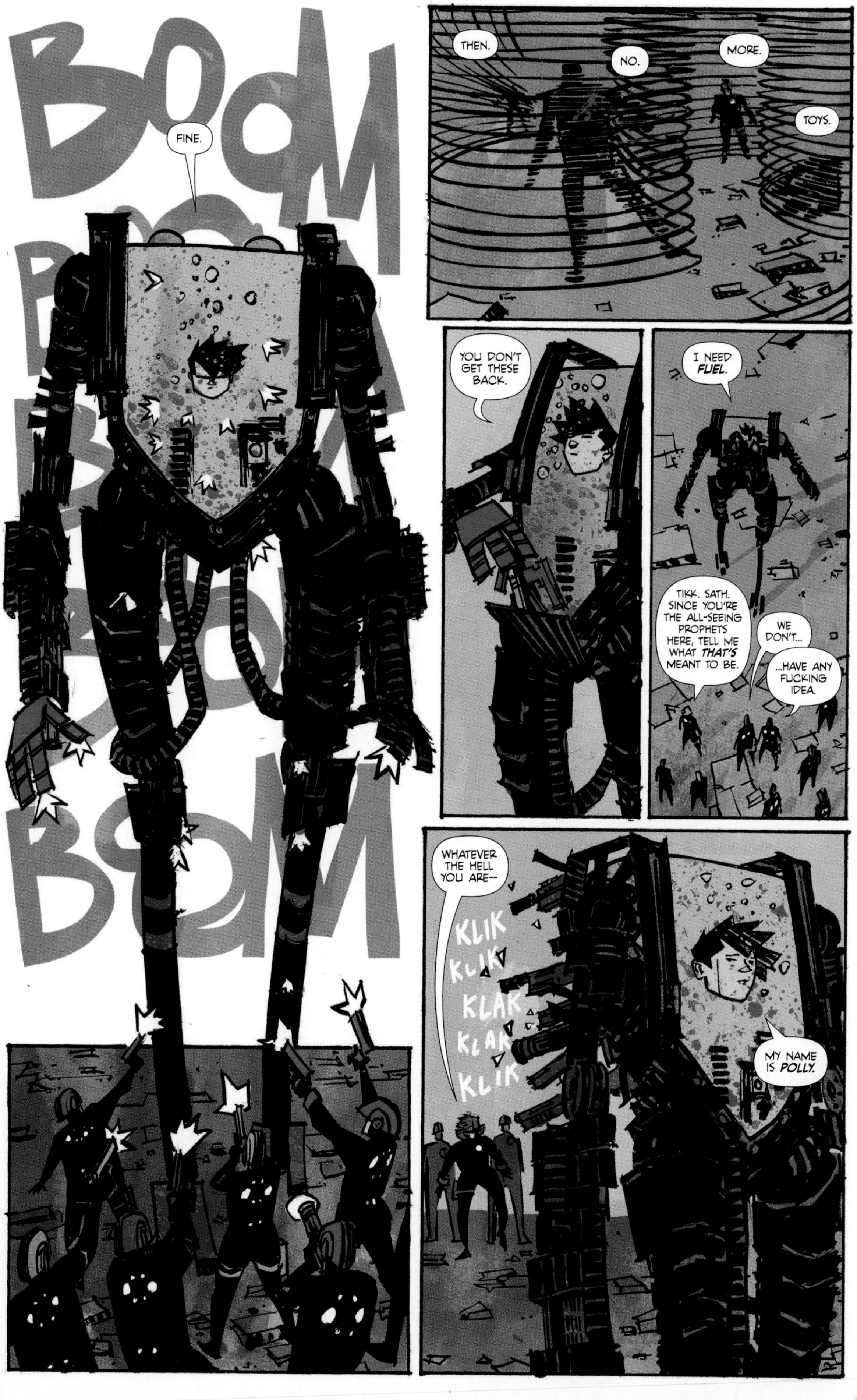
BOOM
FINE.
BOOM
THEN.
NO.
MORE.
TOYS.
YOU DON'T GET THESE BACK.
I NEED *FUEL.*
TIKK. SATH. SINCE YOU'RE THE ALL-SEEING PROPHETS HERE, TELL ME WHAT *THAT'S* MEANT TO BE.
WE DON'T...
...HAVE ANY FUCKING IDEA.
WHATEVER THE HELL YOU ARE--
KLIK
KLIK
KLAK
KLAK
KLIK
MY NAME IS *POLLY.*

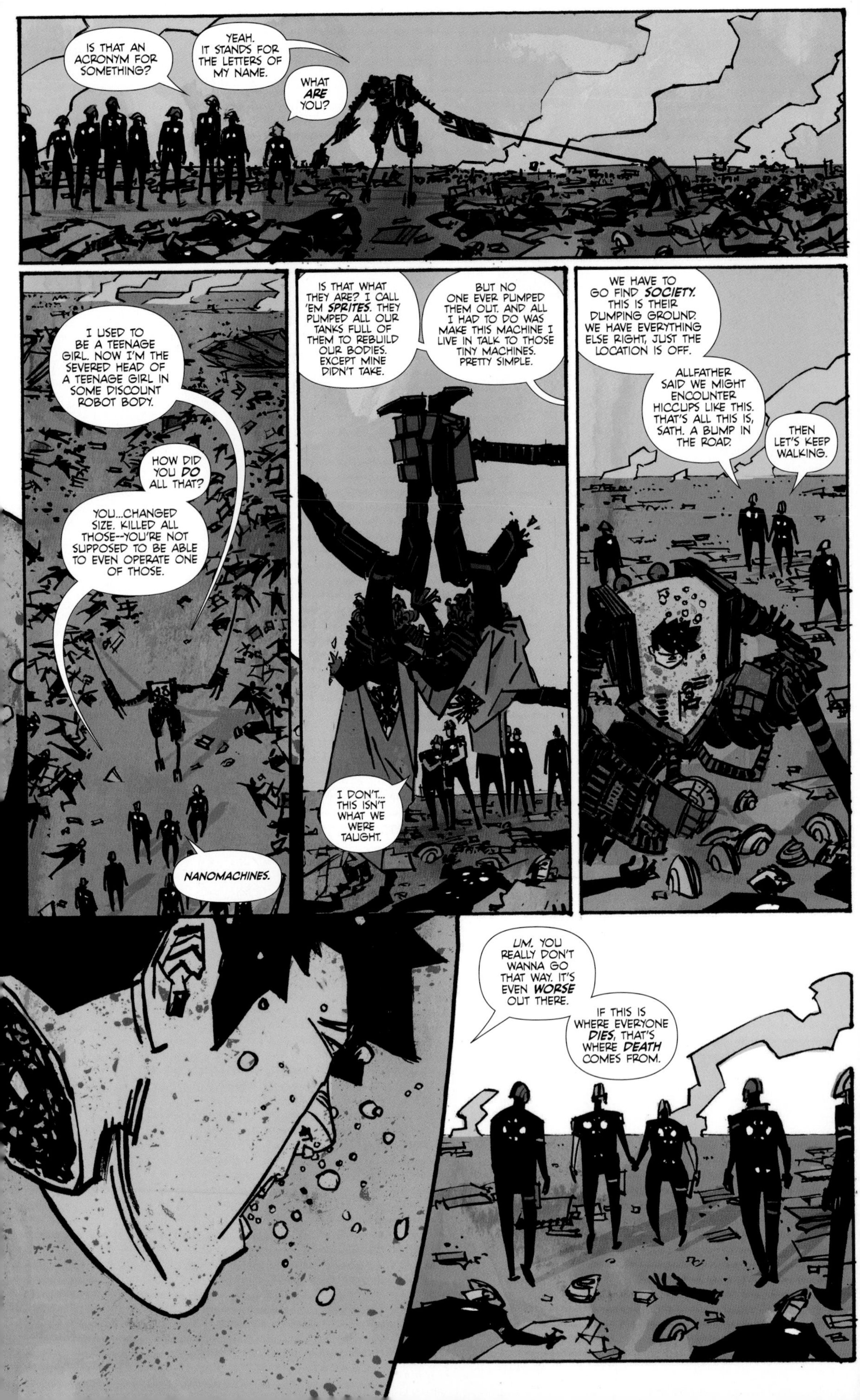

IS THAT AN ACRONYM FOR SOMETHING?
YEAH. IT STANDS FOR THE LETTERS OF MY NAME.
WHAT ARE YOU?
I USED TO BE A TEENAGE GIRL. NOW I'M THE SEVERED HEAD OF A TEENAGE GIRL IN SOME DISCOUNT ROBOT BODY.
HOW DID YOU DO ALL THAT?
YOU...CHANGED SIZE. KILLED ALL THOSE--YOU'RE NOT SUPPOSED TO BE ABLE TO EVEN OPERATE ONE OF THOSE.
NANOMACHINES.
IS THAT WHAT THEY ARE? I CALL 'EM SPRITES. THEY PUMPED ALL OUR TANKS FULL OF THEM TO REBUILD OUR BODIES. EXCEPT MINE DIDN'T TAKE.
BUT NO ONE EVER PUMPED THEM OUT. AND ALL I HAD TO DO WAS MAKE THIS MACHINE I LIVE IN TALK TO THOSE TINY MACHINES. PRETTY SIMPLE.
I DON'T... THIS ISN'T WHAT WE WERE TAUGHT.
WE HAVE TO GO FIND SOCIETY. THIS IS THEIR DUMPING GROUND. WE HAVE EVERYTHING ELSE RIGHT, JUST THE LOCATION IS OFF.
ALLFATHER SAID WE MIGHT ENCOUNTER HICCUPS LIKE THIS. THAT'S ALL THIS IS, SATH. A BUMP IN THE ROAD.
THEN LET'S KEEP WALKING.
UM. YOU REALLY DON'T WANNA GO THAT WAY. IT'S EVEN WORSE OUT THERE.
IF THIS IS WHERE EVERYONE DIES, THAT'S WHERE DEATH COMES FROM.

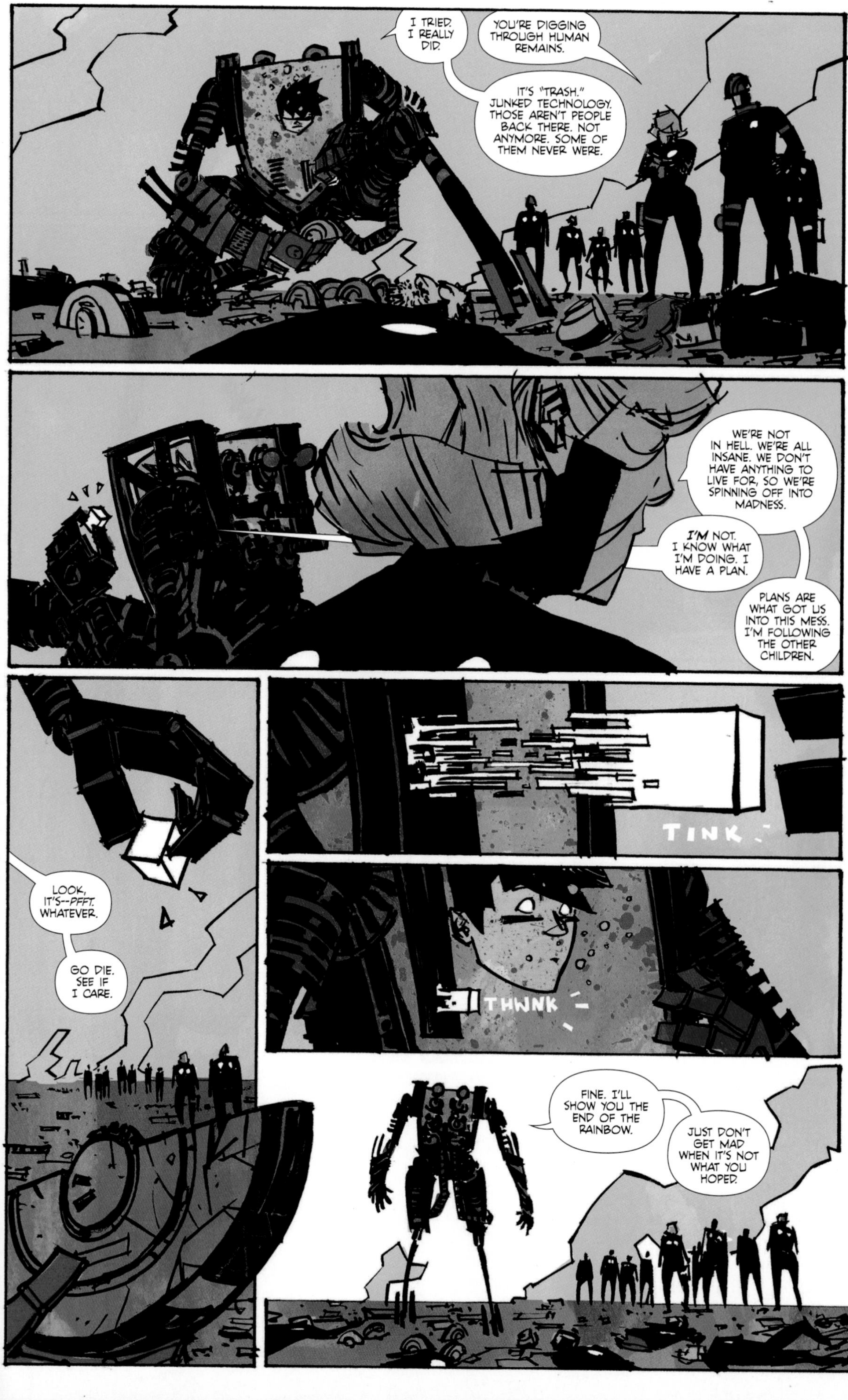
I TRIED. I REALLY DID.
YOU'RE DIGGING THROUGH HUMAN REMAINS.
IT'S "TRASH." JUNKED TECHNOLOGY. THOSE AREN'T PEOPLE BACK THERE. NOT ANYMORE. SOME OF THEM NEVER WERE.
WE'RE NOT IN HELL. WE'RE ALL INSANE. WE DON'T HAVE ANYTHING TO LIVE FOR, SO WE'RE SPINNING OFF INTO MADNESS.
I'M NOT. I KNOW WHAT I'M DOING. I HAVE A PLAN.
PLANS ARE WHAT GOT US INTO THIS MESS. I'M FOLLOWING THE OTHER CHILDREN.
LOOK, IT'S--PFFT. WHATEVER.
GO DIE. SEE IF I CARE.
TINK
THWNK
FINE. I'LL SHOW YOU THE END OF THE RAINBOW.
JUST DON'T GET MAD WHEN IT'S NOT WHAT YOU HOPED.

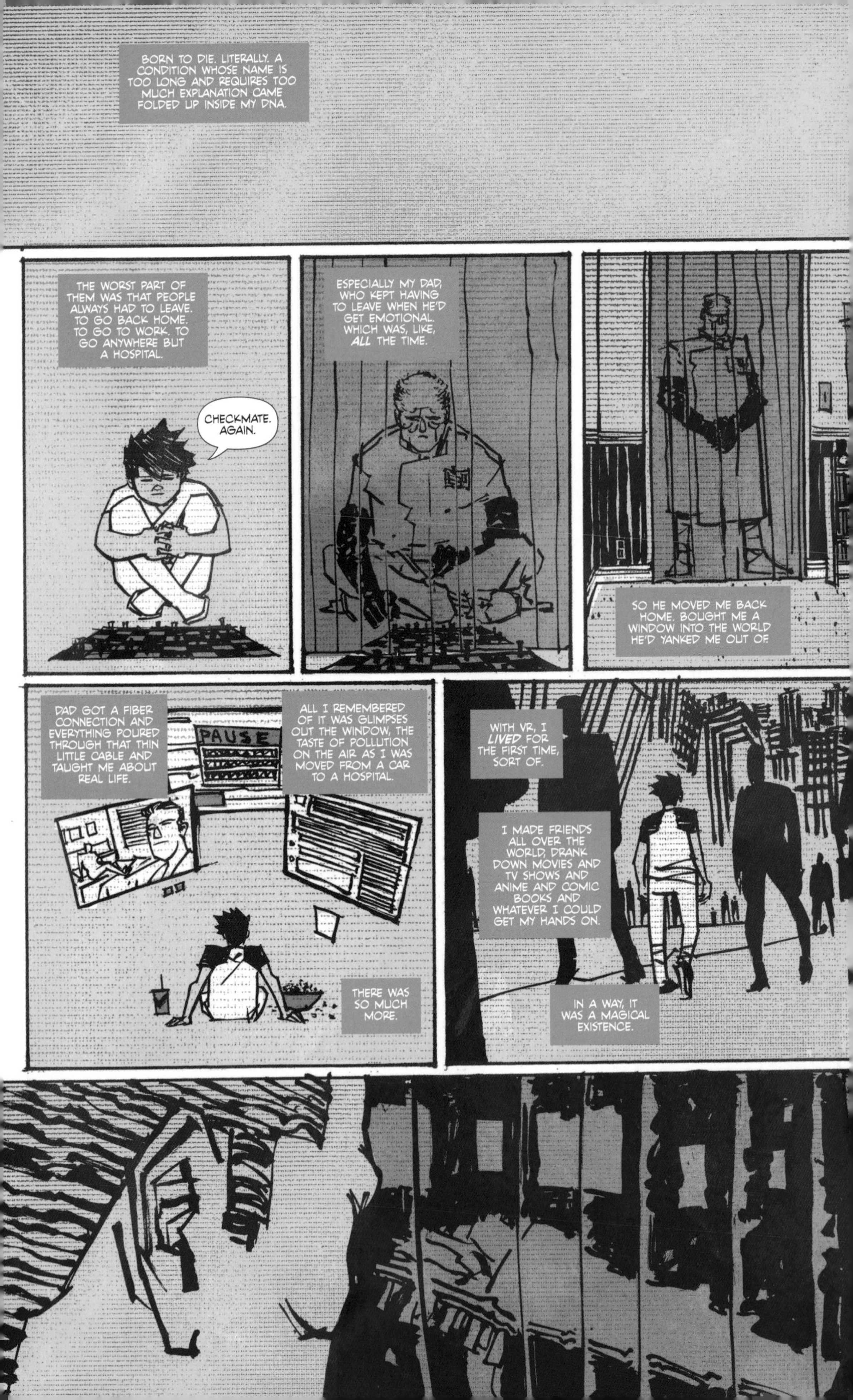
BORN TO DIE. LITERALLY. A CONDITION WHOSE NAME IS TOO LONG AND REQUIRES TOO MUCH EXPLANATION CAME FOLDED UP INSIDE MY DNA.
THE WORST PART OF THEM WAS THAT PEOPLE ALWAYS HAD TO LEAVE. TO GO BACK HOME. TO GO TO WORK. TO GO ANYWHERE BUT A HOSPITAL.
CHECKMATE. AGAIN.
ESPECIALLY MY DAD, WHO KEPT HAVING TO LEAVE WHEN HE'D GET EMOTIONAL. WHICH WAS, LIKE, *ALL* THE TIME.
SO HE MOVED ME BACK HOME. BOUGHT ME A WINDOW INTO THE WORLD HE'D YANKED ME OUT OF.
DAD GOT A FIBER CONNECTION AND EVERYTHING POURED THROUGH THAT THIN LITTLE CABLE AND TAUGHT ME ABOUT REAL LIFE.
PAUSE
ALL I REMEMBERED OF IT WAS GLIMPSES OUT THE WINDOW, THE TASTE OF POLLUTION ON THE AIR AS I WAS MOVED FROM A CAR TO A HOSPITAL.
THERE WAS SO MUCH MORE.
WITH VR, I *LIVED* FOR THE FIRST TIME, SORT OF.
I MADE FRIENDS ALL OVER THE WORLD, DRANK DOWN MOVIES AND TV SHOWS AND ANIME AND COMIC BOOKS AND WHATEVER I COULD GET MY HANDS ON.
IN A WAY, IT WAS A MAGICAL EXISTENCE.

I KNEW WHAT A HOSPITAL WAS BEFORE SCHOOLS OR PLAYGROUNDS OR VIDEO GAMES.

I'D NEVER SEE IT AGAIN, NOT IN PERSON.

I DIDN'T NEED TO. I HAD THE WORLD RUNNING DIRECTLY INTO MY HEAD. A LIFE I COULD PICK, CHOOSE, EDIT AND SKIN THE WAY I WANTED TO.

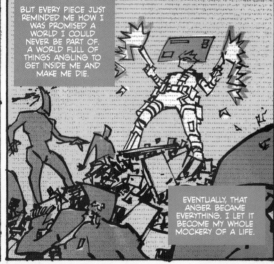
BUT EVERY PIECE JUST REMINDED ME HOW I WAS PROMISED A WORLD I COULD NEVER BE PART OF. A WORLD FULL OF THINGS ANGLING TO GET INSIDE ME AND MAKE ME DIE.

EVENTUALLY, THAT ANGER BECAME EVERYTHING. I LET IT BECOME MY WHOLE MOCKERY OF A LIFE.

BECAUSE AT SOME POINT, IT WOULD TURN OFF. SERVICE WOULD HICCUP. BIOLOGY AND DAD'S CURFEW INSISTED I SLEEP, AND I'D BE PLUNGED BACK TO REALITY.

THE PRISON I LIVED IN. THAT CELL THAT WAS MY BODY. ALL I WANTED WAS TO BE *FREED*. TO DIE AND LEAVE THIS WORLD.

GO SOMEWHERE BETTER.

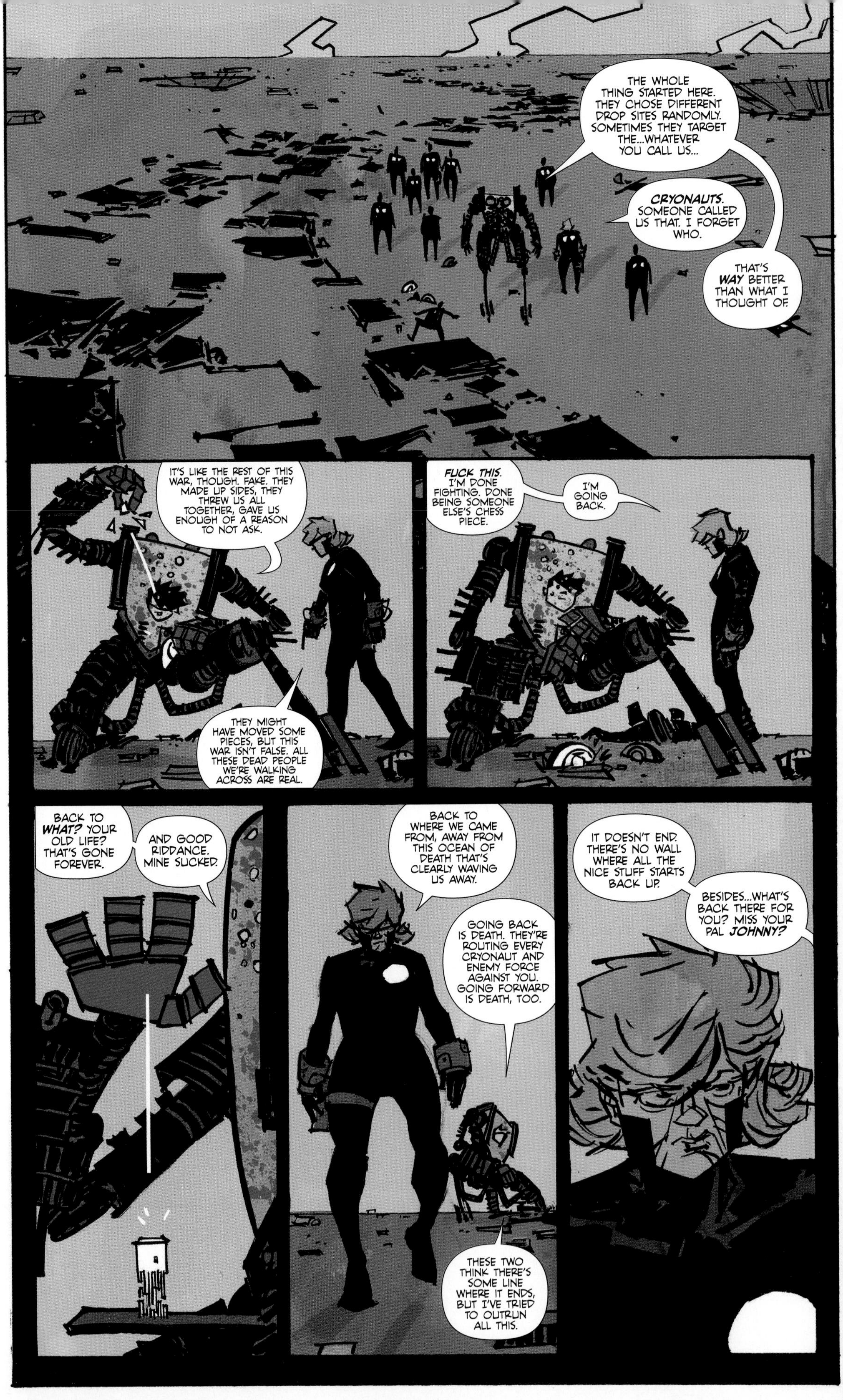

THE WHOLE THING STARTED HERE. THEY CHOSE DIFFERENT DROP SITES RANDOMLY. SOMETIMES THEY TARGET THE...WHATEVER YOU CALL US...
CRYONAUTS. SOMEONE CALLED US THAT. I FORGET WHO.
THAT'S WAY BETTER THAN WHAT I THOUGHT OF.
IT'S LIKE THE REST OF THIS WAR, THOUGH. FAKE. THEY MADE UP SIDES, THEY THREW US ALL TOGETHER, GAVE US ENOUGH OF A REASON TO NOT ASK.
THEY MIGHT HAVE MOVED SOME PIECES, BUT THIS WAR ISN'T FALSE. ALL THESE DEAD PEOPLE WE'RE WALKING ACROSS ARE REAL.
FUCK THIS. I'M DONE FIGHTING. DONE BEING SOMEONE ELSE'S CHESS PIECE.
I'M GOING BACK.
BACK TO WHAT? YOUR OLD LIFE? THAT'S GONE FOREVER.
AND GOOD RIDDANCE. MINE SUCKED.
BACK TO WHERE WE CAME FROM, AWAY FROM THIS OCEAN OF DEATH THAT'S CLEARLY WAVING US AWAY.
GOING BACK IS DEATH. THEY'RE ROUTING EVERY CRYONAUT AND ENEMY FORCE AGAINST YOU. GOING FORWARD IS DEATH, TOO.
THESE TWO THINK THERE'S SOME LINE WHERE IT ENDS, BUT I'VE TRIED TO OUTRUN ALL THIS.
IT DOESN'T END. THERE'S NO WALL WHERE ALL THE NICE STUFF STARTS BACK UP.
BESIDES...WHAT'S BACK THERE FOR YOU? MISS YOUR PAL JOHNNY?

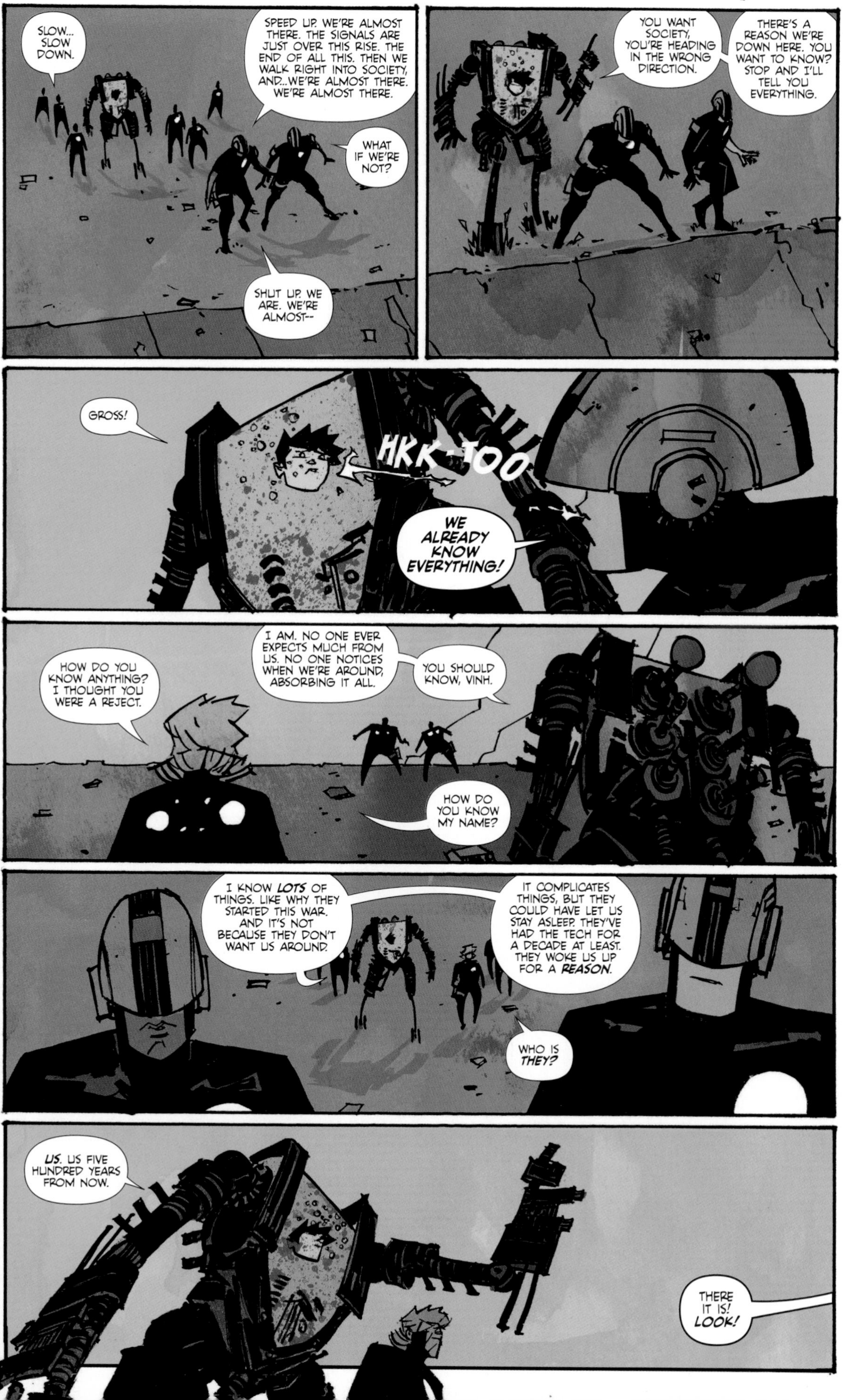
SLOW... SLOW DOWN.
SPEED UP. WE'RE ALMOST THERE. THE SIGNALS ARE JUST OVER THIS RISE. THE END OF ALL THIS. THEN WE WALK RIGHT INTO SOCIETY, AND...WE'RE ALMOST THERE. WE'RE ALMOST THERE.
WHAT IF WE'RE NOT?
SHUT UP. WE ARE. WE'RE ALMOST--
YOU WANT SOCIETY, YOU'RE HEADING IN THE WRONG DIRECTION.
THERE'S A REASON WE'RE DOWN HERE. YOU WANT TO KNOW? STOP AND I'LL TELL YOU EVERYTHING.
GROSS!
HKK-TOO
WE ALREADY KNOW EVERYTHING!
HOW DO YOU KNOW ANYTHING? I THOUGHT YOU WERE A REJECT.
I AM. NO ONE EVER EXPECTS MUCH FROM US. NO ONE NOTICES WHEN WE'RE AROUND, ABSORBING IT ALL.
YOU SHOULD KNOW, VINH.
HOW DO YOU KNOW MY NAME?
I KNOW LOTS OF THINGS. LIKE WHY THEY STARTED THIS WAR. AND IT'S NOT BECAUSE THEY DON'T WANT US AROUND.
IT COMPLICATES THINGS, BUT THEY COULD HAVE LET US STAY ASLEEP. THEY'VE HAD THE TECH FOR A DECADE AT LEAST. THEY WOKE US UP FOR A REASON.
WHO IS THEY?
US. US FIVE HUNDRED YEARS FROM NOW.
THERE IT IS! LOOK!

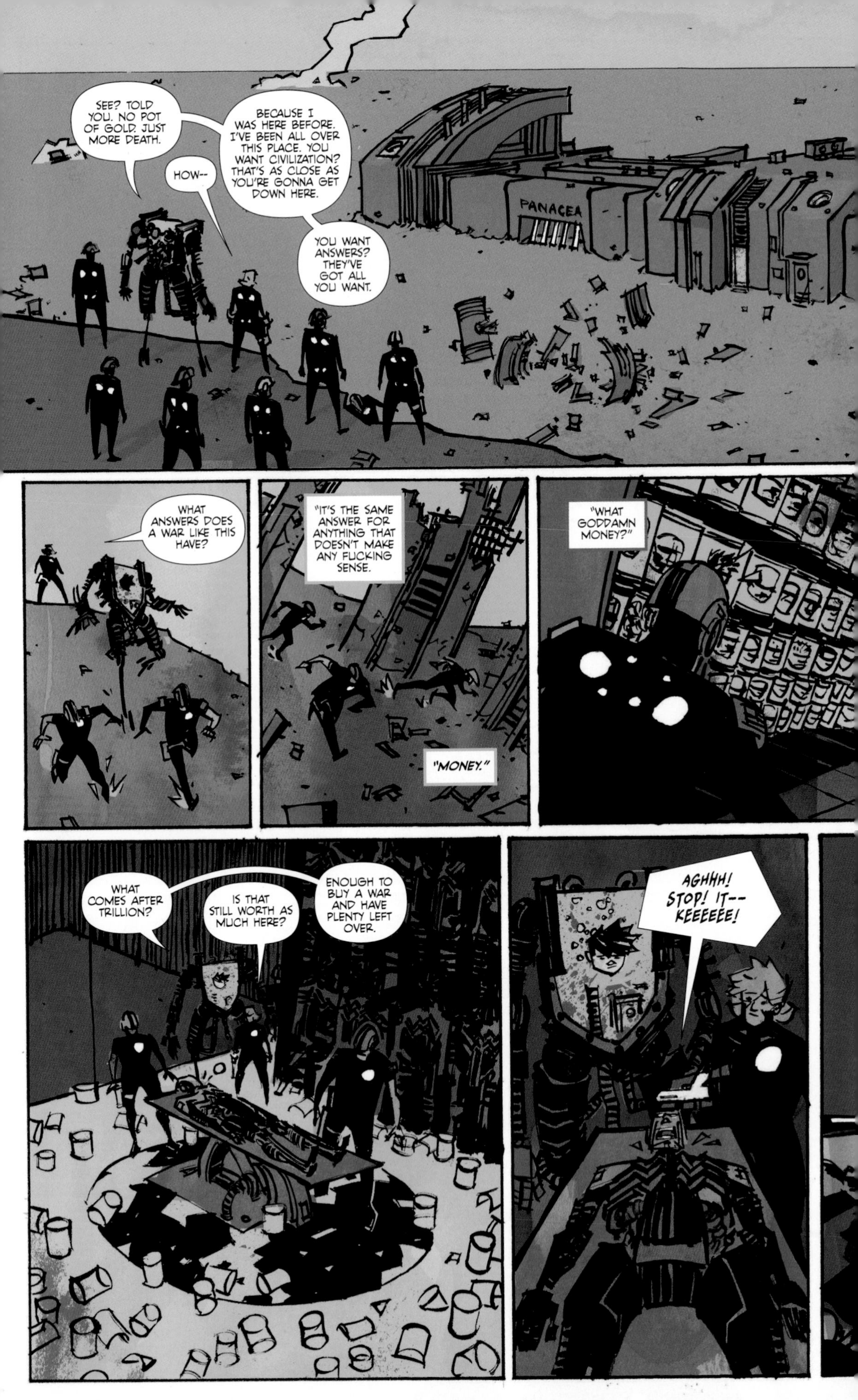
SEE? TOLD YOU. NO POT OF GOLD. JUST MORE DEATH.
HOW--
BECAUSE I WAS HERE BEFORE. I'VE BEEN ALL OVER THIS PLACE. YOU WANT CIVILIZATION? THAT'S AS CLOSE AS YOU'RE GONNA GET DOWN HERE.
YOU WANT ANSWERS? THEY'VE GOT ALL YOU WANT.
PANACEA
WHAT ANSWERS DOES A WAR LIKE THIS HAVE?
"IT'S THE SAME ANSWER FOR ANYTHING THAT DOESN'T MAKE ANY FUCKING SENSE.
"MONEY."
"WHAT GODDAMN MONEY?"
WHAT COMES AFTER TRILLION?
IS THAT STILL WORTH AS MUCH HERE?
ENOUGH TO BUY A WAR AND HAVE PLENTY LEFT OVER.
AGHHH! STOP! IT-- KEEEEEE!

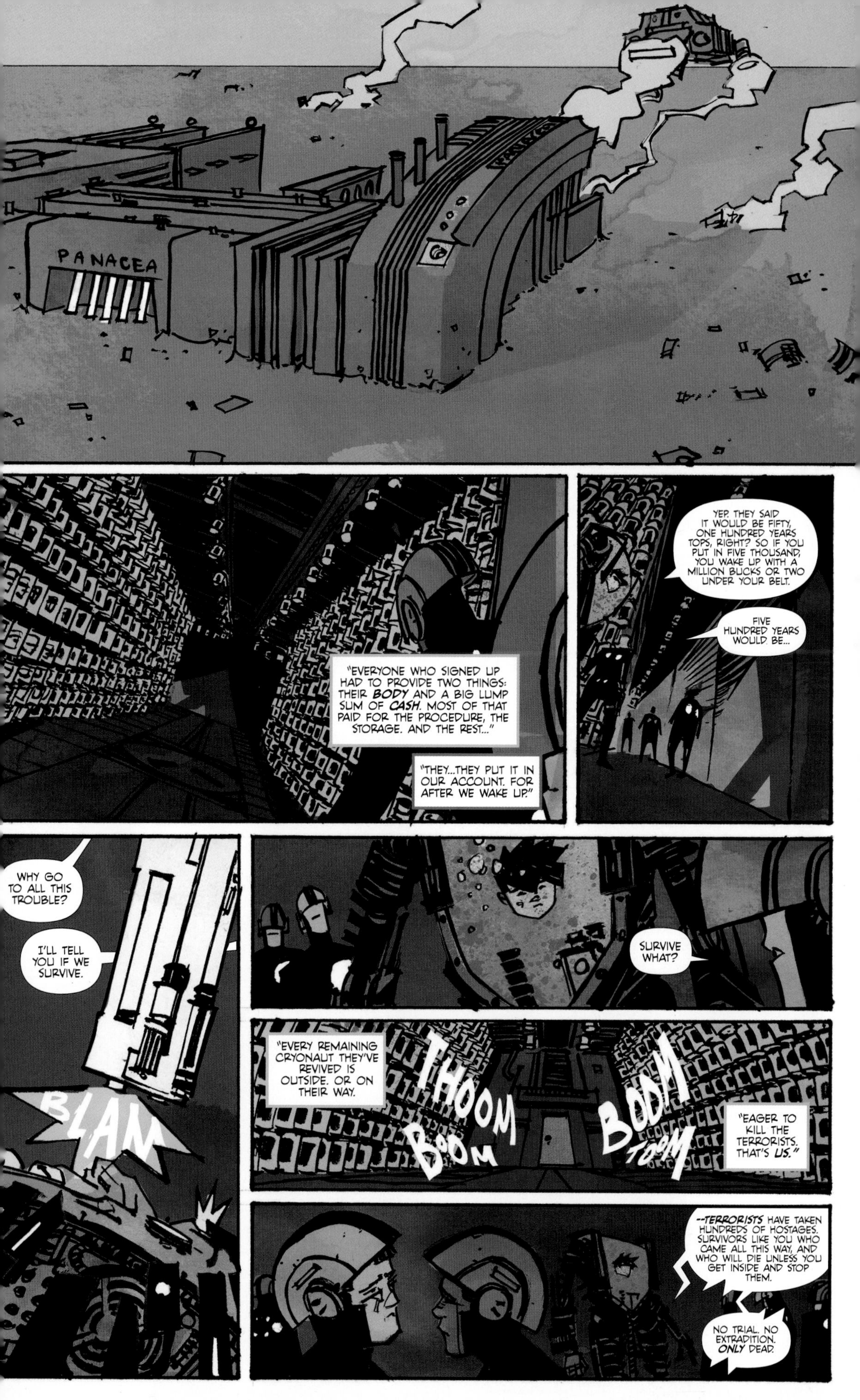
PANACEA
"EVERYONE WHO SIGNED UP HAD TO PROVIDE TWO THINGS: THEIR BODY AND A BIG LUMP SUM OF CASH. MOST OF THAT PAID FOR THE PROCEDURE, THE STORAGE. AND THE REST..."
"THEY...THEY PUT IT IN OUR ACCOUNT. FOR AFTER WE WAKE UP."
YEP. THEY SAID IT WOULD BE FIFTY, ONE HUNDRED YEARS TOPS, RIGHT? SO IF YOU PUT IN FIVE THOUSAND, YOU WAKE UP WITH A MILLION BUCKS OR TWO UNDER YOUR BELT.
FIVE HUNDRED YEARS WOULD BE...
WHY GO TO ALL THIS TROUBLE?
I'LL TELL YOU IF WE SURVIVE.
BLAM
SURVIVE WHAT?
"EVERY REMAINING CRYONAUT THEY'VE REVIVED IS OUTSIDE. OR ON THEIR WAY.
THOOM
BOOM
BOOM
TOOM
"EAGER TO KILL THE TERRORISTS. THAT'S US."
--TERRORISTS HAVE TAKEN HUNDREDS OF HOSTAGES. SURVIVORS LIKE YOU WHO CAME ALL THIS WAY, AND WHO WILL DIE UNLESS YOU GET INSIDE AND STOP THEM.
NO TRIAL. NO EXTRADITION. ONLY DEAD.

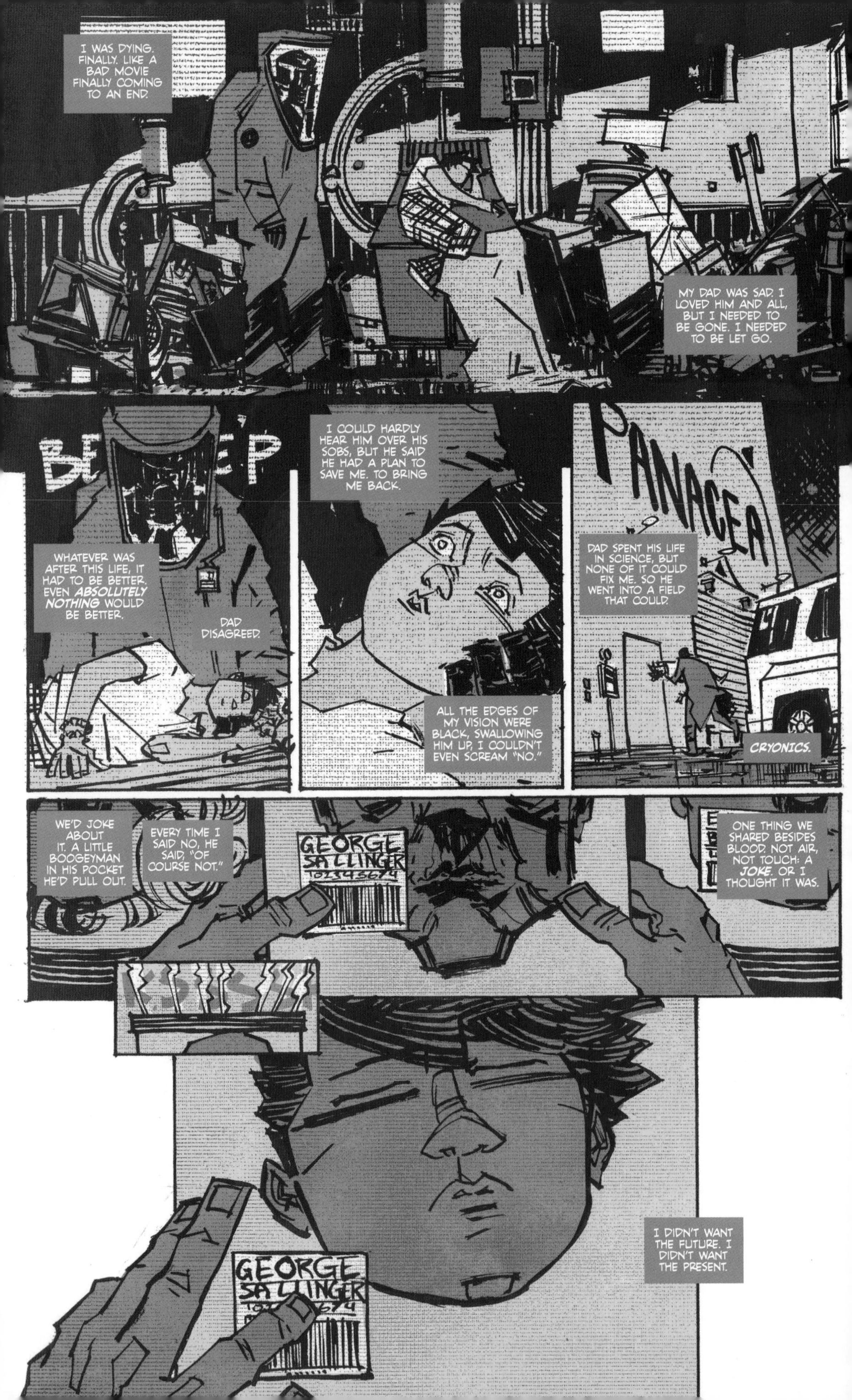
I WAS DYING. FINALLY. LIKE A BAD MOVIE FINALLY COMING TO AN END.
MY DAD WAS SAD. I LOVED HIM AND ALL, BUT I NEEDED TO BE GONE. I NEEDED TO BE LET GO.
WHATEVER WAS AFTER THIS LIFE, IT HAD TO BE BETTER. EVEN *ABSOLUTELY NOTHING* WOULD BE BETTER.
DAD DISAGREED.
I COULD HARDLY HEAR HIM OVER HIS SOBS, BUT HE SAID HE HAD A PLAN TO SAVE ME. TO BRING ME BACK.
ALL THE EDGES OF MY VISION WERE BLACK, SWALLOWING HIM UP, I COULDN'T EVEN SCREAM "NO."
PANACEA
DAD SPENT HIS LIFE IN SCIENCE, BUT NONE OF IT COULD FIX ME. SO HE WENT INTO A FIELD THAT COULD.
CRYONICS.
WE'D JOKE ABOUT IT. A LITTLE BOOGEYMAN IN HIS POCKET HE'D PULL OUT.
EVERY TIME I SAID NO, HE SAID, "OF COURSE NOT."
GEORGE SALLINGER
ONE THING WE SHARED BESIDES BLOOD. NOT AIR, NOT TOUCH: A *JOKE*. OR I THOUGHT IT WAS.
GEORGE SALLINGER
I DIDN'T WANT THE FUTURE. I DIDN'T WANT THE PRESENT.

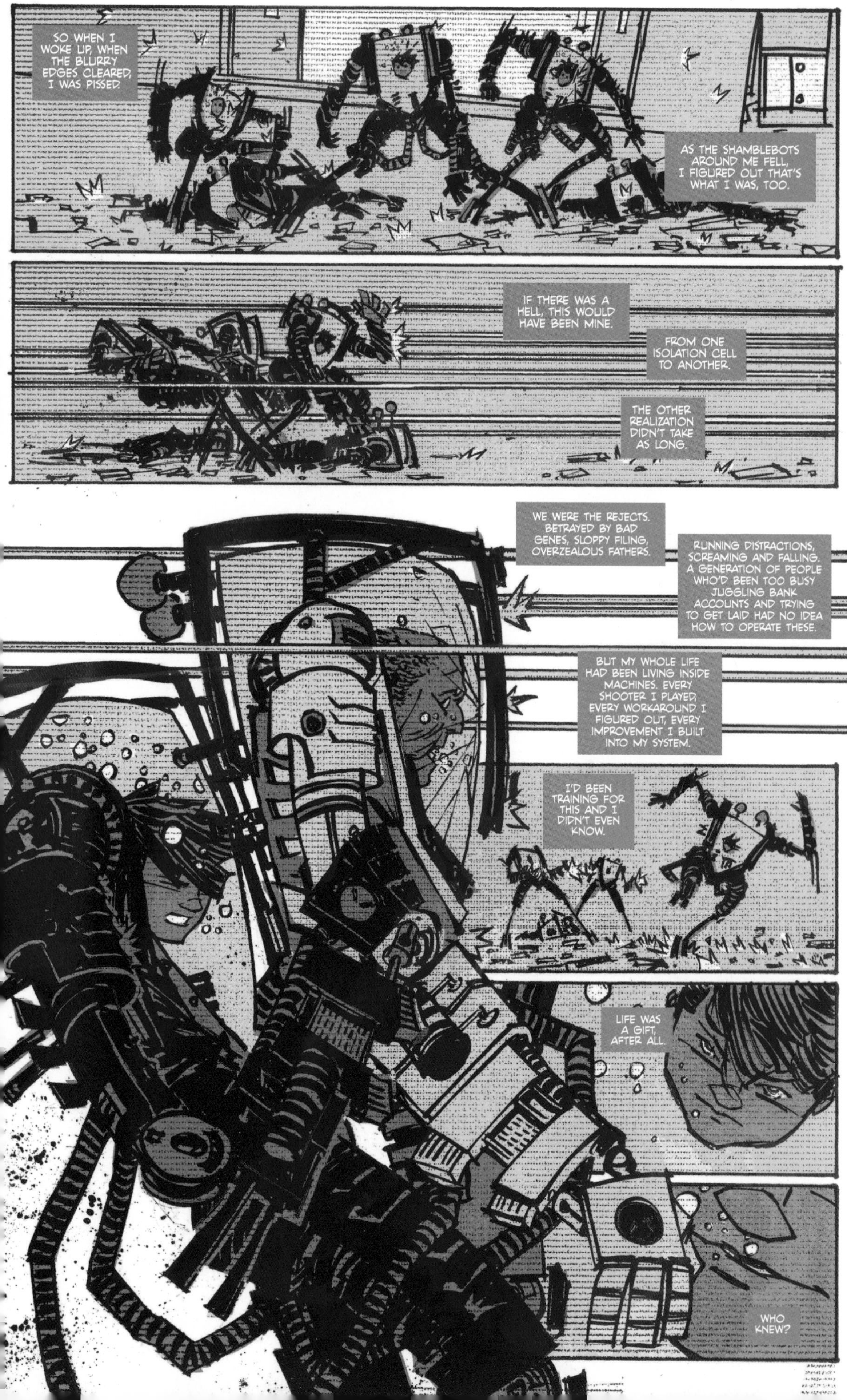
SO WHEN I WOKE UP, WHEN THE BLURRY EDGES CLEARED, I WAS PISSED.
AS THE SHAMBLEBOTS AROUND ME FELL, I FIGURED OUT THAT'S WHAT I WAS, TOO.
IF THERE WAS A HELL, THIS WOULD HAVE BEEN MINE.
FROM ONE ISOLATION CELL TO ANOTHER.
THE OTHER REALIZATION DIDN'T TAKE AS LONG.
WE WERE THE REJECTS. BETRAYED BY BAD GENES, SLOPPY FILING, OVERZEALOUS FATHERS.
RUNNING DISTRACTIONS, SCREAMING AND FALLING. A GENERATION OF PEOPLE WHO'D BEEN TOO BUSY JUGGLING BANK ACCOUNTS AND TRYING TO GET LAID HAD NO IDEA HOW TO OPERATE THESE.
BUT MY WHOLE LIFE HAD BEEN LIVING INSIDE MACHINES. EVERY SHOOTER I PLAYED, EVERY WORKAROUND I FIGURED OUT, EVERY IMPROVEMENT I BUILT INTO MY SYSTEM.
I'D BEEN TRAINING FOR THIS AND I DIDN'T EVEN KNOW.
LIFE WAS A GIFT, AFTER ALL.
WHO KNEW?

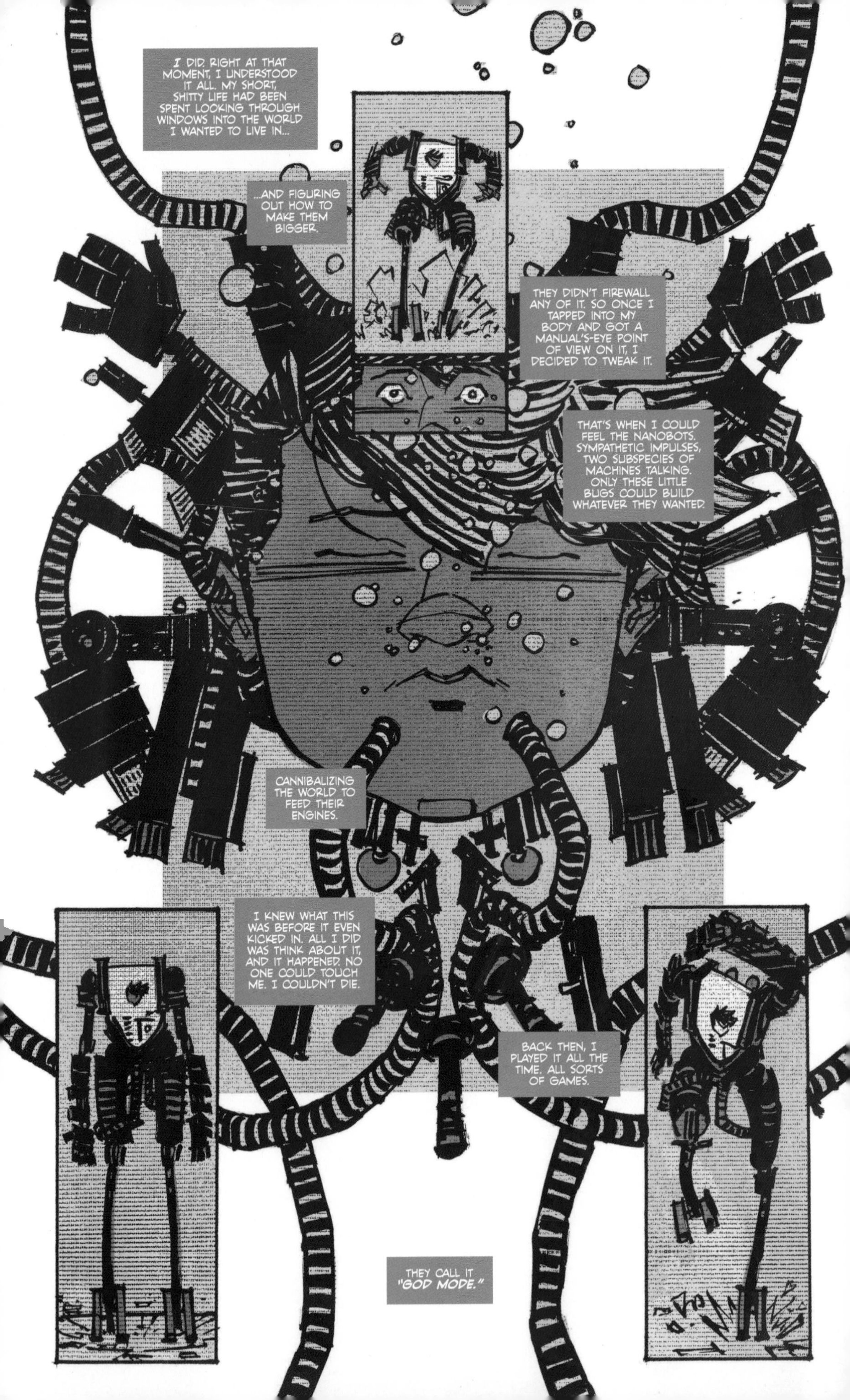
I DID. RIGHT AT THAT MOMENT, I UNDERSTOOD IT ALL. MY SHORT, SHITTY LIFE HAD BEEN SPENT LOOKING THROUGH WINDOWS INTO THE WORLD I WANTED TO LIVE IN...
...AND FIGURING OUT HOW TO MAKE THEM BIGGER.
THEY DIDN'T FIREWALL ANY OF IT. SO ONCE I TAPPED INTO MY BODY AND GOT A MANUAL'S-EYE POINT OF VIEW ON IT, I DECIDED TO TWEAK IT.
THAT'S WHEN I COULD FEEL THE NANOBOTS. SYMPATHETIC IMPULSES, TWO SUBSPECIES OF MACHINES TALKING. ONLY THESE LITTLE BUGS COULD BUILD WHATEVER THEY WANTED.
CANNIBALIZING THE WORLD TO FEED THEIR ENGINES.
I KNEW WHAT THIS WAS BEFORE IT EVEN KICKED IN. ALL I DID WAS THINK ABOUT IT, AND IT HAPPENED. NO ONE COULD TOUCH ME. I COULDN'T DIE.
BACK THEN, I PLAYED IT ALL THE TIME. ALL SORTS OF GAMES.
THEY CALL IT "GOD MODE."

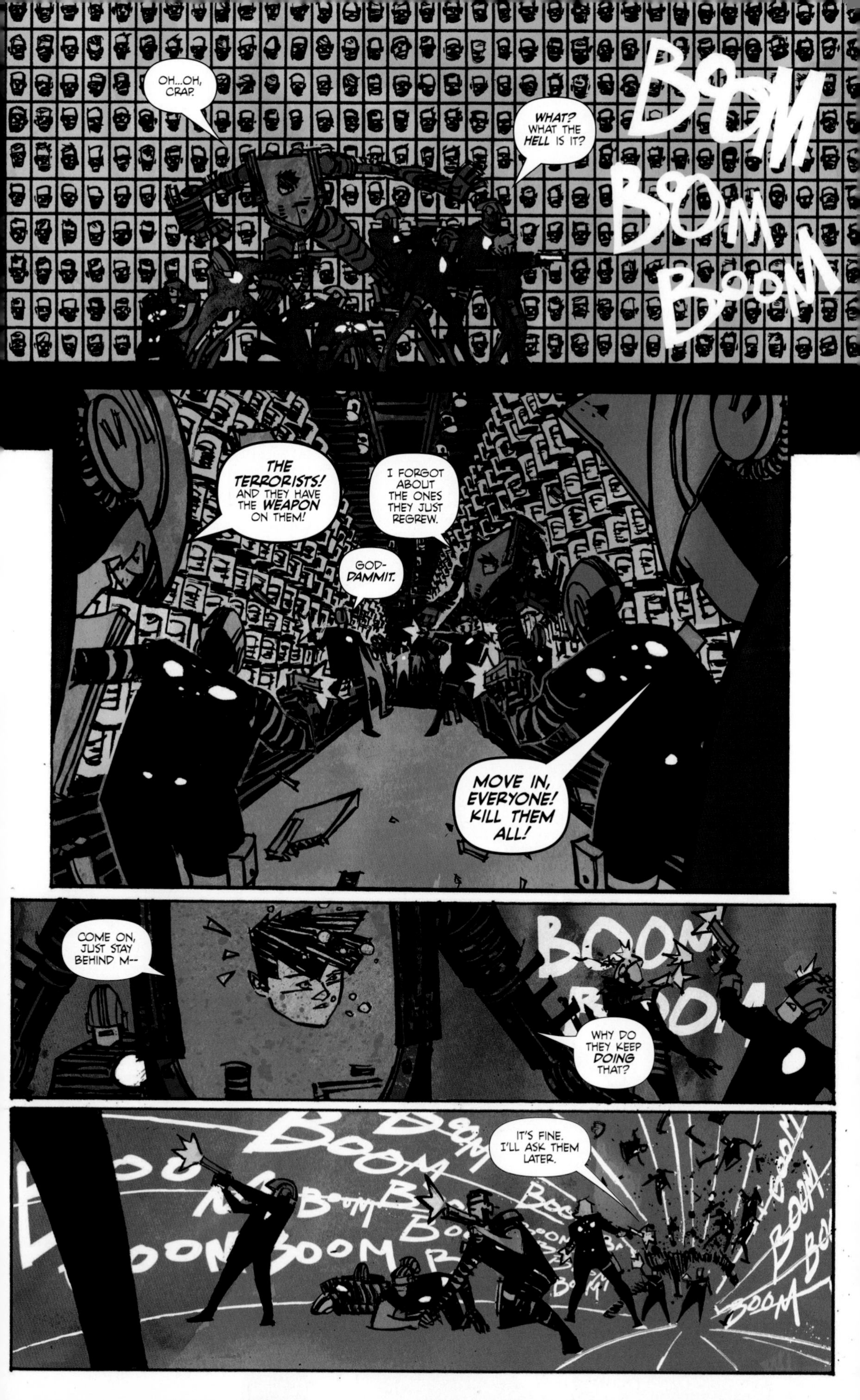
OH...OH, CRAP.
WHAT? WHAT THE HELL IS IT?
BOOM BOOM BOOM
THE TERRORISTS! AND THEY HAVE THE WEAPON ON THEM!
I FORGOT ABOUT THE ONES THEY JUST REGREW.
GOD-DAMMIT.
MOVE IN, EVERYONE! KILL THEM ALL!
COME ON, JUST STAY BEHIND M--
BOOM BOOM
WHY DO THEY KEEP DOING THAT?
IT'S FINE. I'LL ASK THEM LATER.

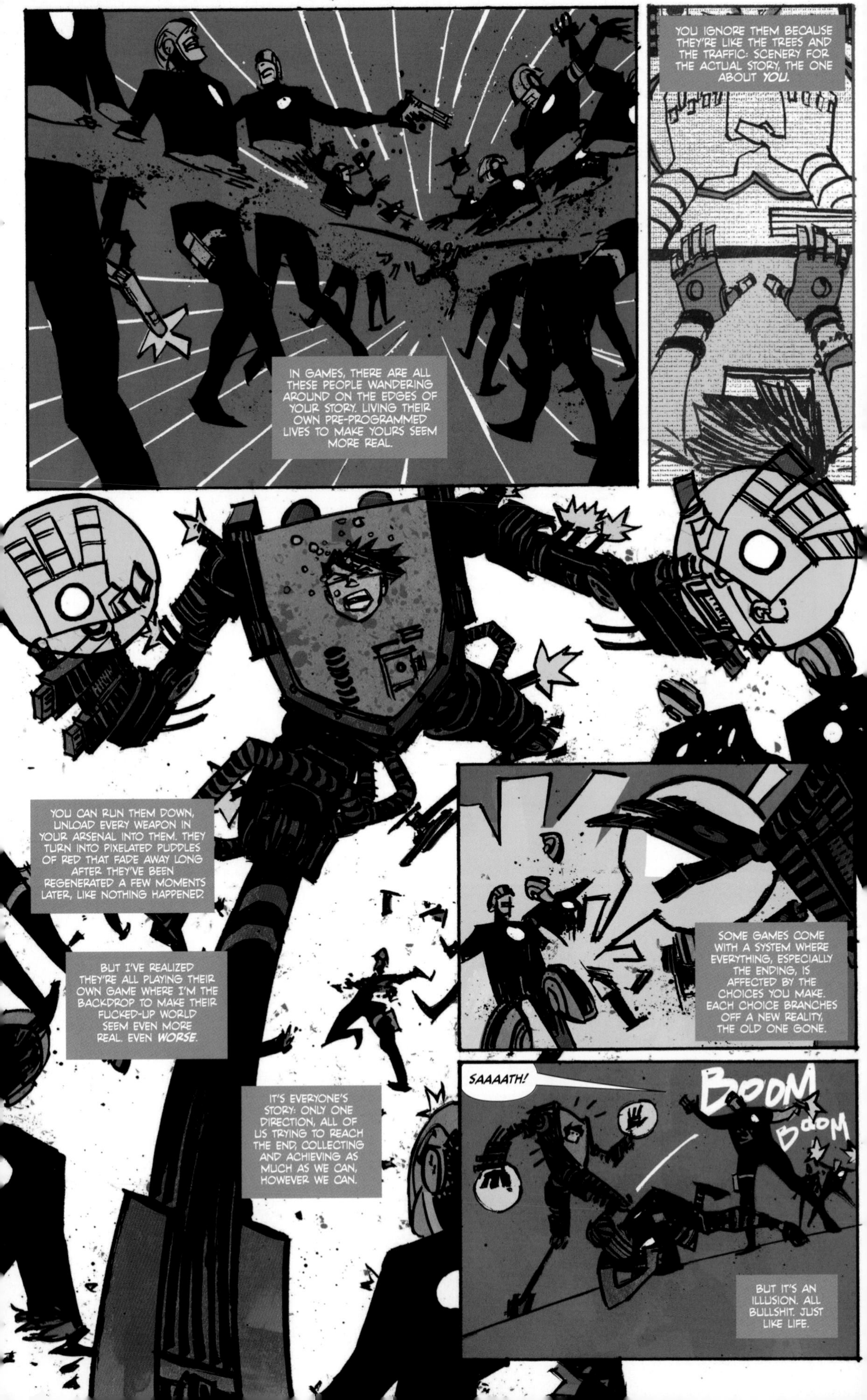
IN GAMES, THERE ARE ALL THESE PEOPLE WANDERING AROUND ON THE EDGES OF YOUR STORY. LIVING THEIR OWN PRE-PROGRAMMED LIVES TO MAKE YOURS SEEM MORE REAL.
YOU IGNORE THEM BECAUSE THEY'RE LIKE THE TREES AND THE TRAFFIC: SCENERY FOR THE ACTUAL STORY, THE ONE ABOUT ***YOU.***
YOU CAN RUN THEM DOWN, UNLOAD EVERY WEAPON IN YOUR ARSENAL INTO THEM. THEY TURN INTO PIXELATED PUDDLES OF RED THAT FADE AWAY LONG AFTER THEY'VE BEEN REGENERATED A FEW MOMENTS LATER, LIKE NOTHING HAPPENED.
BUT I'VE REALIZED THEY'RE ALL PLAYING THEIR OWN GAME WHERE I'M THE BACKDROP TO MAKE THEIR FUCKED-UP WORLD SEEM EVEN MORE REAL. EVEN ***WORSE.***
IT'S EVERYONE'S STORY: ONLY ONE DIRECTION, ALL OF US TRYING TO REACH THE END, COLLECTING AND ACHIEVING AS MUCH AS WE CAN, HOWEVER WE CAN.
SOME GAMES COME WITH A SYSTEM WHERE EVERYTHING, ESPECIALLY THE ENDING, IS AFFECTED BY THE CHOICES YOU MAKE. EACH CHOICE BRANCHES OFF A NEW REALITY, THE OLD ONE GONE.
SAAAATH!
BOOM
BOOM
BUT IT'S AN ILLUSION. ALL BULLSHIT. JUST LIKE LIFE.

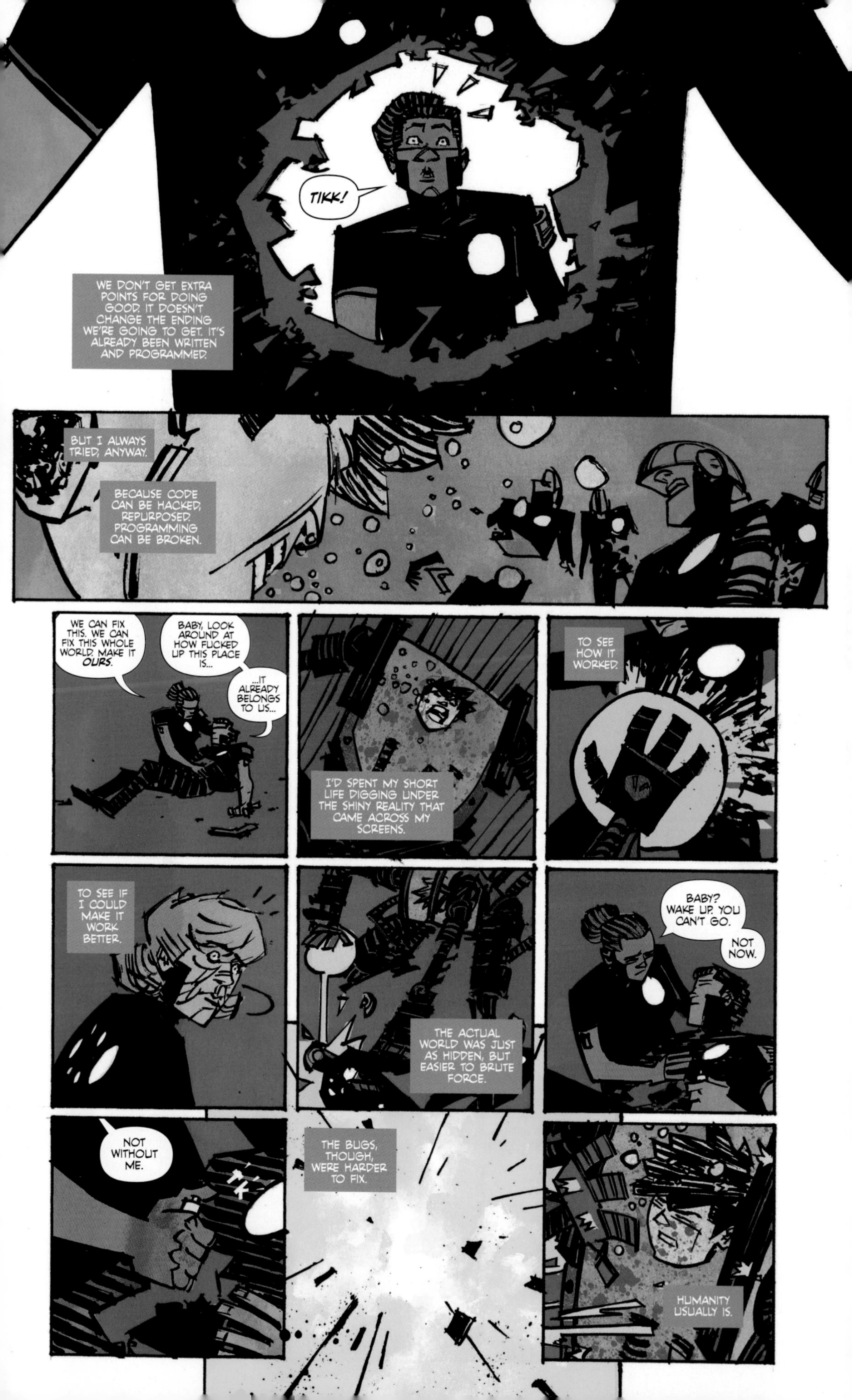
TIKK!
WE DON'T GET EXTRA POINTS FOR DOING GOOD. IT DOESN'T CHANGE THE ENDING WE'RE GOING TO GET. IT'S ALREADY BEEN WRITTEN AND PROGRAMMED.
BUT I ALWAYS TRIED, ANYWAY.
BECAUSE CODE CAN BE HACKED, REPURPOSED. PROGRAMMING CAN BE BROKEN.
WE CAN FIX THIS. WE CAN FIX THIS WHOLE WORLD. MAKE IT *OURS*.
BABY, LOOK AROUND AT HOW FUCKED UP THIS PLACE IS...
...IT ALREADY BELONGS TO US...
I'D SPENT MY SHORT LIFE DIGGING UNDER THE SHINY REALITY THAT CAME ACROSS MY SCREENS.
TO SEE HOW IT WORKED.
TO SEE IF I COULD MAKE IT WORK BETTER.
THE ACTUAL WORLD WAS JUST AS HIDDEN, BUT EASIER TO BRUTE FORCE.
BABY? WAKE UP. YOU CAN'T GO.
NOT NOW.
NOT WITHOUT ME.
TIK
THE BUGS, THOUGH, WERE HARDER TO FIX.
HUMANITY USUALLY IS.

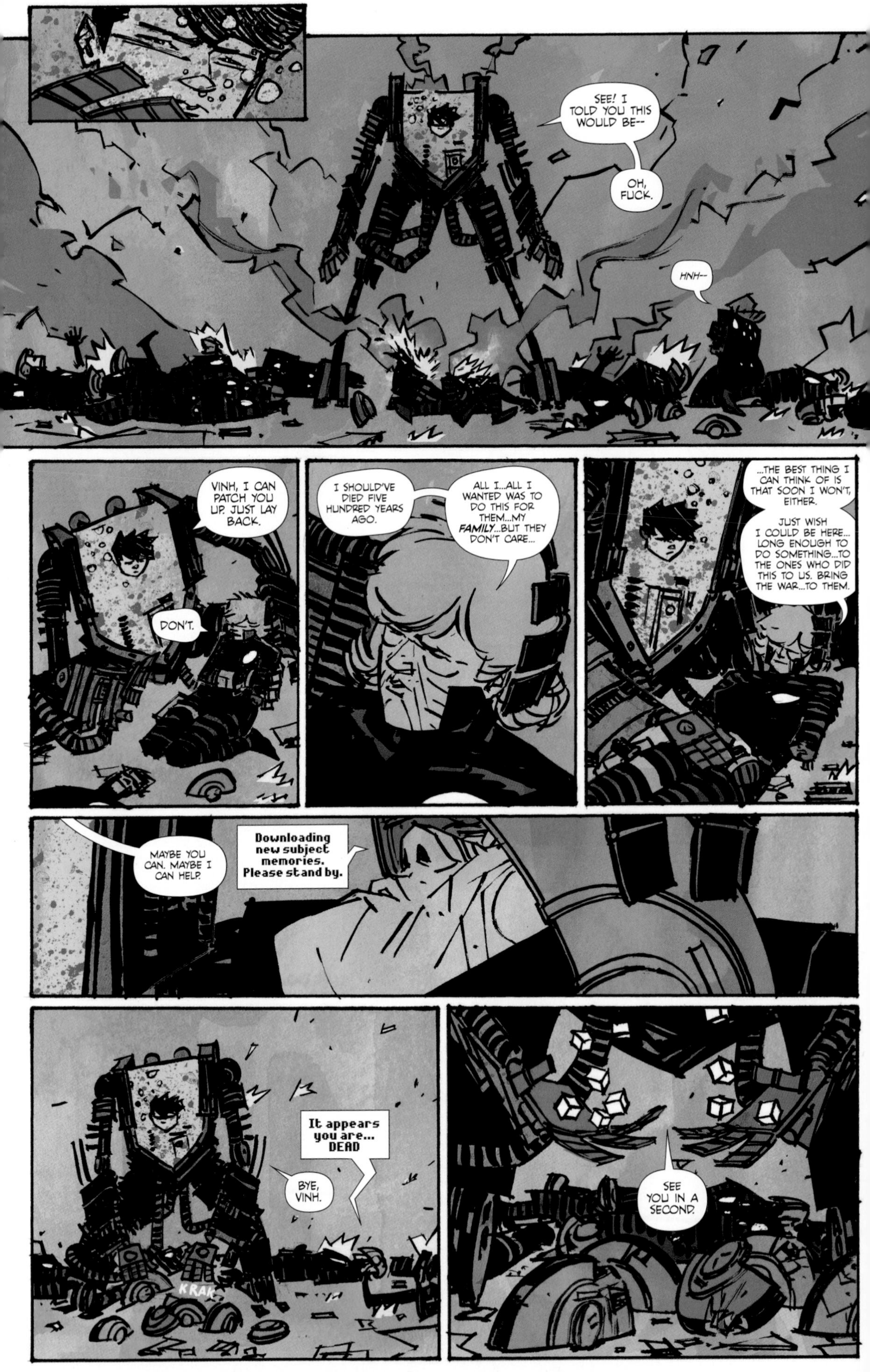
SEE! I TOLD YOU THIS WOULD BE--
OH, FUCK.
HNH--
VINH, I CAN PATCH YOU UP. JUST LAY BACK.
DON'T.
I SHOULD'VE DIED FIVE HUNDRED YEARS AGO.
ALL I...ALL I WANTED WAS TO DO THIS FOR THEM...MY FAMILY...BUT THEY DON'T CARE...
...THE BEST THING I CAN THINK OF IS THAT SOON I WON'T, EITHER.
JUST WISH I COULD BE HERE... LONG ENOUGH TO DO SOMETHING...TO THE ONES WHO DID THIS TO US. BRING THE WAR...TO THEM.
MAYBE YOU CAN. MAYBE I CAN HELP.
Downloading new subject memories. Please stand by.
It appears you are... DEAD
BYE, VINH.
KRAK
SEE YOU IN A SECOND.

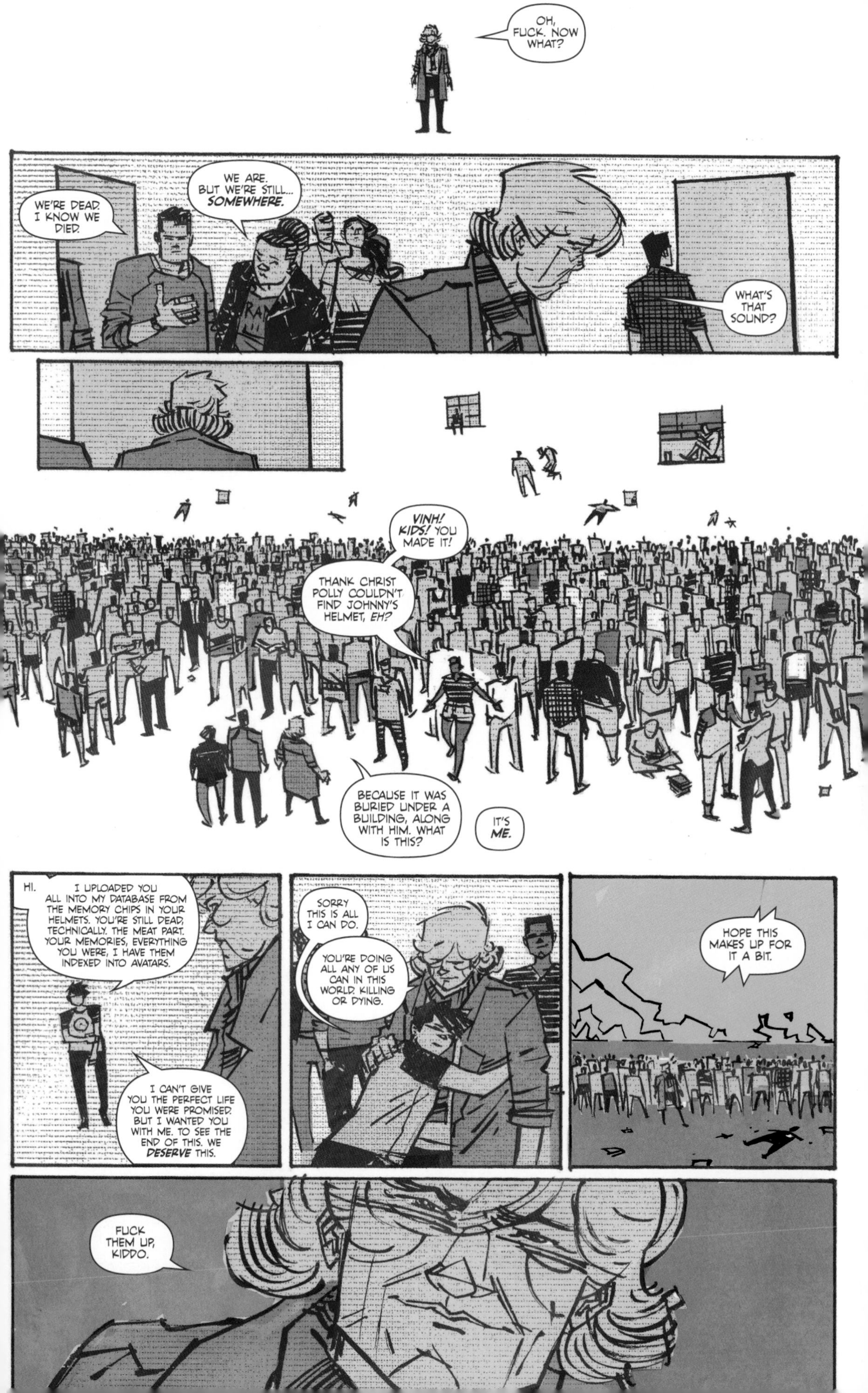

OH, FUCK. NOW WHAT?
WE'RE DEAD. I KNOW WE DIED.
WE ARE. BUT WE'RE STILL... **SOMEWHERE.**
WHAT'S THAT SOUND?
VINH! KIDS! YOU MADE IT!
THANK CHRIST POLLY COULDN'T FIND JOHNNY'S HELMET, *EH?*
BECAUSE IT WAS BURIED UNDER A BUILDING, ALONG WITH HIM. WHAT IS THIS?
IT'S ***ME.***
HI.
I UPLOADED YOU ALL INTO MY DATABASE FROM THE MEMORY CHIPS IN YOUR HELMETS. YOU'RE STILL DEAD, TECHNICALLY. THE MEAT PART. YOUR MEMORIES, EVERYTHING YOU WERE, I HAVE THEM INDEXED INTO AVATARS.
I CAN'T GIVE YOU THE PERFECT LIFE YOU WERE PROMISED. BUT I WANTED YOU WITH ME. TO SEE THE END OF THIS. WE ***DESERVE*** THIS.
SORRY THIS IS ALL I CAN DO.
YOU'RE DOING ALL ANY OF US CAN IN THIS WORLD. KILLING OR DYING.
HOPE THIS MAKES UP FOR IT A BIT.
FUCK THEM UP, KIDDO.

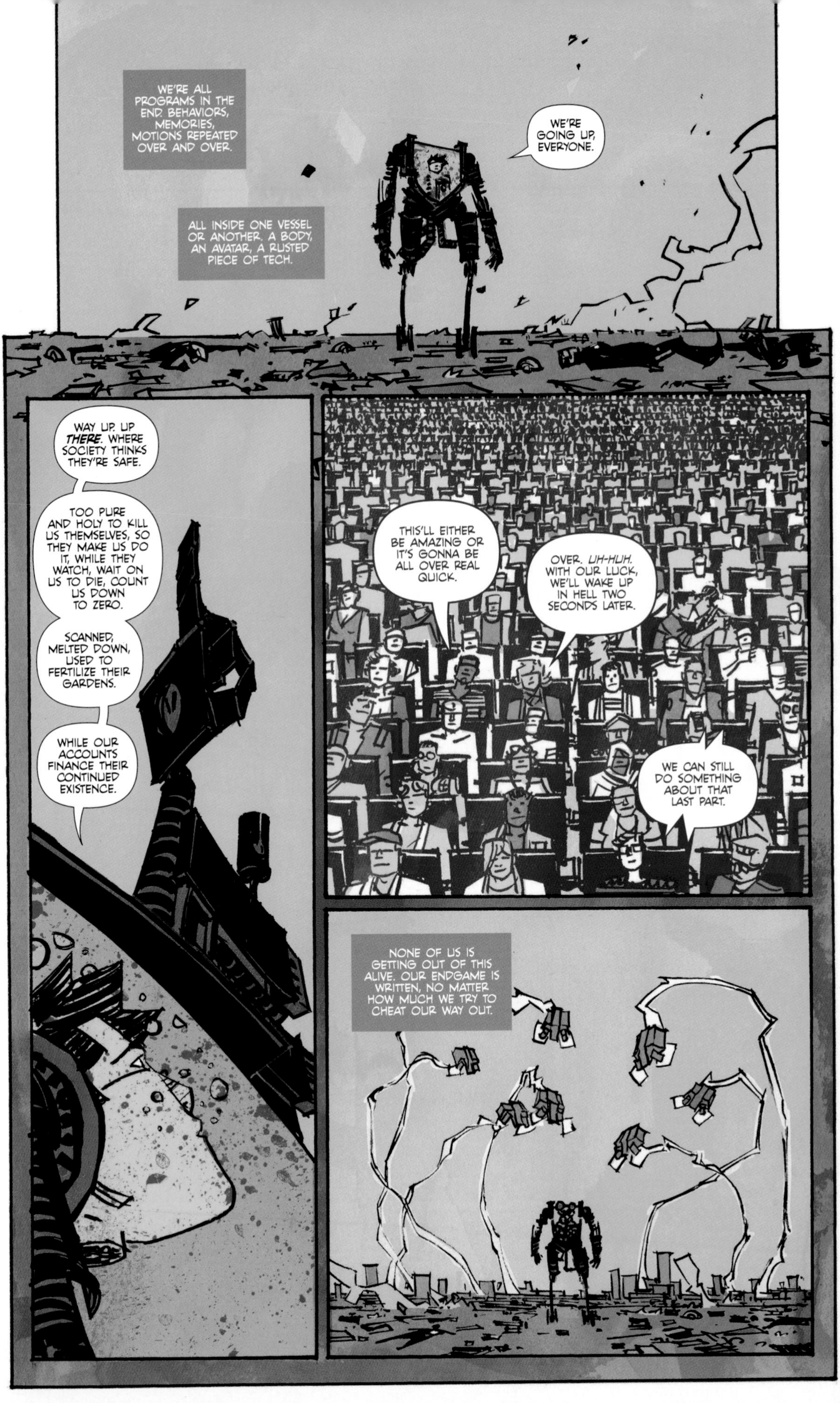
WE'RE ALL PROGRAMS IN THE END. BEHAVIORS, MEMORIES, MOTIONS REPEATED OVER AND OVER.
ALL INSIDE ONE VESSEL OR ANOTHER. A BODY, AN AVATAR, A RUSTED PIECE OF TECH.
WE'RE GOING UP, EVERYONE.
WAY UP. UP *THERE*. WHERE SOCIETY THINKS THEY'RE SAFE.
TOO PURE AND HOLY TO KILL US THEMSELVES, SO THEY MAKE US DO IT, WHILE THEY WATCH, WAIT ON US TO DIE, COUNT US DOWN TO ZERO.
SCANNED, MELTED DOWN, USED TO FERTILIZE THEIR GARDENS.
WHILE OUR ACCOUNTS FINANCE THEIR CONTINUED EXISTENCE.
THIS'LL EITHER BE AMAZING OR IT'S GONNA BE ALL OVER REAL QUICK.
OVER. *UH-HUH.* WITH OUR LUCK, WE'LL WAKE UP IN HELL TWO SECONDS LATER.
WE CAN STILL DO SOMETHING ABOUT THAT LAST PART.
NONE OF US IS GETTING OUT OF THIS ALIVE. OUR ENDGAME IS WRITTEN, NO MATTER HOW MUCH WE TRY TO CHEAT OUR WAY OUT.

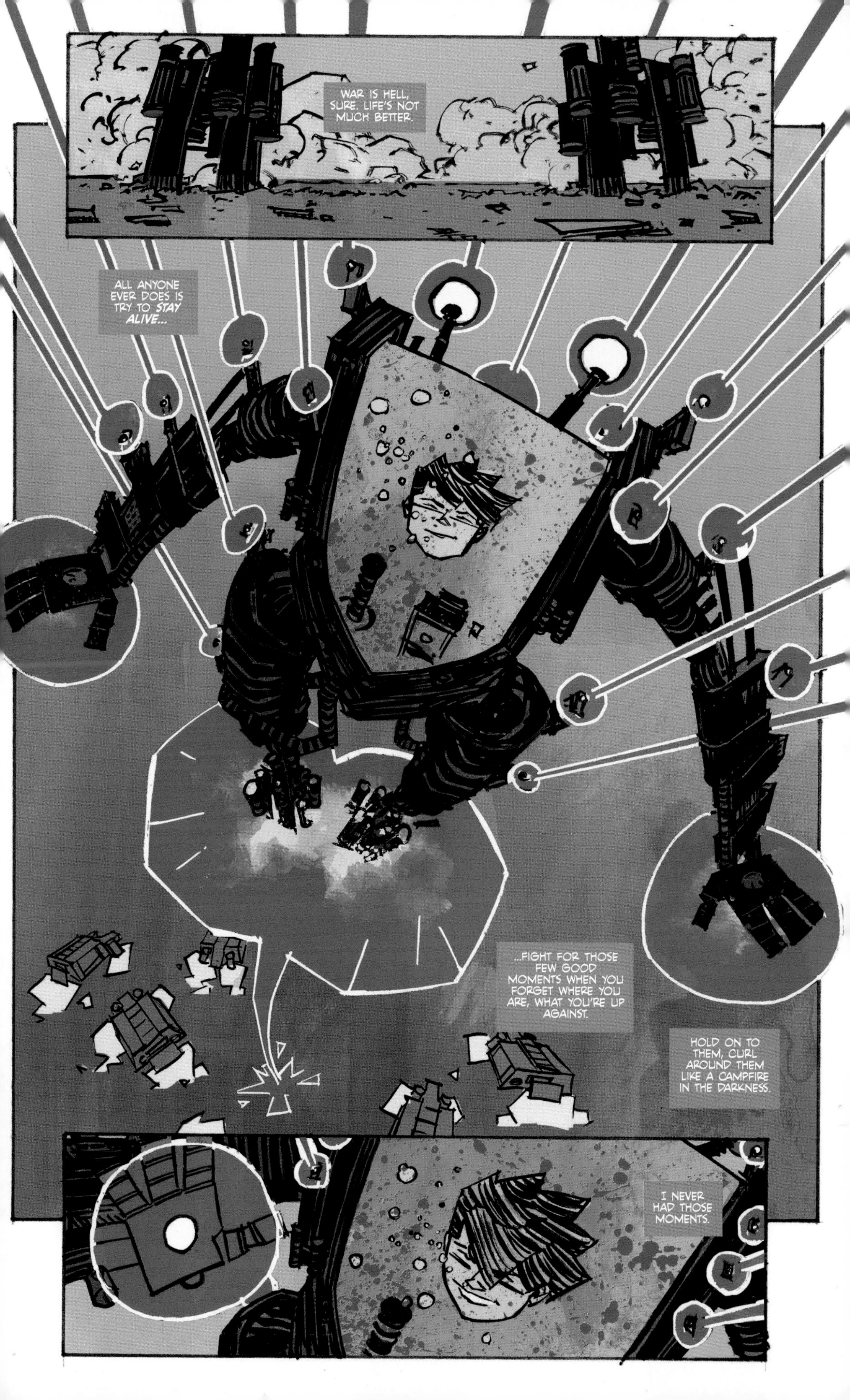
WAR IS HELL, SURE. LIFE'S NOT MUCH BETTER.
ALL ANYONE EVER DOES IS TRY TO *STAY ALIVE*...
...FIGHT FOR THOSE FEW GOOD MOMENTS WHEN YOU FORGET WHERE YOU ARE, WHAT YOU'RE UP AGAINST.
HOLD ON TO THEM, CURL AROUND THEM LIKE A CAMPFIRE IN THE DARKNESS.
I NEVER HAD THOSE MOMENTS.

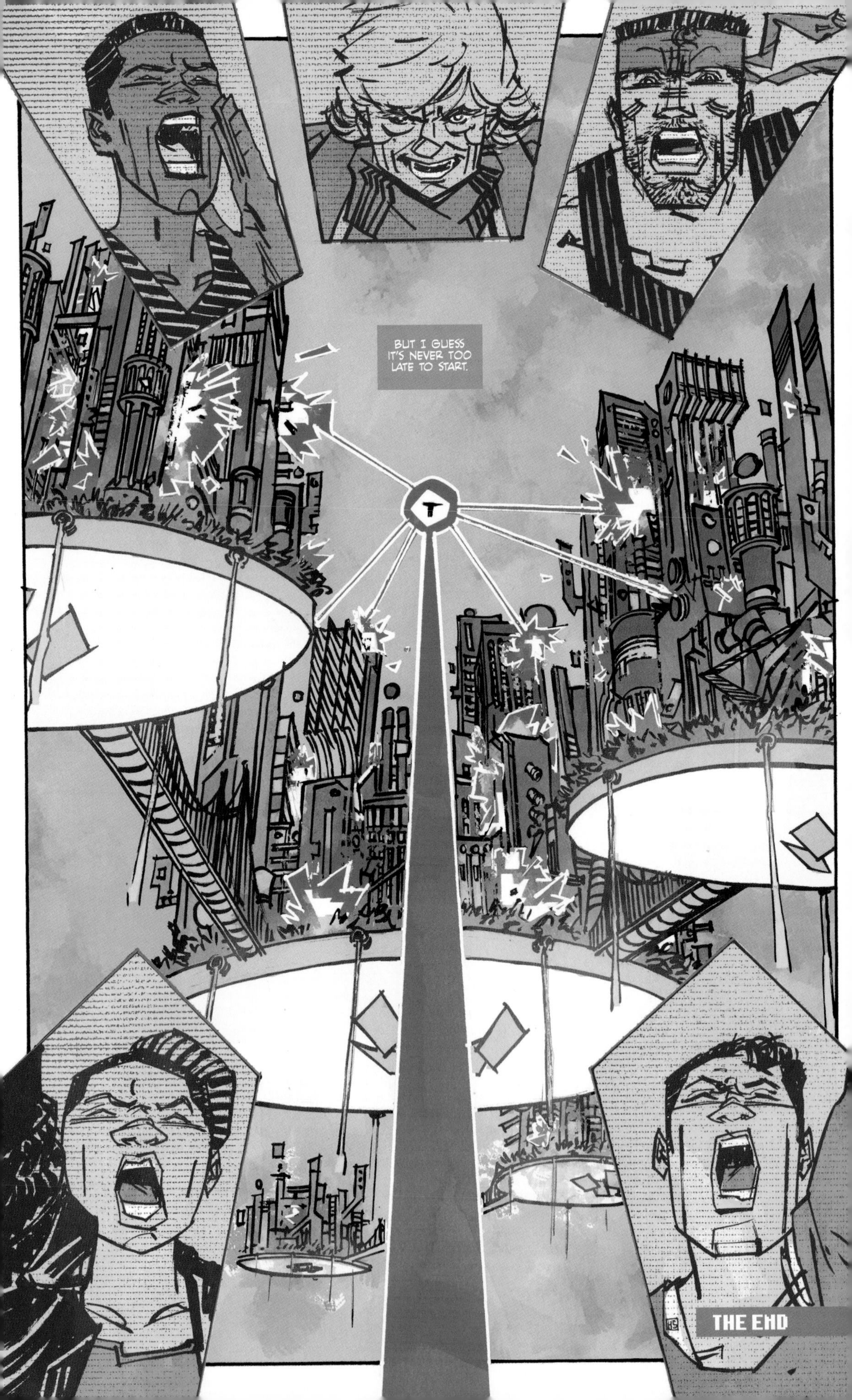
BUT I GUESS IT'S NEVER TOO LATE TO START.
THE END

COVER GALLERY

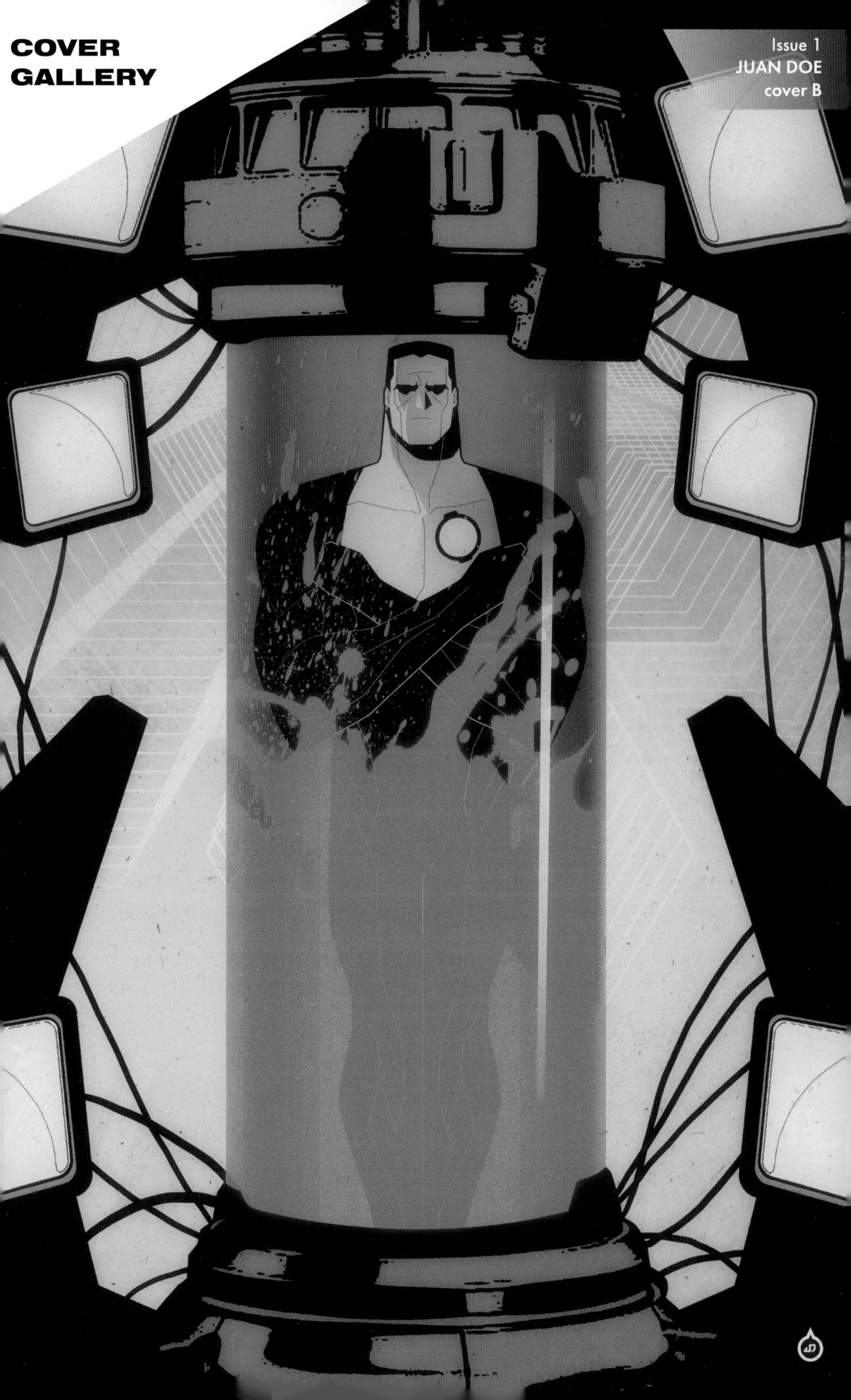
Issue 1
JUAN DOE
cover B

Issue 1
HAYDEN SHERMAN
ComicsPro variant cover

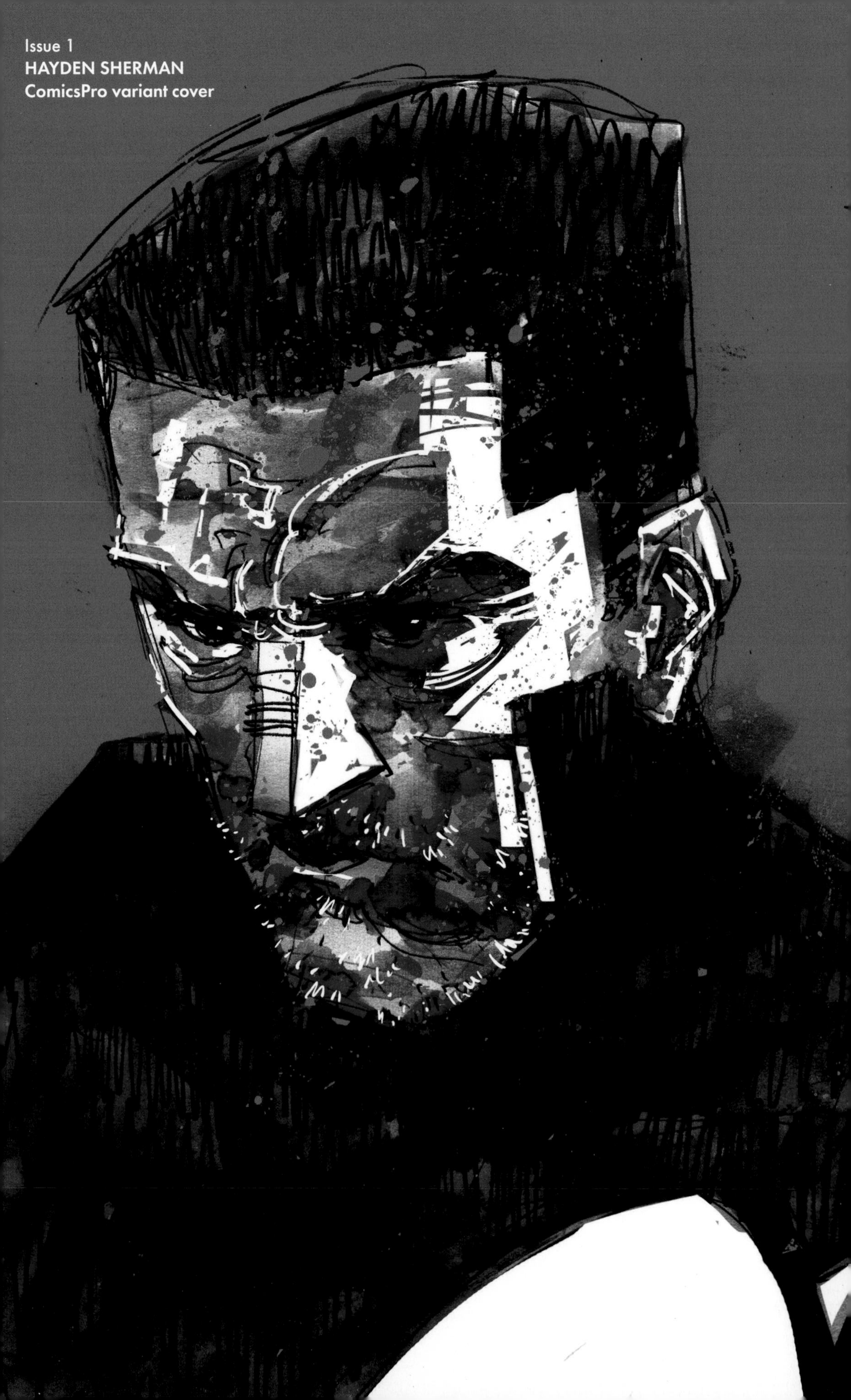

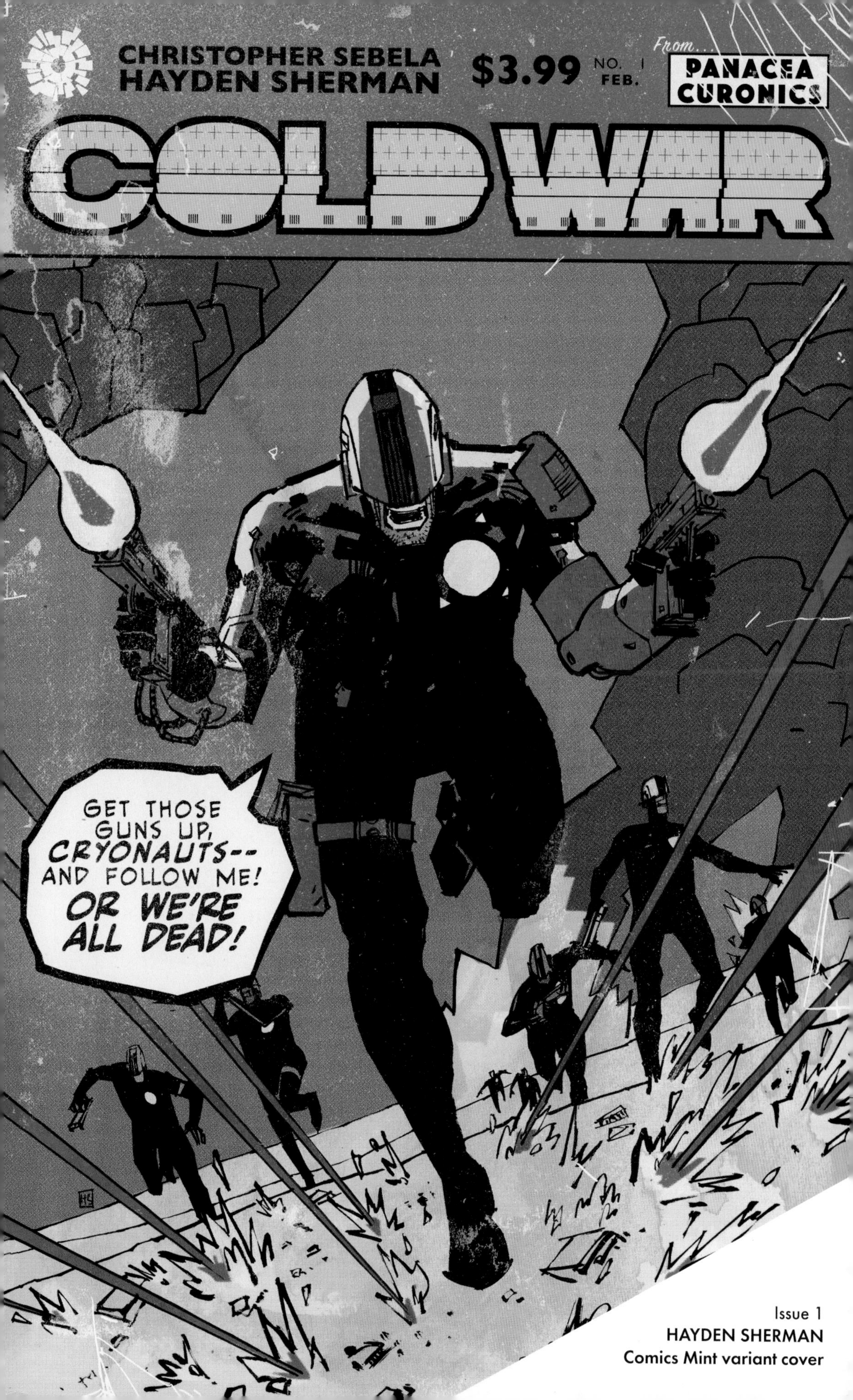
CHRISTOPHER SEBELA
HAYDEN SHERMAN
$3.99
NO. 1
FEB.
From...
PANACEA CURONICS
COLD WAR
GET THOSE GUNS UP, CRYONAUTS-- AND FOLLOW ME! OR WE'RE ALL DEAD!

Issue 1
HAYDEN SHERMAN
Comics Mint variant cover

Series Cover Layouts

1

COLD WAR

2

3

COLD WAR

4

COLD WAR

5

COLD WAR

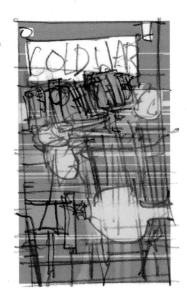

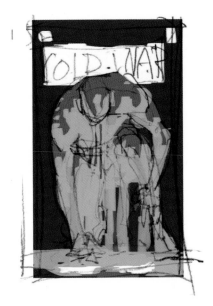

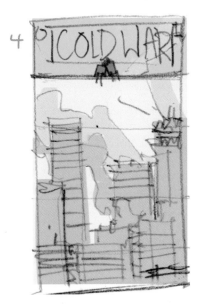

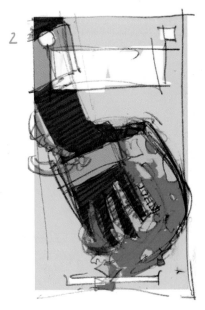

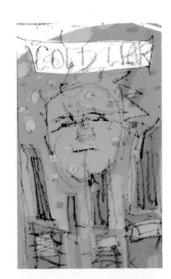

Issue #1 Interior Layouts

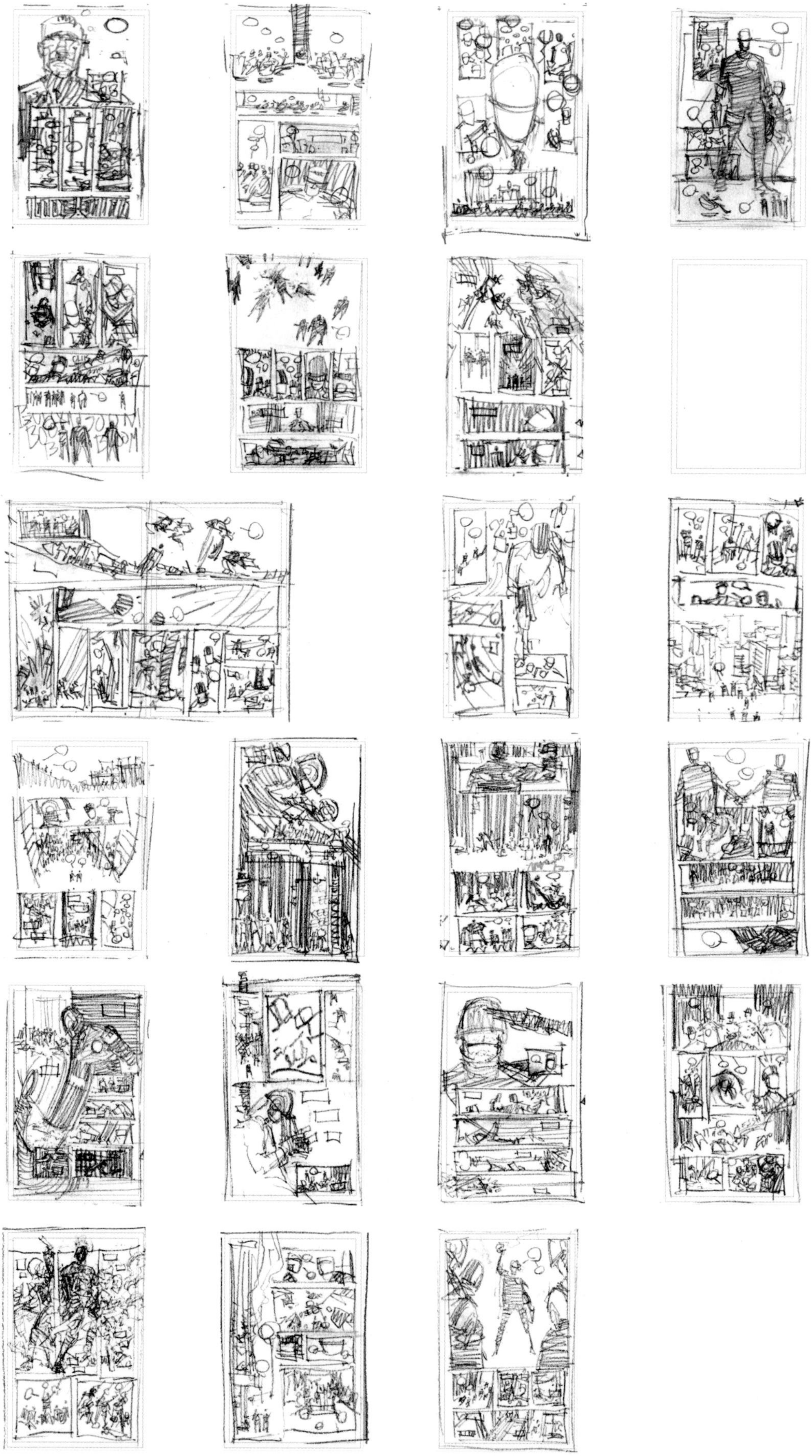

Character Studies & Designs

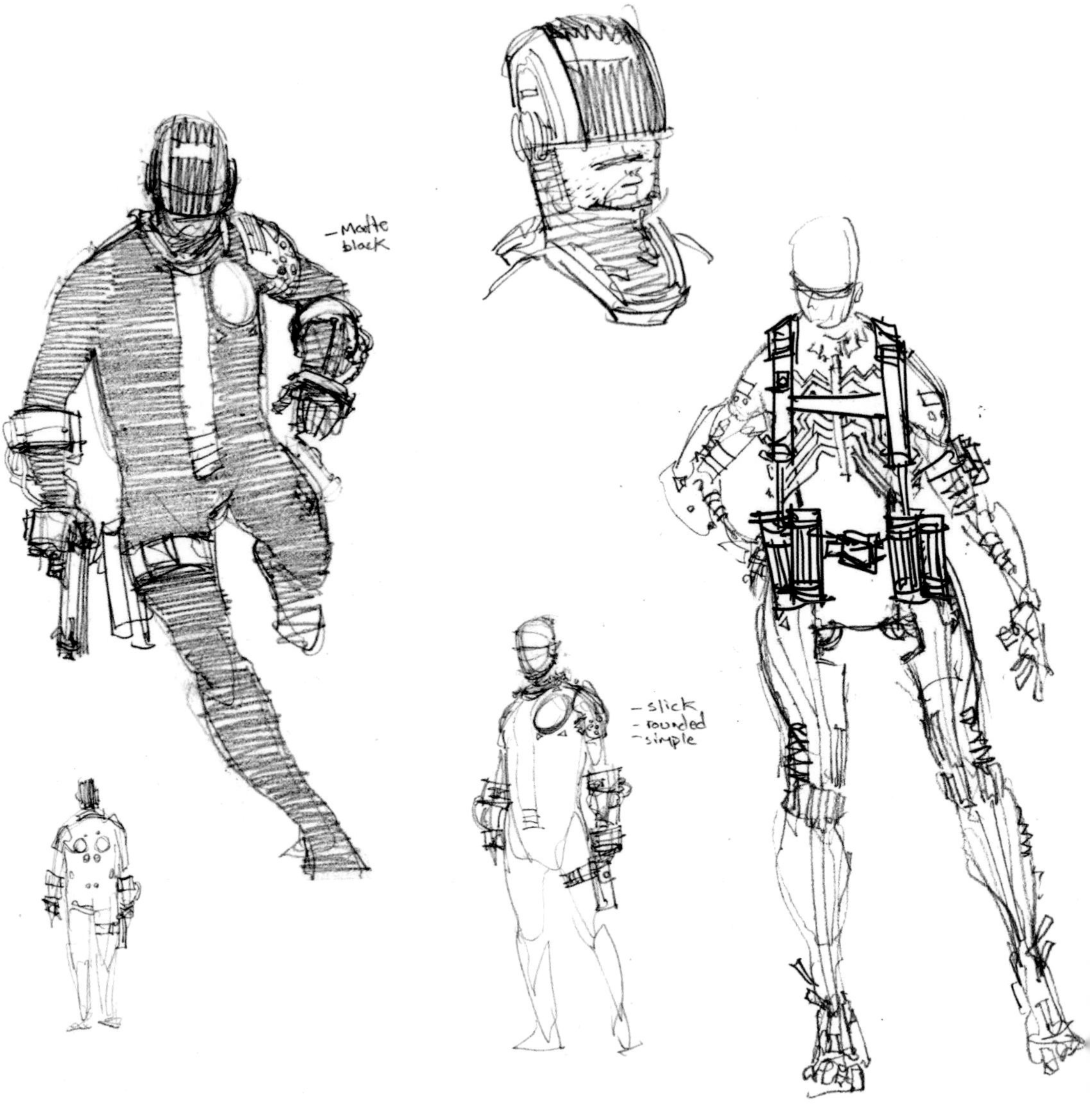
-Matte black
-slick
-rounded
-simple

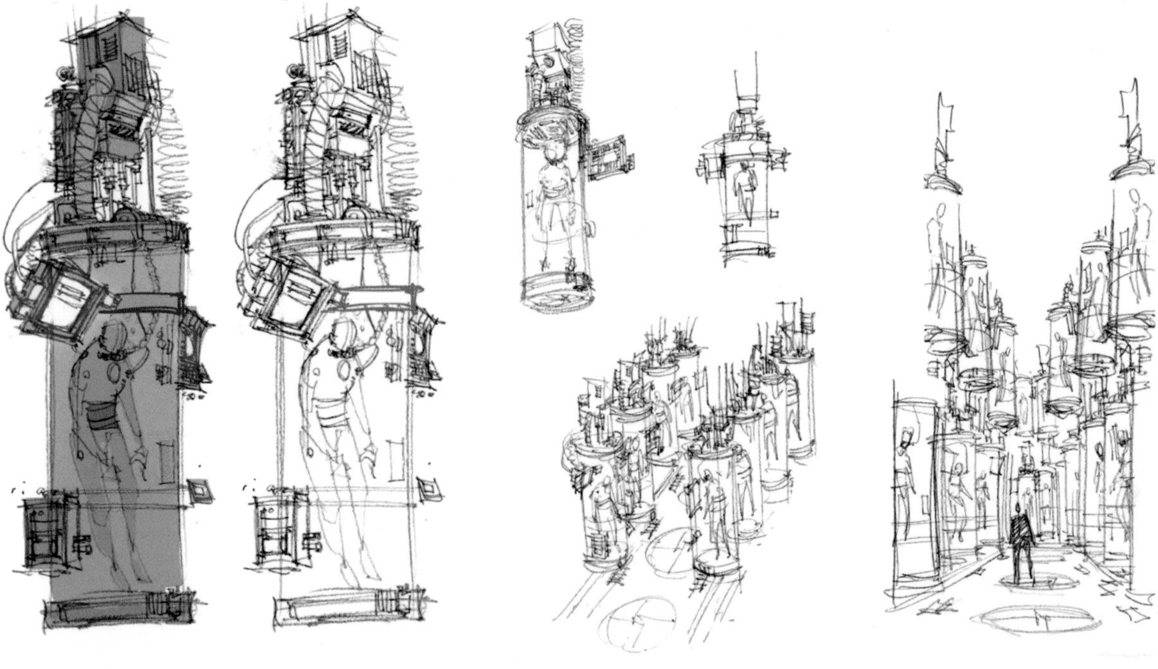

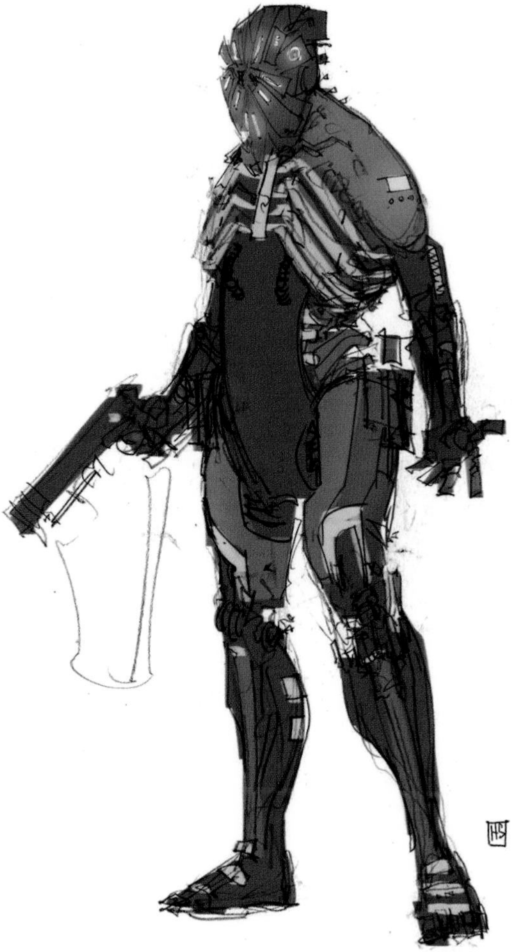

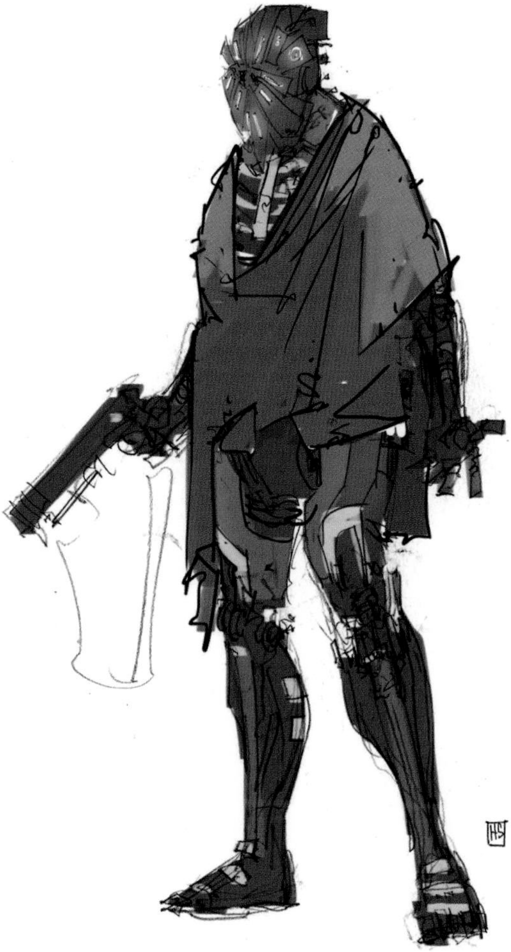

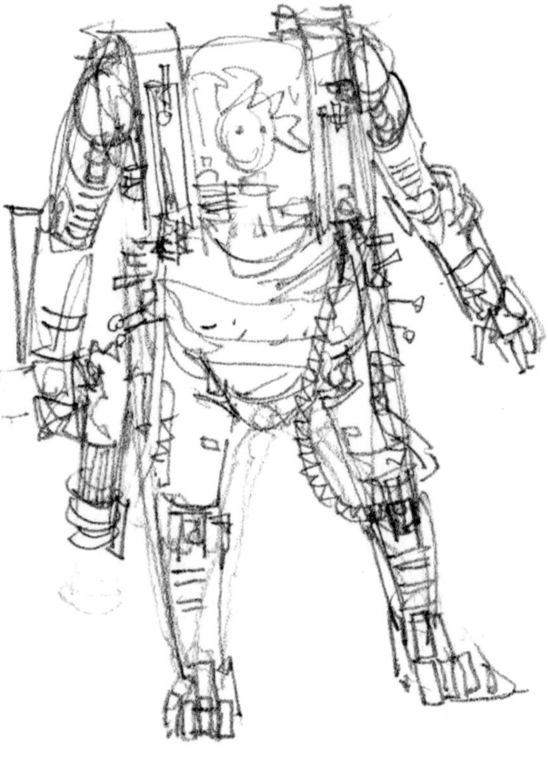

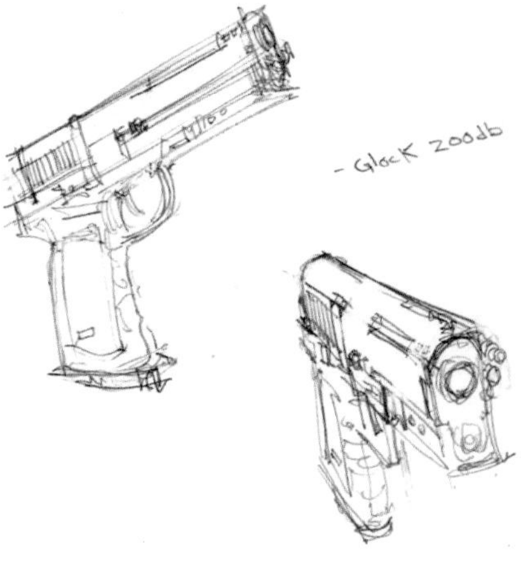
- Glock 200db

Character Studies & Ship Designs

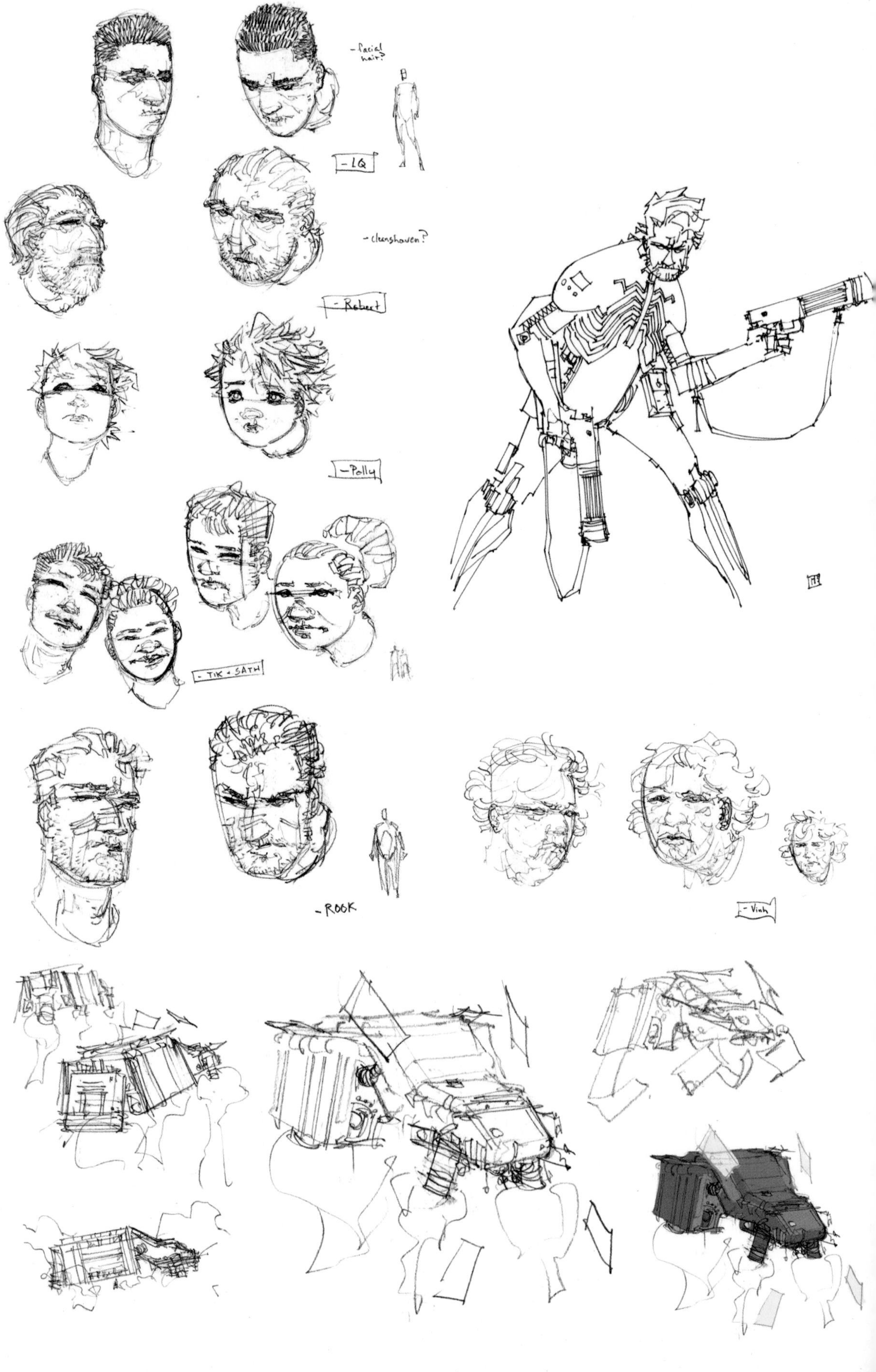
- facial hair?
- LQ
- cleanshaven?
- Robert
- Polly
- TIK + SATH
- ROOK
- Vinh

CHECK OUT THESE GREAT AFTERSHOCK
COLLECTIONS!

ALTERS VOL 1 & VOL 2
PAUL JENKINS / LEILA LEIZ MAR171244 & APR181239

AMERICAN MONSTER VOL 1
BRIAN AZZARELLO / JUAN DOE SEP161213

ANIMOSITY YEAR ONE, VOL 1, VOL 2 & VOL 3
MARGUERITE BENNETT / RAFAEL DE LATORRE FEB181034, JAN171219, AUG171130 & MAY181314

ANIMOSITY: EVOLUTION VOL 1 & VOL 2
MARGUERITE BENNETT / ERIC GAPSTUR MAR181079 & FEB188089

ANIMOSITY: THE RISE HARDCOVER
MARGUERITE BENNETT / JUAN DOE AUG178324

ART OF JIM STARLIN HARDCOVER
JIM STARLIN MAR181077

BABYTEETH VOL 1 & VOL 2
DONNY CATES / GARRY BROWN OCT171087 & APR181225

BLACK-EYED KIDS VOL 1, VOL 2 & VOL 3
JOE PRUETT / SZYMON KUDRANSKI AUG161115, FEB171100 & JAN181152

CAPTAIN KID VOL 1
MARK WAID / TOM PEYER / WILFREDO TORRES APR171231

DARK ARK VOL 1
CULLEN BUNN / JUAN DOE FEB181035

DREAMING EAGLES HARDCOVER
GARTH ENNIS / SIMON COLEBY AUG161114

ELEANOR & THE EGRET VOL 1
JOHN LAYMAN / SAM KIETH DEC171041

FU JITSU VOL 1
AI NITZ / WESLEY ST. CLAIRE APR181241

INSEXTS YEAR ONE, VOL 1 & VOL 2
MARGUERITE BENNETT / ARIELA KRISTANTINA APR181228, JUN161072 & SEP171098

JIMMY'S BASTARDS VOL 1
GARTH ENNIS / RUSS BRAUN DEC171040

PESTILENCE VOL 1
FRANK TIERI / OLEG OKUNEV NOV171154

REPLICA VOL 1
PAUL JENKINS / ANDY CLARKE MAY161030

ROUGH RIDERS VOL 1 & VOL 2
ADAM GLASS / PATRICK OLLIFFE OCT161101 & SEP171097

SECOND SIGHT VOL 1
DAVID HINE / ALBERTO PONTICELLI DEC161186

SHOCK HARDCOVER
VARIOUS MAY161029

SUPERZERO VOL 1
AMANDA CONNER / JIMMY PALMIOTTI / RAFAEL DE LATORRE MAY161029

UNHOLY GRAIL VOL 1
CULLEN BUNN / MIRKO COLAK JAN181151

WORLD READER VOL 1
JEFF LOVENESS / JUAN DOE SEP171096

FIND THESE AT YOUR FAVORITE LOCAL COMIC
BOOK SHOP OR BOOK STORE! MORE INFO:
www.aftershockcomics.com/collections

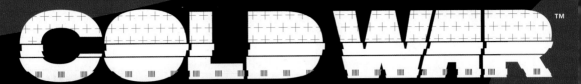

COLD WAR™

CHRISTOPHER SEBELA
writer
🐦 @xTop

Christopher Sebela is a two-time Eisner-nominated writer living and working in Portland, Oregon. He's the co-creator of such books as *Heartthrob*, *High Crimes*, *We(l)come Back*, *Dead Letters* and *Short Order Crooks* as well as having written books like *Blue Beetle*, *Kiss/Vampirella*, *Detective Comics*, *Escape from New York*, *Captain Marvel*, *Injustice: Ground Zero* and *Demonic*. He is a fan of every dog, toxic amounts of coffee, found footage horror movies and writing about himself in the third person.

HAYDEN SHERMAN
artist
🐦 @Cleanlined

Hayden Sherman is a recent addition to the comic industry. So far he's co-created and illustrated *The Few* along with Sean Lewis for Image Comics, as well as illustrating *John Carter: The End* for Dynamite Entertainment and *Civil War II: Kingpin* for Marvel. He currently lives with a couple of oddballs somewhere along the East Coast.